IARIA

AA004024

SENSORDEVICES 2020

The Eleventh International Conference on Sensor Device Technologies and Applications

November 21 - 25, 2020

SENSORDEVICES 2020 Editors

Arkady Zhukov, Dpto. Fisica de Materiales, UPV/EHU, San Sebastian, Spain
Oana Dini, IARIA, USA/EU
Janez Trontelj ml., Univesity of Ljubljana, Faculty of Electrical Engineering, Slovenia
Manuela Vieira, CTS-ISEL, Portugal

José Miguel Jiménez, Universitat Politecnica de Valencia, Spain

Printed from e-media with permission by:

Curran Associates, Inc.
57 Morehouse Lane
Red Hook, NY 12571

Some format issues inherent in the e-media version may also appear in this print version.

International Academy, Research, and Industry Association (IARIA)
412 Derby Way
Wilmington, DE 19810

Phone: (408) 893-6407
Fax: (408) 527-6351

petre@iaria.org

Additional copies of this publication are available from:

Curran Associates, Inc.
57 Morehouse Lane
Red Hook, NY 12571 USA
Phone: 845-758-0400
Fax: 845-758-2633
Email: curran@proceedings.com
Web: www.proceedings.com

Table of Contents

SENSORDEVICES 2020

Forward

The Eleventh International Conference on Sensor Device Technologies and Applications (SENSORDEVICES 2020), held on November 21-25, 2020, continued a series of events focusing on sensor devices themselves, the technology-capturing style of sensors, special technologies, signal control and interfaces, and particularly sensors-oriented applications. The evolution of the nano-and microtechnologies, nanomaterials, and the new business services make the sensor device industry and research on sensor-themselves very challenging.

Most of the sensor-oriented research and industry initiatives are focusing on sensor networks, data security, exchange protocols, energy optimization, and features related to intermittent connections. Recently, the concept of Internet-of-things gathers attention, especially when integrating IPv4 and IIPv6 networks. We welcomed technical papers presenting research and practical results, position papers addressing the pros and cons of specific proposals, such as those being discussed in the standard fora or in industry consortia, survey papers addressing the key problems and solutions on any of the above topics short papers on work in progress, and panel proposals.

We take here the opportunity to warmly thank all the members of the SENSORDEVICES 2020 technical program committee, as well as all the reviewers. The creation of such a high quality conference program would not have been possible without their involvement. We also kindly thank all the authors who dedicated much of their time and effort to contribute to SENSORDEVICES 2020. We truly believe that, thanks to all these efforts, the final conference program consisted of top quality contributions.

We also thank the members of the SENSORDEVICES 2020 organizing committee for their help in handling the logistics and for their work that made this professional meeting a success.

We hope that SENSORDEVICES 2020 was a successful international forum for the exchange of ideas and results between academia and industry and to promote further progress in the area of sensor devices technologies and applications.

SENSORDEVICES 2020 Chairs

SENSORDEVICES 2020 General Chair
Sandra Sendra, Universitat Politecnica de Valencia, Universidad de Granada, Spain

SENSORDEVICES 2020 Publicity Chair
Daniel A. Basterretxea, Universitat Politecnica de Valencia, Spain
Jose Luis García, Universitat Politecnica de Valencia, Spain

SENSORDEVICES 2020

Committee

SENSORDEVICES 2020 General Chair

Sandra Sendra, Universitat Politecnica de Valencia, Universidad de Granada, Spain

SENSORDEVICES 2020 Publicity Chair

Daniel A. Basterretxea, Universitat Politecnica de Valencia, Spain
Jose Luis García, Universitat Politecnica de Valencia, Spain

SENSORDEVICES 2020 Technical Program Committee

Jorge Marcos Acevedo, University of Vigo, Spain
Ahmed Alfadhel, Rochester Institute of Technology, USA / Research Products Development Company, Saudi Arabia
Jesús B. Alonso Hernández, Institute for Technological Development and Innovation in Communications (IDeTIC) | University of Las Palmas de Gran Canaria (ULPGC), Spain
Darius Andriukaitis, Kaunas University of Technology (KTU), Lithuania
Francisco Arcega, University of Zaragoza, Spain
Ripendra Awal, Prairie View A&M University, USA
Valerio Baiocchi, "Sapienza" University of Rome, Italy
Camelia Bala, University of Bucharest, Romania
Jose Barata, NOVA University of Lisbon, Portugal
Yoseph Bar-Cohen, Jet Propulsion Laboratory | NASA, USA
Michal Borecki, Warsaw University of Technology | Institute of MIcroelectronics and Optoelectronics, Poland
Manuel José Cabral dos Santos Reis, IEETA / University of Trás-os-Montes e Alto Douro, Portugal
Juan-Carlos Cano, Universitat Politecnica de Valencia, Spain
Vítor Carvalho, 2Ai Lab- School of Technology - IPCA / Algoritmi Research Center - Minho University, Portugal
Paula María Castro Castro, University of A Coruña, Spain
Fulvio Re Cecconi, Politecnico di Milano, Italy
Irinela Chilibon, National Institute of Research and Development for Optoelectronics - INOE-2000, Romania
Nan-Fu Chiu, National Taiwan Normal University, Taiwan
Chi-Wai Chow, National Chiao Tung University, Hsinchu, Taiwan
Sazzadur Chowdhury, University of Windsor, Canada
Juan M. Corchado, University of Salamanca, Spain
Marco Crescentini, Advanced Research Center on Electronic Systems - "ARCES E. De Castro" | University of Bologna - Cesena Campus, Italy
Francesco G. Della Corte, Università degli Studi Mediterranea, Italy
Emiliano Descrovi, Norwegian University of Science and Technology (NTNU), Trondheim, Norway / Polytechnic University of Turin, Torino, Italy

Copyright Information

Distanced Observation of Magnetic Field Anomalies During Periods of Power Failure and Applications in Remote Classification of Electrical Activity

Christopher Duncan, MS
Computational and Data Sciences
George Mason University
Fairfax, VA 22030
Email: cduncan@masonlive.gmu.edu

Olga Gkountouna, PhD
Computational and Data Sciences
George Mason University
Fairfax, VA 22030
Email: ogkounto@gmu.edu

Ron Mahabir, PhD
Computational and Data Sciences
George Mason University
Fairfax, VA 22030
Email: rmahabir@masonlive.gmu.edu

***Abstract*—During research focusing on radio frequency field transmission detection from broadcasters on known frequencies at known time and transmission in the magnetic field, anomalies were detected in frequencies outside of the frequency scope of the original research. Analysis of these anomalies indicated they were linked to an ongoing power issue in which a fuse had failed in a power transformer located approximately 1.3 miles from the magnetic field sensor system and antenna. The research crew, through the use of digital signal processing software, were able to diagnose the problem and assist electrical crews with fixing the issue while observing the anomaly at a distance that typically would be outside of the range of detection. The results supplemented previous research indicating magnetic field behavior is dissimilar to companion electronic field behavior during propagation by demonstration the collection of the magnetic field from an RF broadcaster located within a Faraday cage. The magnetic field was collected for analysis while the RF was undetectable. This incidental researched supported the potential for use of magnetic fields in remote sensing and remote classification of electronic activity. Further data analysis, including a meta-analysis of previously conducted studies which also produced anomalies validated that at a distance the magnetic field may be a viable candidate remote sensing of electrical activity, such as power outages, or radio frequency activity, when a standard electrical field antenna is less suitable.**

Keywords–computational; science; magnetic; fields; low frequency; human; activity; remote; sensing.

I. Introduction

The broader field of remote sensing is typically associated with the identification of vegetation and features of a given area using active sensors to annotate and compare the reflectance curve signature of varying bands of the electromagnetic spectrum. Although typically relegated to passive sensors, it may be possible to remotely sense and classify activity using passive sensors to detect activity from varying emission sources and algorithms for classification. The particular interest of this research was the observation of such emissions and anomalies in the magnetic field at atypical distances and the potential for use in remote sensing and classification applications. The intent of this research is the validate the potential for magnetic fields to serve as a potential dimension of remote sensing and classification of activities, particularly so when frequencies are lower than standard use and common electrical field antennas become cumbersome due to size requirements.

There are numerous examples of the influence of magnetic fields on biological tissue and activity. For example, studies have shown that grazing animals typically align north and south when undisturbed, but near power lines (and subsequently the associated magnetic fields), the alignment changed [1], and there is even a correlation with the increase in stroke in some populations during geomagnetic storming [2]. Previous research has identified the possibility of magnetic fields to penetrate a Faraday cage, as well as their ease of detectability when compared to the associated electrical field and the accompanying antenna size requirements of electrical field detection [3].

Some of the data collected in this research was unintended and is based on anomaly observations and identification in the magnetic field while conducting other research in the magnetic field. Initially the study was setup to collect signatures of basic electrical activity at a distance, in a controlled environment, when an anomaly occurred nearby, the focus was changed to gather data on the anomaly. Consequent to the observation and identification of the anomalies, research teams were able to assist local utilities in the identification and repair of power lines at a distance of approximately 13 miles.

In Section 2, we will describe the testing setup and methodology of the original research being conducted. The section focuses on physical setup, sensor calibration and the data collection. In Section 3, the paper focuses on the observation of anomalies, which changed the focus of the original research and the processing of the data, including visual analysis of the anomalies over time in comparison to observed activities. Section 4 primarily focuses on a forensic scrub of previously collected data in which anomalies were observed and a comparison of those anomalies to known events, and in Section 5 we present our conclusions.

II. The Testing

The original setup of the sensor includes RF shielded boxes to limit interference, fiber optic cable, and battery power for both the computer and all other equipment. The sensors are calibrated using Helmholtz coils to create a uniform magnetic field, and the data is handled by custom created digital signal processing software, which displays the entire collection band and all 6 axes of the sensors on a waterfall display at once. The software sample rate is adjusted by the band used, and the software enables record and life Fourier transform and spectral

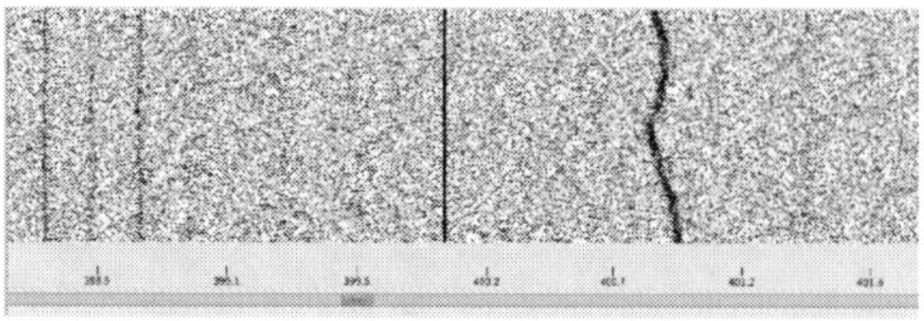

Figure 1. The live signal waterfall collection screen view from the digital signal processing computers.

density processing as well as audiometric analysis (in the case where a signal is a suspected audio transmission). More details of the setup are provided below.

A. The Setup

Routine research was being conducted in an isolated desert environment to reduce the man-made electromagnetic interference. The intent of the research was waveform analysis of radio signals transmitted at the UHF band from radios transmitted at ground level from a distance of approximately 15 miles.

The sensors were battery powered magnetic loop antennas placed on the ground, on a ridge approximately 500 feet in altitude above the ground level, isolated in radio frequency shielded boxes, and fed fiber optic cabling to reduce the likelihood of interference. Two battery powered Linux powered computers dedicated to digital signal processing were located within a battery powered trailer and used for digital signal processing to monitor the entire spectrum of frequencies which the antenna was able to monitor.

B. Sensor Calibration

To ensure the proper calibration of the sensors and software in the magnetic field, a standard two coil Helmholtz coil was used, spaced apart approximately 3 feet. The coils were powered by uniform frequency electricity to create a uniform magnetic field between the two coils. The sensor was placed between the coils while inside the radio frequency shield box, and calibration adjustments were made to ensure the frequency of the detected uniform magnetic field matched the frequency of electricity powering the coils. Sensors were calibrated each day before the tests were conducted [3].

C. Data Collection and Handling

Data collected by the sensors is displayed as shown in Figure 1. The display shows a live feed from the antennas in the entire band, with darker colors indicating stronger signals. The x axis indicates frequency while the y axis is time, with the current time being at the top of the screen. The darker lines signify a strong signal detected in the frequency (x axis) [3]. The system allows for isolate of specific frequencies and conversion to wave form via Fast Fourier transform. Darker or more condensed dark points appear on the screen (typically in line form) in areas of stronger frequency presence. A strong radio signal would place a dark line from top to bottom of the screen in the frequency of the broadcast and for the duration of the broadcast. Figure 2 illustrates the the setup and placement of sensors in relation to power lines and transformers for the duration of the collection. Exact measurements were made using Google Maps functionality.

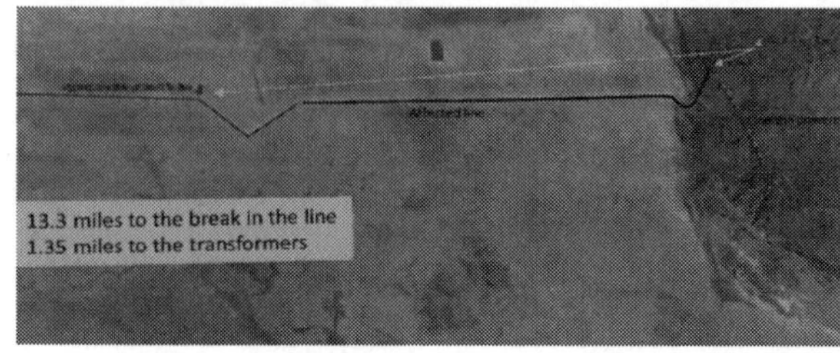

Figure 2. The layout and measurement of the original research site including distances from power lines and transformer boxes that were the source of the magnetic anomalies.

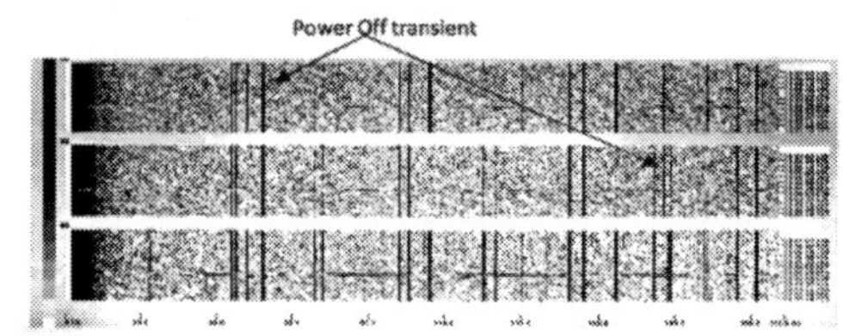

Figure 3. Waterfall display of frequency density.

III. Anomaly Observation and Post Fourier Transform Analysis

The anomaly in question was noticed during routine research as shown in Figure 3. The X axis represents frequency ranging from .1 Hz to 1000 Hz, and Y axis representing time, with the most recent being at the top of each waterfall. Each band represents a different axis of the Cube antenna. The center band (Y2) shows a total disruption of frequencies at the time of power loss with the top band (Y1) showing a likely spectral density loss at time of power loss at approximately 60 Hz. The reduction of spectral density was significant enough to warrant further examination, particularly given that spectral density from human activity is often detected in the 50 and 60 Hz range [4], and a power reduction or loss at one location would not necessarily ensure a total loss of frequency detection on the display. Prior to the power outage, the signal and decibel level are stable and appear as expected.

A. Visual Analysis of Power Outage

Shortly after the anomalies were noticed in the waterfall observation screen, a power truck was observed approaching a power line approximately 13 miles away. Times were noted and the data was recorded for analysis as the power company began working to isolate the problem. A post-Fourier transform analysis of the incident as shown in Figure 4, focusing on a single frequency, revealed a clear disruption in power and violent shifts in both amplitude of the signal and frequency.

B. Visual Analysis of First Fix Attempt

An initial attempt by the power company to re-energize the power lines, similar to a circuit breaker system, appeared to have some effect for a few seconds, as shown in Figure 5, but the power almost immediately failed. Power crews continued working to identify and isolate the problem. Figure 5 also demonstrates that while the decibel level dropped drastically, there was still signal to be detected, although it was relatively unstable.

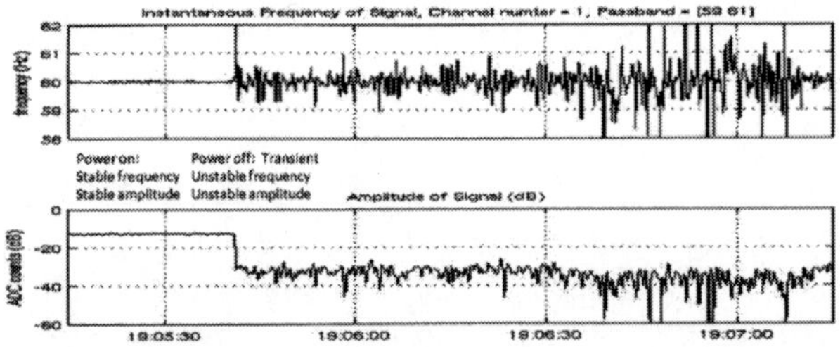

Figure 4. Wave form and decibel variation after loss of power due to blown fuse.

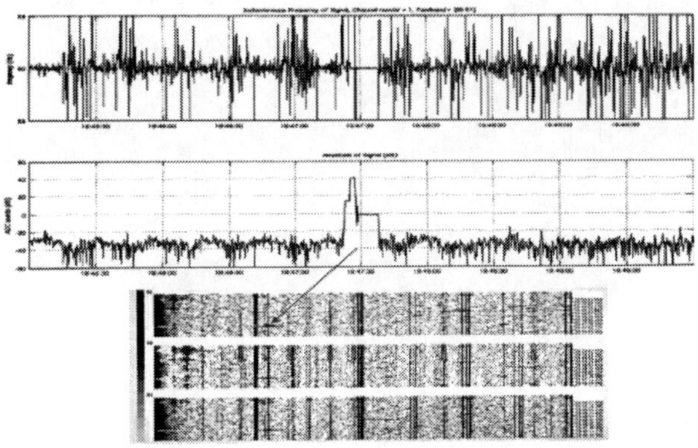

Figure 5. Changes in wave form, decibel level and frequency presence during the first attempt to restore power with a blown fuse.

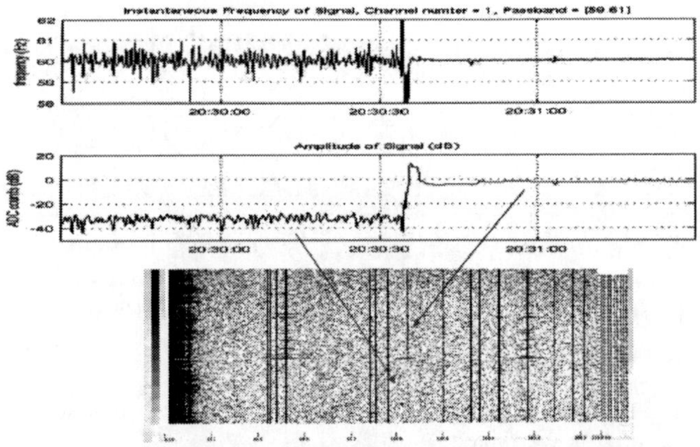

Figure 6. Frequency and decibel level normalize after restoration of power following a fuse change. The change is also depicted on the waterfall.

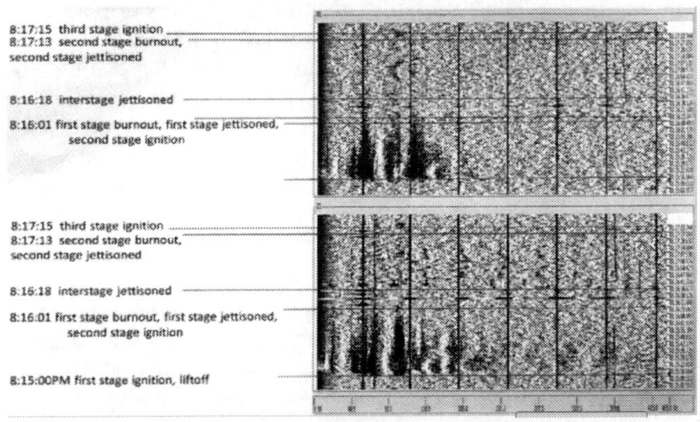

Figure 7. Waterfall image of the 2013 Wallops Island launch of a Minotaur I on the 20th of November.

C. *Visual Analysis of Fuse Replacement*

Research crews monitoring the sensor and anomalies made contact with the testing range and power crew, and based on wave form activity and axis location shown in Figures 3 and 4, as well as post-fix attempt activity shown in Figure 5, speculated that it was likely a fuse that needed replacing. Crews replaced the fuse located in the transformer box approximately 1.3 miles from the sensor as shown in Figure 2. The attempt to restore power following the fuse change was successful as shown in Figure 6. The return to normal decibel level and frequency matched the frequency and decibel level of the power line prior to the blown fuse.

IV. Prior Data Comparison

Following the incidental research, a data scrub for comparison was conducted that revealed similar results of much greater magnitude.

A. *Wallops Island Launch*

On the 20th of November, 2013 research in the magnetic field was being conducted on Wallops Island against a known launch of a Minotaur I rocket from Wallops Island, VA. Once sensor was located approximately 4 miles from the launch site, while the second was located 50 miles from the launch site. Collection from the site located 50 miles away was intermittent and not saved as it was unreliable at best, while data collection at the 4 mile location was remarkably clear and is displayed in Figure 7 with an offset of 16 seconds from actual launch, with times aligning with actual recorded times with a uniform offset of 16 seconds. The bulk of the detections appear between 46 and 140 Hz. Detections of the flight were made slightly beyond 3rd stage ignition which would place the rocket at approximately 120 Km above the surface of the earth and 170 Km in linear distance away from the launch site.

It was originally assumed that the detections were likely emissions from rocket but following the analysis of the data of the power outage, a further review was conducted. To ensure the frequencies detected were not radio or computer hardware and no hardware or electronics were found to match frequencies of detection as shown in Figure 8. Given the frequency of detection compared to the frequencies used in Figure 8, it is possible the signals detected were the result electromagnetic field induction by the rocket passing through the earths magnetic field.

V. Conclusion

Previous research documented the apparent ability of magnetic fields associated with a radio frequency broadcast to penetrate a Faraday cage [3], while the associated radio frequency remained undetectable. The previous conclusion warranted further research into the propagation of magnetic fields. The results of this inadvertent study serve to validate the original premise that magnetic fields appear to behave

SOURCE	1	2	3	4	5
Function	Command Destruct	Tracking Transponder	Tracking Transponder	Launch Vehicle	Instrumentation on Telemetry (Optional)
Receive/Xmit	Receive	Transmit	Receive	Transmit	Transmit
Band	UHF	C-Band	C-Band	S-Band	S-Band
Frequency (MHz)	416.5 or 425.0	5765	5690	2288.5	2269.5
Bandwidth	N/A	N/A			
Power Output	N/A	400 W (peak)	N/A	10 W	10 W
Sensitivity	-107 dB		-70 dB		
Modulation	Tone	Pulse Code	Pulse Code	PCM/FM	PCM/FM

Figure 8. Table 4-12 from the Minotaur I users guide, showing operating, radio and telemetry frequencies during the use of the Minotaur I [5]

differently than their electrical field partners and that further research is warranted.

Specifically in this case, waveform and spectral density coupled with visual isolation were adequate to remotely classify or "remotely sense" electrical activity. To further research the viability of this phenomena and its applicability in the field of remote sensing, research should move to blind testing methods, as well as electromagnetically challenging environments. Further research should also include duplication of this event in varying electromagnetic environments to test against algorithms for detection when compared to similar but intentional disruptive events. Results may serve to determine if a difference in a blown fuse and induced events such as a light switch can be determined amongst the varying levels of environmental noise.

Finally, if validated, the potential for characterization of space launches by electromagnetic field detection via magnetic loop antennas offers yet another axis of data collection in the field of remote sensing of human activity and potentially in electronic activity classification. The potential has a wide variety of public safety applications, such as alternative and supplementary geo-location of aircraft travel, including potentially those who have lost power in emergency situations resulting in a loss of radio and transponder broadcast.

ACKNOWLEDGMENT

Christopher would like to thank like to thank the public school system for inspiring him to do better.

The authors collectively would like to thank the College of Science, the Department of Computational and Data Sciences and our fans.

REFERENCES

[1] S. Reebs, "Misaligned by Power Lines." Natural History 118, no. 5 (June 1, 2009): 14. http://search.proquest.com/docview/210652836/ retrieved: September, 2020

[2] V. L. Feigin et al., "Geomagnetic Storms Can Trigger Stroke: Evidence from 6 Large Population-Based Studies in Europe and Australasia," Stroke 45, no. 6, June 2014, pp. 1639–1645

[3] C. Duncan, O. Gkountouna, and R. Mahabir, "Theoretical Application of Magnetic Fields at Tremendously Low Frequency in Remote Sensing and Electronic Activity Classification", Advances in Computer Vision and Computational Biology, 2020, pp 308-312

[4] Z. Nieckarz, Imprints of Natural Phenomena and Human Activity Observed During 10 Years of ELF Magnetic Measurements at the Hylaty Geophysical Station in Poland. Acta Geophysica, 64(6), pp. 2591–2608. https://doi.org/10.1515/acgeo-2016-0101 retrieved: September, 2020

[5] Orbital Sciences. Minotaur Users Guide. Minotaur Users Guide, US Air Force, 2002.

Dynamic Mode AFM Measurement of CMUT Diaphragm Deflection Profile

Sazzadur Chowdhury
Department of Electrical and Computer Engineering
University of Windsor
Windsor, ON, N9B 3P4, Canada
e-mail: sazzadur@uwindsor.ca

Abstract—**Atomic Force Microscopy (AFM) measurement results of the deflection shape and ISO 25178 roughness parameters of the diaphragm of an adhesive wafer bonded Silicon-on-Insulator (SOI) based Capacitive Micromachined Ultrasonic Transducer (CMUT) has been presented. The AFM measurements were carried out using the dynamic mode operation of an atomic force microscope to achieve higher resolution. The measurement results were used to construct the 3D deflection shape of the CMUT diaphragm with actual height parameters. The measured deflection shape of the CMUT diaphragm can be used to determine the stiffness, residual stress, and other physical parameters in a CMUT diaphragm to facilitate more accurate calibration and CMUT sensitivity.**

Keywords-CMUT; SOI; AFM; Dynamic mode; Residual stress.

I. INTRODUCTION

Capacitive Micromachined Ultrasonic Transducers (CMUT) are advantageous over the piezoelectric ultrasonic transducers as they offer superior sensitivity, better temporal and axial resolution, higher fractional bandwidth, and higher energy transduction efficiency [1]. CMUTs also offer lower mechanical impedance, lower self-heating, lower dielectric loss, lower internal loss, and better thermal dissipation than their piezoelectric counterparts [1]-[4]. All of these positive features of CMUTs translate into better image quality as has been experimentally verified in [5]-[7]. Additionally, unlike the piezoelectric transducers, the CMUTs can be batch fabricated with sub-micrometer resolution using CMOS compatible highly matured conventional microelectronic fabrication techniques to reduce per unit production cost [7].

The CMUTs rely on electrostatic or acoustic vibration of a thin diaphragm which is separated from a fixed backplate by a thin airgap or vacuum space to generate ultrasound in a surrounding medium (transmit mode) or to generate an electrical signal corresponding to an incident ultrasound wave on the diaphragm (receive mode) [1]-[3]. As the CMUTs rely on the vibration of a diaphragm to transmit or receive ultrasound, accurate measurement of the deflection profile (shape) of the diagram and surface roughness is crucial for proper characterization of transducer operation [8].

The deflection profile of a diaphragm depends on the stiffness of the diaphragm that in turn depends on the shape of the diaphragm, support conditions, homogeneity of the diaphragm material, residual stress, Poisson ratio, diaphragm thickness uniformity and the shape of the cavity. The CMUT cavity is either a sealed vacuum entity or filled with atmospheric air if the diaphragm has perforations.

A CMUT diaphragm experiences different types of stresses, such as tensile or compressive residual stress due to the fabrication process, stress due to atmospheric pressure indentation (vacuum cavity), and stress due to the expansion of the trapped residual gas in the sealed cavity during fabrication [9]. Fabrication process induced imperfections may also contribute to cavity shape alternations, diaphragm thickness variation, and the quality of the diaphragm. Consequently, such structural imperfections affect the electrostatic pressure generation during transmit operation or capacitive readout during ultrasound reception. A measurement of the diaphragm deflection profile and surface roughness can be used to determine proper balance of laminate thickness of different materials used to fabricate the diaphragm, improve thickness uniformity of the diaphragm, material properties adjustments by modifying fabrication process parameters and steps to achieve optimized residual stress. All of these will contribute to superior yield, superior array operation, and better imaging resolution.

Optical profilometry is one of the widely used techniques for surface characterization in microfabrication applications. White Light Interferometry (WLI), Confocal Laser Scanning (CLS) microscopy, and Confocal Grid Structured Illumination (CGSI) microscopy are commonly used techniques to characterize thinfilm thickness, reflectivity, and height measurement. Stylus based contact profilometry techniques are also used but that needs additional fabrication steps to prepare the sample and imposes risk of device damage. Possible uses of different optical profilometry techniques for CMUT characterization are available in [9].

In this context, this paper presents initial results of the dynamic (tapping) mode AFM characterization of the deflection profile of a CMUT diaphragm [10][11]. The measurements were carried out using a FlexAFM™ with C3000 controller from Nanosurf™ [10]. Relative advantages and disadvantages of AFM as compared to optical systems have also been discussed in the context of CMUT diaphragm deflection profile characterization.

The rest of the paper has been organized in the following way: In Section II, major specifications of the measured CMUT sample are given. Section III provides a brief theoretical description of the dynamic mode AFM, Section IV provides AFM measurement set up and data processing and finally Section V makes the concluding remarks.

II. CMUT Specifications

A cross section of the measured CMUT sample is shown in Figure 1 and the device specifications are provided in Table I. The CMUT was fabricated using an adhesive wafer bonding technique using BCB as the dielectric spacer and the device layer of an SOI wafer was used to realize the CMUT diaphragm [12].

Figure 2 shows a Scanning Electron Microscope (SEM) image of one of the diced CMUT cell array. The array was fabricated for an automotive collision avoidance application. Detailed description of the fabrication process is available in [12].

TABLE I. CMUT Cell Specifications

Parameter	Value	Unit
Diaphragm laminate thickness	800	nm
Gold layer thickness	100	nm
Silicon device layer thickness	700	nm
Cavity thickness	1	µm
Cavity width	28	µm
Sidewall width	10	µm
Bottom wafer thickness	500	µm

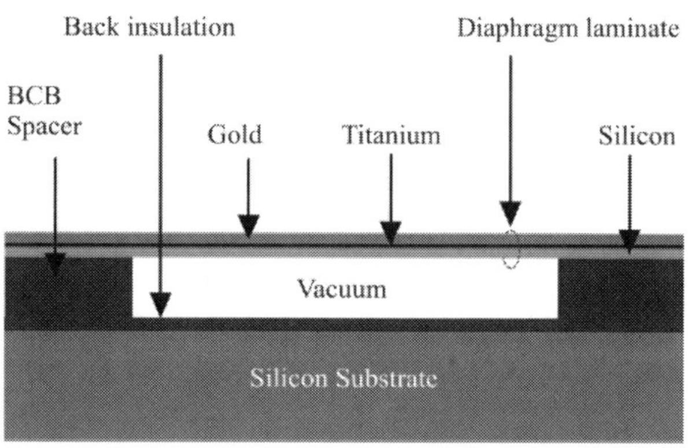

Figure 1. Cross-section of the measured CMUT cell.

The array has 40 x 40 CMUT cells with specifications as listed in Table I in a footprint area of 1870 x 1870 μm^2.

Figure 2. SEM image of a singulated CMUT die.

III. AFM Dynamic Mode Operation

An AFM technique creates a 3D topography of the sample's surface using a cantilever probe with a sharp tip as the probe or the sample is scanned in x-y plane [10][11]. As an AFM provides the vertical height data directly from measurements, the technique is very different from an optical imaging microscope, which measures a two-dimensional projection of a sample's surface [13].

Despite the advantages of the optical systems as summarized in [13], as a two-dimensional image from an optical system does not have any height information in it, such images must infer the height information from the image or rotate the sample to see feature heights [13]. The AFM also provides various types of surface measurements and can generate images at atomic resolution with angstrom scale resolution height information for both conducting and insulating surfaces with minimum sample preparation [14]. In [15], it has been mentioned that the spatial and "*Z*" resolution of the AFM is much better than that could be obtained by an optical profilometer whatever optical system is used. In [15], it has also been mentioned that the AFM images are more faithful to nanoscale surface topographic variations compared to optical profilometers. Furthermore, an AFM measuring system is free of any errors related to optical focusing, depth of field adjustment, or sample illumination angles. Consequently, an AFM allows one to measure surface topography with unprecedented resolution and accuracy [16]. As the capacitance change during the CMUT diaphragm vibration is very small (attofarad to femtofarad range) corresponding to picometer range deflection of the CMUT diaphragm, precision measurement of the diaphragm deflection profile is crucial for proper characterization of CMUT operation to improve imaging resolution.

For the current research work, the AFM measurements were done using a FlexAFM™ from Nanosurf™ operating in dynamic mode. The dynamic mode was chosen over the static mode due to the fact that the static mode AFM does not achieve atomic resolution due to the mesoscopic properties of the tip, which induces a contact zone dispersed over many atoms as opposed to a single atom [11]. Additionally, the dynamic mode offers the following advantages: (1) gentle interaction of the probe tip with the surface during tapping to preserve the sharpness of the tip to improve accuracy, (2) minimized torsional forces between the probe and the sample, and (3) by using the cantilever's oscillation amplitude as the feedback parameter, the user is able to fine-tune the interaction between probe and sample between different regimes- such as attractive and repulsive ones- to control the tip–surface distance on an atomic scale [10].

The dynamic mode operation of an AFM is illustrated conceptually in Figure 3. During operation, the cantilever is forced to vibrate at its resonance frequency using a piezo element. As the oscillating cantilever is brought closer to the sample surface, it experiences a repulsive force that increases the resonance frequency of the cantilever.and its vibration amplitude decreases [10]. The vibration amplitude of the

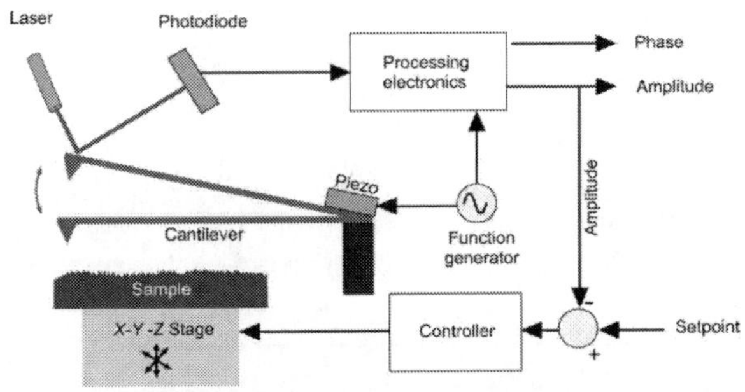

Figure 3. AFM dynamic mode operation.

cantilever is detected using a laser and photodiode based detection system as shown in Figure 3.

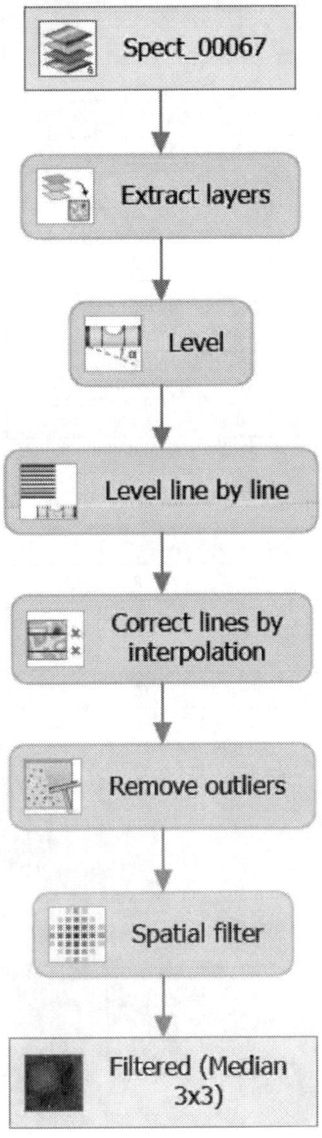

Figure 4. FlexAFM Spect-0067 data processing steps.

The measured laser beam deflection or cantilever vibration amplitude is then used as an input for a feedback loop that keeps the tip–sample interaction constant by changing the tip height. The output of this feedback loop thus corresponds to the local sample height. This amplitude reduction is a direct measure of the feature height on the sample surface that is mapped in a 2-D *x-y* plane [10][11].

IV. THE AFM MEASUREMENT SET UP FOR CMUT

The AFM measurements of the CMUT sample were done using FlexAFM™ with C3000 controller from Nanosurf™ operating in dynamic mode with active vibration isolation and acoustic isolation.

An ACLA™ cantilever with nominal spring constant of 58 N/m was used to collect the data. The ACLA™ probes are silicon probes with long cantilevers used for tapping mode and other applications that allow for larger laser clearance, and have aluminum coating on the reflex side to increase laser signal quality. Detailed measurement setup instructions are available in [17].

Once the AFM measurement was done, the height data was processed following standard AFM data processing steps as shown in Figure 4. The generated pseudo-color view of the surface is shown in Figure 5. The Gwyddion™ [18] AFM data processing software has been used next to generate a 3-D height image of the surface as shown in Figure 6. The statistical roughness parameters following IS0 25178 have been extracted using Gwyddion™ and provided in Table II.

As the AFM data are usually collected as line scans along the *x* axis that are concatenated together to form a two-dimensional image, the scanning speed in the *x* direction is considerably higher than the scanning speed in the *y* direction. As a result, the *x* profiles are less affected by low frequency noise and thermal drift of the sample as compared to the *y* profile [18].

Consequently, standardized one dimensional roughness parameters are considered more accurate [18]. Accordingly, the one dimensional roughness parameters for a scan line centered approximately at the middle of the CMUT diaphragm along the y-axis direction as shown in Figure 7 was extracted using Gwyddion™ and are plotted in Figure 8.

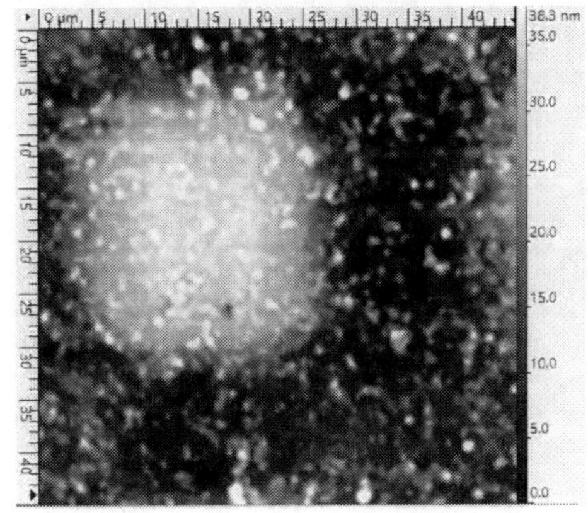

Figure 5. Pseudo-color image of the sample.

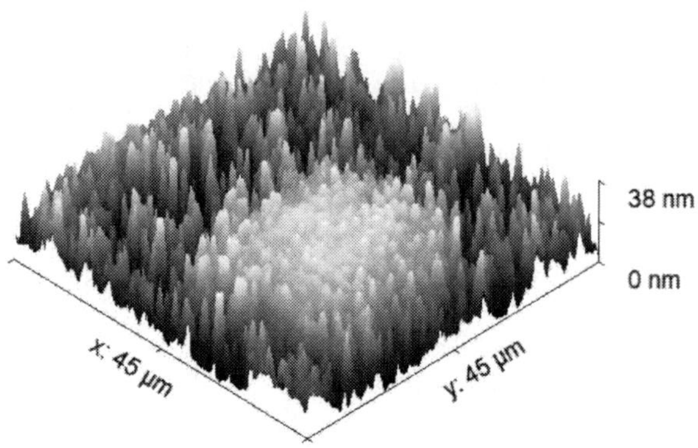

Figure 6. 3D height image of the sample.

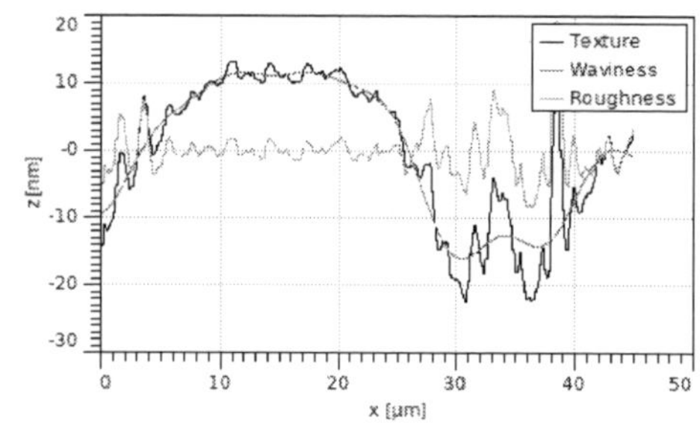

Figure 8. Roughness, texture, and waviness profile along an x-directional scan line as shown in Figure 7.

TABLE II. STATISTICAL ROUGHNESS PARAMETERS

Parameter	Value	Unit
RMS roughness, S_q	10.50	nm
Mean-sqaure roughness, S_a	9.08	nm
Skew (S_{sk})	0.06925	
Excess kurtosis	-1.185	
Maximum peak height, S_p	19.24	nm
Maximum pit depth, S_V	19.01	nm
Maximum height, S_Z	38.25	nm
Projected area:	2025	µm²
Surface area	2026	µm²
Volume	38.50	µm³

Corresponding texture and waviness data are also shown. Detailed roughness parameters along this scan line are provided in Table III. The waviness average along this particular scanning line as determined from Gwyddion™ is 8.77 nm with a cut-off wavelength of 7.69 µm. The same measurement was carried out along a y-axis scanning line as shown in Figure 9 and the corresponding texture, roughness, and waviness parameters are shown in Figure10. Finally, the waviness parameters are plotted for an arbitrary diagonal direction as shown in Figure 11 and the corresponding waviness profile is shown in Figure 12.

TABLE III. ONE DIMENSIONLA ROUGHNESS PARAMETERS

Parameter	Value	Unit
Cut-off	7.69	µm
Roughness average (R_a)	3.09	nm
Root mean square roughness (R_q)	4.87	nm
Maximum height of the roughness (R_t)	34.58	nm
Maximum roughness valley depth (R_v)	10.67	nm
Maximum roughness peak height (R_p)	23.91	nm
Average maximum height of the roughness (R_{tm})	17.92	nm
Average maximum roughness valley depth (R_{vm})	6.97	nm
Average maximum roughness peak height (R_{pm})	10.95	nm
Average third highest peak to third lowest valley height (R_{3z})	20.34	nm
Average third highest peak to third lowest valley height (R_{3z} ISO)	14.38	nm
Average maximum height of the profile (R_z)	20.83	nm
Average maximum height of the roughness (R_z ISO)	17.92	nm
Maximum peak to valley roughness ($R_y = R_{max}$)	34.58	nm
Skewness (R_{sk})	1.87	
Kurtosis (R_{ku})	10.46	
Waviness average (W_a)	8.77	nm
Root mean square waviness (W_q)	10.16	nm

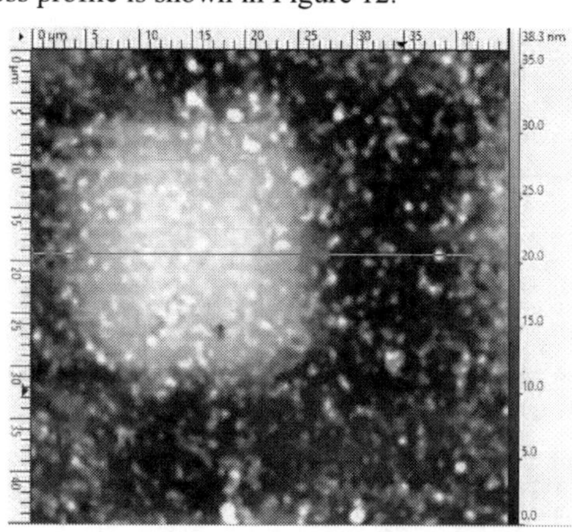

Figure 7. Scan line to determine standardized roughness parameters along the x-axis direction.

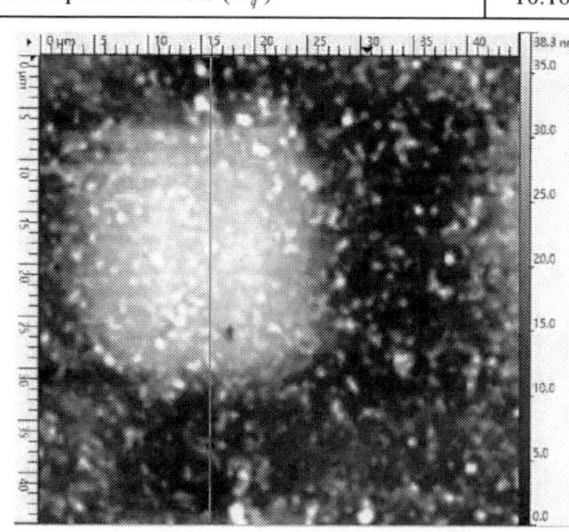

Figure 9. Scan line to determine standardized roughness parameters along the y-axis direction.

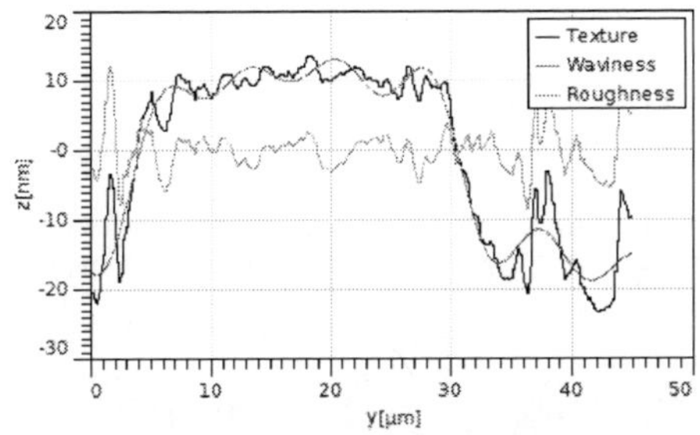

Figure 10. Roughness, texture, and waviness profile along an y-directional scan line as shown in Figure 9.

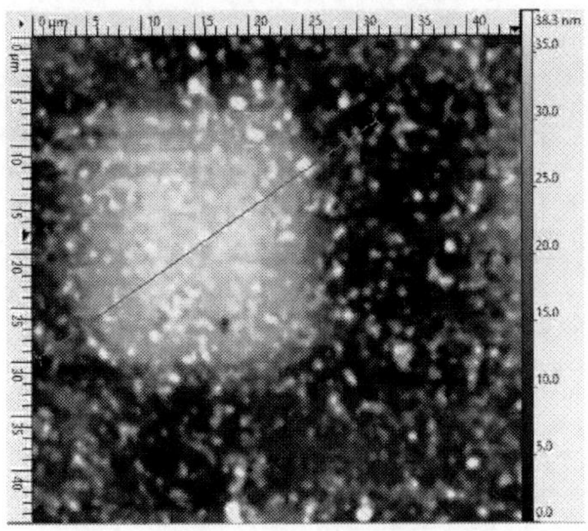

Figure 11. Scan line to determine standardized roughness parameters along an arbitrary diagnonal direction.

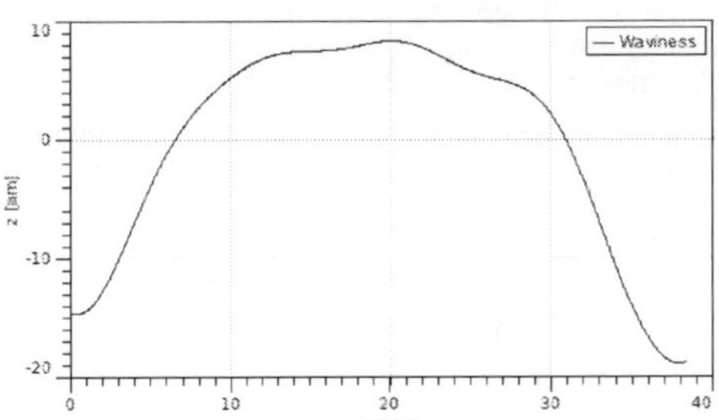

Figure 12. Waviness profile along an arbitrary diagnonal direction as shown in Figure 11.

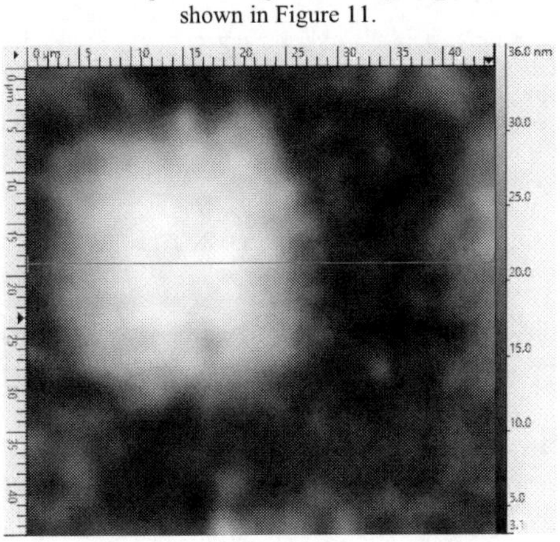

Figure 13. Pseudo-color image of the surface after applying a Gaussian filter.

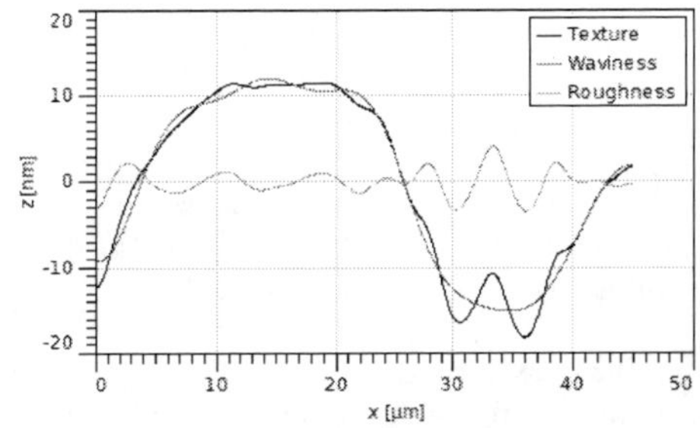

Figure 14. Roughness, texture, and waviness profile along the *x*-directional scan as shown in Figure 13 after applying a Gaussian filter.

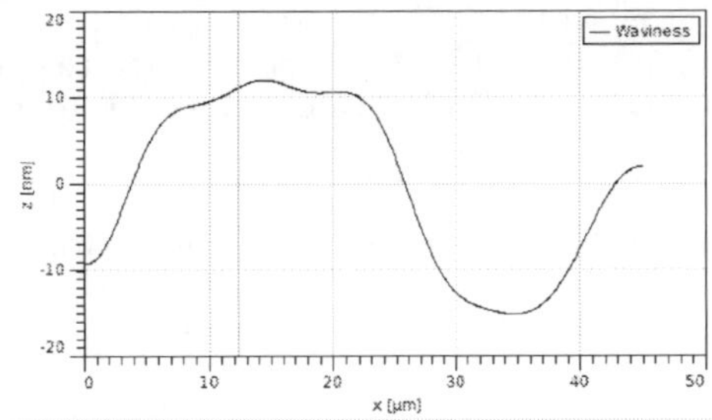

Points	X [μm]	Y [nm]	Length [μm]	Height [nm]	Angle [deg]
	12.32	11.18			
	19.98	10.67	7.66	-0.51	-0.00

Figure 15. Waviness profile measurement over a length on filtered data.

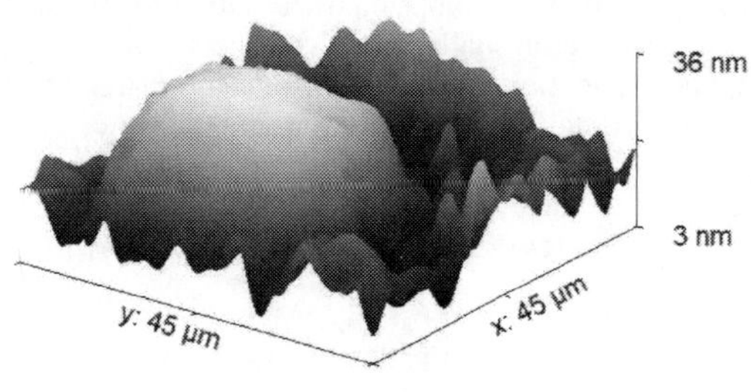

Topview

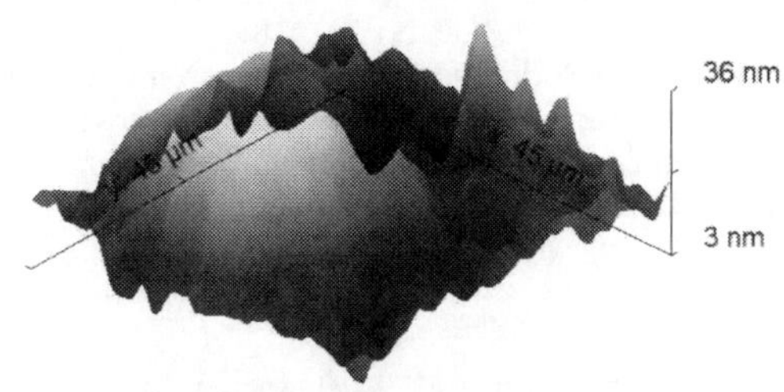

Bottom view

Figure 16. 3D top and bottom views of the deflection profile after Gaussian filtering.

Figures 7-12 show that using an AFM it is extremely convenient to measure the CMUT diaphragm deflection profile with a very high degree of precision along any direction from which physical properties such as stiffness, residual stress, etc. of the diaphragm laminate can be extracted using appropriate mathematical models.

Further processing of the AFM data using a Gaussian filter removes the high frequency roughness artifacts further and provides a smoothed out deflection shape of the CMUT diaphragm along an x directional scan line as shown in Figure 13. A 40 pixel magnitude Gaussian filter was used.

The smoothed texture, roughness, and waviness profiles are provided in Figure 14 for comparison. Corresponding waviness values over a length of 7.66 micrometers (two red markers) are shown in Figure 15. The waviness average height (W_a) for this scanned profile is 8.85 nm and maximum height is 11.18 nm to 10.67 nm over this range shows almost a flat surface. Corresponding top and bottom view of the 3D deflection profile are shown in Figure 16.

V. CONCLUSIONS

The presented dynamic mode AFM measurement and data analysis of a CMUT diaphragm appears to be a valuable method to evaluate the deflection profile of a CMUT diaphragm with a very high degree of precision. Main advantage of the proposed method is that the height data is measured directly with nanometer scale precision instead of inferring from a 2D projection of an optical image. Such deflection profiles can be used to determine the residual stress and other physical parameters of a CMUT diaphragm to aid in fine tuning of the process parameters to optimize CMUT diaphragm vibrational characteristics to obtain high quality images. Additionally, the dynamic mode enables to measure the deflection shape of insulating materials, thus enabling to measure the diaphragm shapes where the diaphragm has an insulating top surface. Overall, the dynamic mode AFM can provide high accuracy high resolution nanometer scale measurements to characterize CMUT surfaces.

ACKNOWLEDGMENT

This research work was supported by the Natural Science and Engineering Research Council of Canada (NSERC)'s discovery grant number RGPIN 293218. The authors also greatly acknowledge the generous measurement support provided by Nanosurf™. The authors also acknowledge the collaborative research support provided by the IntelliSense Corporation, Lynnfield, MA, Remcom, PA, Angstrom Engineering, ON, and the CMC Microsystems, Canada.

REFERENCES

[1] A. Ergun, G. Yaralioglu; and B. T. Khuri-Yakub, "Capacitive Micromachined Ultrasonic Transducers: Theory and Technology," *Journal of Aerospace Engineering*, vol. 16, no. 2, pp. 76-84, Apr. 2003,

[2] B. T. Khuri-Yakub and Ö. Oralkan, "Capacitive Micromachined Ultrasonic Transducers for Medical Imaging and Therapy," *Journal of Micromech .and Microeng*, vol. 21, no. 5, pp. 054004–054014, May, 2011.

[3] M. Klemm, "Acoustic Simulation and Characterization of Capacitive Micromachined Ultrasonic Transducers," Ph.D. dissertation, Dresden University of Technology, TUD Press, Dresden, Germany, 2017.

[4] S. Berg, "Capacitive Micromachined Ultrasonic Transducers," Ph.D. Dissertation, Dept. of Electronics and Telecommunications, Norwegian University of Science and Technology, Trondheim, Norway, 2012.

[5] E. Cianci, et al., "Fabrication Techniques in Micromachined Capacitive Ultrasonic Transducers and their Applications," in MEMS/NEMS Handbook, Springer, Boston, MA, C. Leondes (eds), 2006, pp. 353-382.

[6] S. Savoia, G. Caliano, and M. Pappalardo, "A CMUT Probe for Medical Ultrasonography: From Microfabrication to System Integration," *IEEE Transactions on Ultrasonics, Ferroelectrics, and Frequency Control*, vol. 59, no. 6, pp. 1127-1138, Jun.2012.

[7] A, Unamuno, "New Applications for Ultrasound Technology Through CMUTs," Fraunhofer IPMS, Presentations at the joint event MNBS 2013 and EPoSS general assembly annual forum 2013/eposs-annual-forum-2013-26-september-2013, [Online]. Available from: http://www.smart-systems-integration.org Accessed on: Oct. 5, 2020.

[8] M. Rahman, J. Hernandez, and S. Chowdhury, "An Improved Analytical Method to Design CMUTs with Square Diaphragms," *IEEE Transactions on Ultrasonics, Ferroelectrics, and Frequency Control*," vol. 60, no. 4, pp. 834-845, Apr. 2013.

[9] A. Bakhtazad and S. Chowdhury, "An evaluation of optical profilometry techniques for CMUT characterization," *Microsystem Technologies*, Springer, vol. 25, pp. 3627-3642, Sep. 2019.

[10] Nanosurf AG, Switzerland, "Flex-Axiom The most flexible AFM for materials research," [Online]. Available from: https://www.nanosurf.com/downloads/Nanosurf-Flex-Axiom-Brochure.pdf, Accessed on: Oct 2, 2020.

[11] L. Chaurette, N. Cheng, and B. Stuart, "Atomic Force Microscopy," University of British Columbia, [Online]. Available from: https://phas.ubc.ca/~berciu/TEACHING/PHYS502/PROJECTS/AFM16.pdf, Accessed on: Oct 2, 2020.

[12] A. Bakhtazad, R. Manwar, and S. Chowdhury, "Fabrication and Characterization of Sealed Cavities Realized by Adhesive Wafer Bonding with Dry Etched Cyclotene," *Microsystem Technologies*, Springer, vol. 21, issue 11, pp. 1-8, Jan. 2015.

[13] Biomedical Engineering Reference In-Depth Information, "Atomic Force Microscopy, " [Online]. Available from: http://what-when-how.com/Tutorial/topic-55iija/Atomic-Force-Microscopy-10.html, Accessed on: Sep. 4, 2020.

[14] Park Systems, "How AFM Woks, [Online]. Available from: https://parksystems.com/medias/nano-academy/how-afm-works, Accessed on: Oct. 4, 2020.

[15] C. Serra-Rodríguez, Re: Can we compare average roughness values obtained from AFM and Optical Profilometer? [Online]. Available from: https://www.researchgate.net/post/Can_we_compare_average_roughness_values_obtained_from_AFM_and_Optical_Profilometer2/52d6cd50d2fd64580c8b45c3/citation/download. 2014, Accessed on: Sep. 10, 2020.

[16] M. Raposo, Q. Ferreira, and P. Ribeiro, "A Guide for Atomic Force Microscopy Analysis of Soft-Condensed Matter", *Modern Research and Educational Topics in Microscopy*," vol. 1, pp. 758-769, Jan. 2007.

[17] Nanosurf AG, Switzerland, Nanosurf FlexAFM Operating Instructions for SPM Control Software, Version 3.1, July 2012. [Online]. Available from: http://www.uel.br/proppg/portalnovo/pages/arquivos/arquivos_gerais/espec/Nanosurf%20FlexAFM%20Operating%20Instructions.pdf, Accessed on: Sep. 5, 2020.

[18] P. Klapetek, D. Ne˘cas, and C. Anderson, "Gwyddion user guide," [Online]. Available from: http://gwyddion.net/documentation /user-guide-en/, Accessed on: Sep. 4, 2020.

Design and Modelling of a Piezoelectric Road Energy Harvester

Bin Wei
Department of Computer Science and Technology
Algoma University
Sault Ste Marie, Canada
Email: bin.wei@algomau.ca

Rahul Iyer
Department of Mechanical Engineering
University of Windsor
Windsor, Canada
Email: iyer112@uwindsor.ca

***Abstract*— The physical model of a piezoelectric road energy harvester is successfully illustrated in this work. The principle governing the design of the piezoelectric elements of the harvester has been explained in detail. The design of the piezoelectric elements has been determined by various simulations in Matlab, and the plots of which have been represented thoroughly. Based on the Matlab results, a physical model of the piezoelectric energy harvester has been successfully designed using SolidWorks. The dynamic analysis of the harvester is used to elucidate the operation of the design. Finally, the stress and displacements plots are used to validate the proposed design of the piezoelectric road energy harvester.**

Keywords - piezoelectric; road energy harvester; modelling.

I. INTRODUCTION

With the increase in fossil fuel usage, the imminent depletion of non-renewable sources of energy and the negative costs associated with it occurred as a consequence of the overall ecology [1]. The need for environmentally friendly and renewable energy sources has been on the rise for the best part of the past two decades. While solar and wind energies have proved to be immensely promising in being able to suffice more applications than previously envisioned [2]-[5], their true potential remains untapped by some countries that cannot boast of the same geological advantages as comparing to others [6]. Consequently, to remedy some of these difficulties, kinetic energy harvesting has garnered tremendous attention in recent years aided by the advancements made in the field of piezoelectricity.

A popular application of kinetic energy harvesting using the principles of piezoelectricity is the piezoelectric road energy harvester. The idea is to utilize the wasted kinetic energy emanated by vehicles on the road (vibrations) by converting it to electrical energy which may be used for other applications. The ability of piezoelectric materials to generate electric potential when subjected to ambient vibrations has been well documented in numerous pieces of past research [7]-[9].Piezoelectric energy generation from kinetic energy can be obtained by two major approaches: the cantilever beam tactic and the impact-based approach.

Piezoelectric cantilever beams have been found to be highly sensitive to minute ambient vibrations, thus generating power at a small scale, making it a viable option for potentially powering low power motion sensors, radar systems and speed detectors [10]. While the previous study considered the use of the principle of impedance matching to maximize power output from the piezoelectric cantilever beams, studies considering the use of piezoelectric beams fixed at both ends [11] have shown to produce much larger deformations and thus, marginally improving the power output of the energy harvesting system. Moreover, the efficiency of these harvesters is heavily dependent on the speed of the vehicles on the road which indicated the scope for improvement in terms of frequency tuning for covering larger distances. Apart from the vehicle velocity analysis, other practical considerations such as the position of the harvester along particular length of road, as well as the effect of road surface irregularities on power generation of a piezoelectric road harvester has given rise to new perspectives with regards to improving the efficiency of such harvesting systems [12]. Cantilever beam based piezoelectric energy harvesters also offer numerous opportunities for further research with regards to altering its individual components, especially the tip mass. The use of a single tip mass for multiple piezoelectric cantilevers [13] illustrates a much simpler circuit structure as it eliminated the use of multiple rectifier circuits, as well as made the system behaviour more lucid as the cantilever oscillations became much more predictable. As a result, power estimation for the system is readily obtainable.

The scientific inquiry into piezoelectric road energy harvesters has also led to improvements being made in the digital space, wherein empirical data may be easily compared with digitally computed results from software packages [14] that are specially dedicated to analysing and accruing road, environmental and piezoelectric material data over numerous years and thus, providing an increased degree of validity, which can aid future applications. Various pieces of research have also focused on the materials most suitable to amass maximum energy from the road harvesters, with complex composite films providing one of the best results in this domain [15].

Apart from piezoelectricity, electromagnetic approaches that can convert kinetic energy into usable forms of electricity (as road harvesters) have also been studied extensively in the past [16]. Moreover, these approaches have been further extended into the mobile domain as opposed to the stationary domain (road harvesters) wherein the heat energy dissipated by vehicle suspension systems especially, the shock absorbers has been electromagnetically converted into electrical energy by incorporating regenerative shock absorbers [17].

In this paper, the aim is to evaluate the performance of an impact based piezoelectric energy harvester consisting of cylindrical piezoelectric elements that are embedded into a robust steel structure that can endure the forces exerted by various vehicles passing on the road, which is the main contribution of this study. The actuation of the harvester is done through a separate hydraulic mechanism [18] with minor changes, which transmits the forces exerted by the vehicles into a hydraulic piston, which then stresses the piezoelectric block to cause electricity generation.

The structure of the paper is organized as follows: Section 2 presents the principle of the piezoelectric road energy harvester; analysis of the proposed piezoelectric road energy harvester is conducted in Section 3; Section 4 illustrates the design process of the piezoelectric module; stress analysis of the piezoelectric road energy harvester is conducted in Section 5; and finally the conclusion is given in Section 6.

II. THE PRINCIPLE

The piezoelectric material has been used in the form of a transformer model [19] as shown in Figure 1:

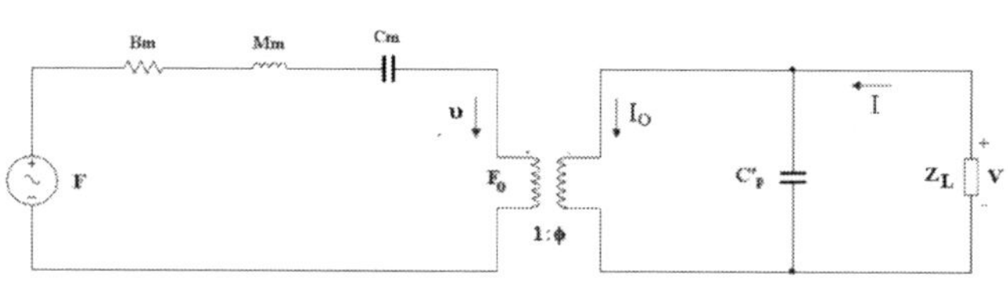

Figure 1. The piezoelectric generator transformer model

The transformer model illustrates two sides: the primary side and the secondary side. The primary side of the transformer uses the mechanical and dynamic properties of the piezoelectric material to model an analogous electrical representation, in which the damping constant of the piezoelectric material B_m is considered as a resistance, mass M_m as an inductor and the mechanical compliance C_m as a capacitor. The input source on the primary side is the input force F, which is induced mechanically. The resultant current on the primary side is the velocity of the piezoelectric layers caused due to the mechanical deformation corresponding to the applied force F. Fo represents the internal force responsible for the electrical energy generation on the secondary side of the transformer model.

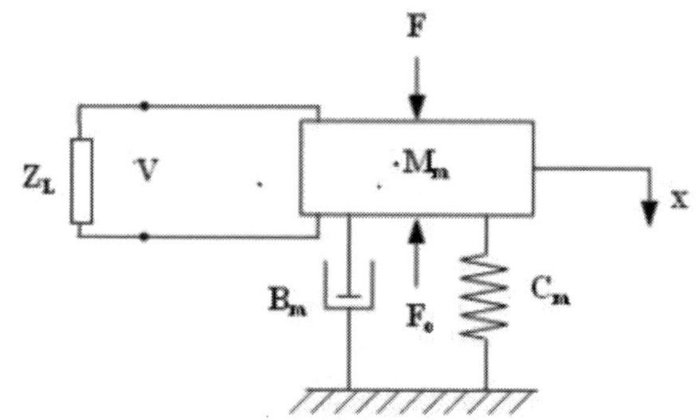

Figure 2. Mechanical realization of piezoelectric generator model

On the secondary side, Z_L represents the load connected to the piezoelectric model. C_P' is the blocked capacitance while V is the potential difference across the load Z_L. I is the resultant current generated while I_O is the current corresponding to the internal force Fo of the piezoelectric material. The mechanical realization of this model is shown in Figure 2.

III. ANALYSIS

The design of the piezoelectric cylinders is based on the simulations performed in Matlab. These simulations are performed taking the maximum possible force that can be exerted on the piezoelectric energy harvesting system into consideration, i.e., the force exerted by the weight of a loaded truck. The input force is in the form of two pulses, assuming that only the first two sets of wheels have passed over the piezoelectric energy harvesting system. Thus in theory, the bigger the vehicle, the larger is the power generated. However, the corresponding mechanical structure of the piezoelectric energy harvester has to be robust to endure the stresses exerted by such heavy vehicles, which will be discussed further in Section 5. The energy harvesting system considers six piezoelectric cells being embedded in one mechanical assembly.

A circular cross section for the piezoelectric material is deemed most appropriate for the piezoelectric energy harvester. This is because a cylindrical structure is much easier to manufacture for future mass production without incurring excessive production costs. The initial iterations take into consideration different diameters and thicknesses based on which power and voltage are calculated. For thickness ranging from 1 to 10 cm, the power plot is discontinuous as the curve would go back to zero soon after the first impact. Moreover, the plot for power generated for diameters ranging from 1 to 10 cm also shows tremendous variations. Hence, the thickness to area ratio is a critical factor in determining the optimum power generated, which is helpful in determining the dimensions of the piezoelectric cylinder.

The goal is to achieve sustained oscillations for the piezoelectric cylinder after impact in order to generate continuous power and thus facilitate continuous energy generation, which can later be used in various applications. Hence, further iterations are conducted by varying the thickness of the piezoelectric cylinder to up to 20 cm. The diameter of the cylinder is restricted to a value below 10 cm.

The most suitable results are obtained when the piezoelectric material is designed according to dimensions mentioned in Table 1, the result of which will be used to determine the resultant mean power over the time interval [0, 200] seconds.

TABLE 1. DIMENSIONS OF THE PIEZOELECTRIC CYLINDER

Diameter	6.5 cm
Thickness	18 cm

The resultant plots for input force, voltage and power generated versus time are shown in Figure 3.

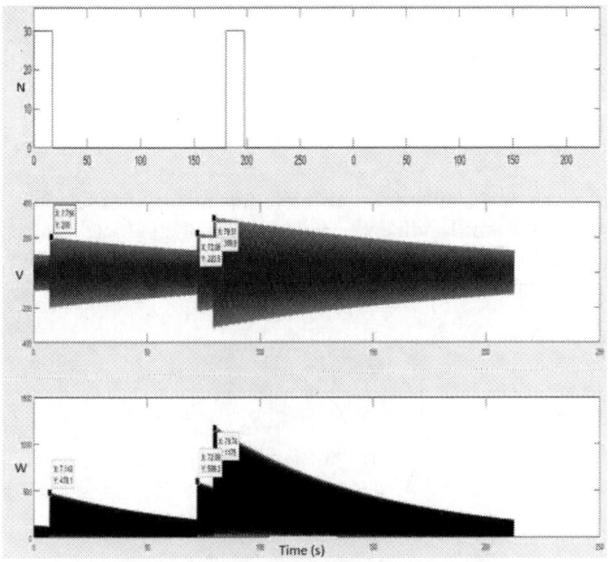

Figure 3. Input force, voltage, power versus time

The peak values obtained from Figure 4 for voltage and power at first impact are listed in Table 2.

TABLE II. RESULTANT PEAK VALUES FOR VOLTAGE AND POWER

Voltage	200 V
Power	478.1 W

According to the Table 1, the resultant mean power over the time interval [0, 200] seconds is also calculated as shown in Figure 4.

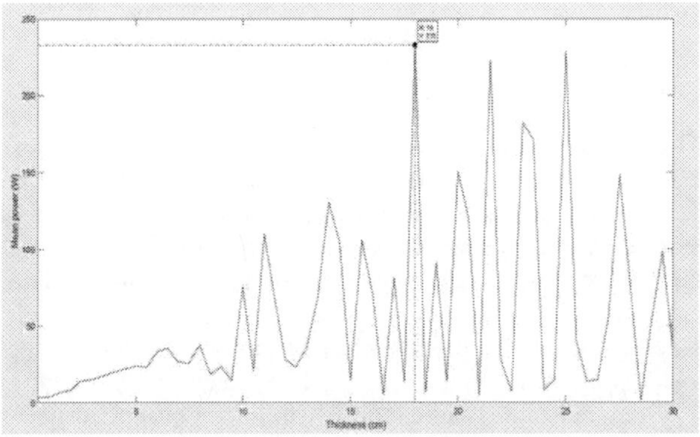

Figure 4. Calculation of mean power

Thus from Figure 4, it is clear that at thickness 18 cm, the mean power obtained is 233W. Further, using the optimization curve function in Matlab, Figure 3 is replotted to obtain the optimized values for power and voltage, which is shown in Figure 5 below.

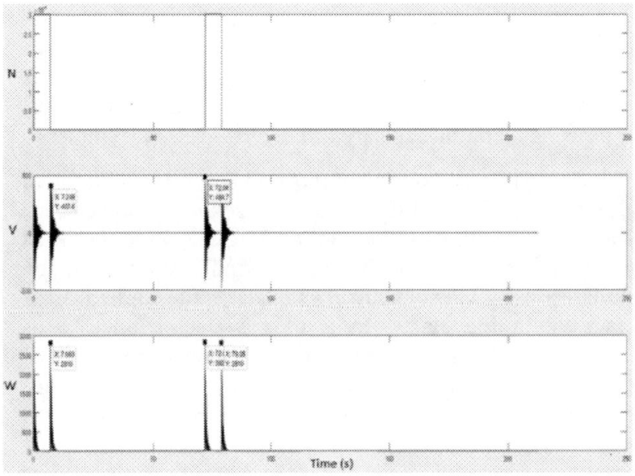

Figure 5. Optimized voltage and power versus time

TABLE III. RESULTANT PEAK VALUES FOR OPTIMIZED VOLTAGE AND POWER

Voltage	407.6V
Power	2810W

The optimized values of voltage and power after the first impact obtained from Figure 5 is shown in Table 3. For a value of maximum possible input force (weight of the vehicle), the corresponding power and voltage outputs are successfully calculated using Matlab.

IV. DESIGN OF THE PIEZOELECTRIC MODULE

The actual force exerted by the vehicle is a complex calculation owing to the effect of vehicle suspension systems and that of the module itself. The initial design of the piezoelectric road energy harvester are inclusive of a spring system which aided the movement of the pressuring plate back to its initial position. However, a problem identified with this design being that the tendency of the springs that causes an oscillating effect to the pressuring plate and thus, making the system unstable with poor feasibility. Consequently, a solution identified to this problem being that the inclusion of dampers so as to disintegrate the oscillations produced by the springs, and stabilize the spring back motion of the pressuring plate. Thus, the dynamic action of the entire system is more controlled with added protection offered to the piezoelectric cylinders through energy dissipation carried out by the dampers.

However, the power generation potential of the piezoelectric cylinders is predicated mainly on the impact-based approach of the pressuring plate caused by the movement of vehicles on the road. The inclusion of dampers causes the movement of the pressuring plate to slow down with the entire scenario liable to be analysed in a quasi-static state rather than an impulsive impact based state. This affects the power generation capacity of the piezoelectric cylinders.

The best solution to combat this problem is to make use of an embedded system of thick steel block and piezoelectric cylinders. The elasticity modulus of steel could be used favourably to perform the spring and damping action simultaneously. This of course, depends on the applied stress being within the elastic limit of the steel. Hence, it is imperative to design the steel block in a manner in which its height exceeded that of the piezoelectric cylinders. Due to this fact, the pressuring plate would first make contact with the steel during the impact while causing it to elastically compress and gradually exposing the piezoelectric cylinders to the input stress. This ensures the durability of the piezoelectric cylinders by preventing cracking and sudden buckling due to high value of the input stress (impulse). The proposed method thus advocates the use of cheap and easily available grade of steel, which can be easily replaced as part of planned and regular maintenance routines.

The grade of steel used for the steel block is AISI 304 stainless steel. This grade of stainless steel is the most commonly used and cheapest grade of steel available commercially. The material properties for AISI 304 stainless steel is shown in Table 4.

TABLE IV. PROPERTIES OF AISI 304 STAINLESS STEEL

	Physical properties	metric
1.	Density	8 g/cc
2.	Hardness B	70
3.	Ultimate tensile strength	505 Mpa
4.	Yield tensile strength	215 Mpa
5.	Modulus of elasticity	200 Gpa
6.	Poisson's ratio	0.29
7.	Shear modulus	86 Gpa

The material used for the piezoelectric cylinders is PZT-5H. The material properties for PZT-5H is shown in Table 5.

TABLE V. MATERIAL PROPERTIES OF PZT-5H

1.	Density	7.4 g/cc
2.	D33	585e-12
3.	K33	0.59
4.	K(eff)	0.53
5.	Modulus of Rupture	61.5 MPa
6.	Damping Constant	5e-8

The selection of the PZT-5H material is based on the comparatively higher values of D33 (piezoelectric coefficient), K33 (piezoelectric coupling coefficient) and K(eff) (effective piezoelectric coupling coefficient) against the other grades of commercially available piezoelectric material [20]. The material PZT-5H is specifically picked considering the application used in this study.

4.1. Dynamics of the system

In order to calculate the acceleration of the piezoelectric bodies within the module when stressed by the vehicle above, it is essential to consider the following 2-DOF mass and spring damper system, as shown in Figure 6.

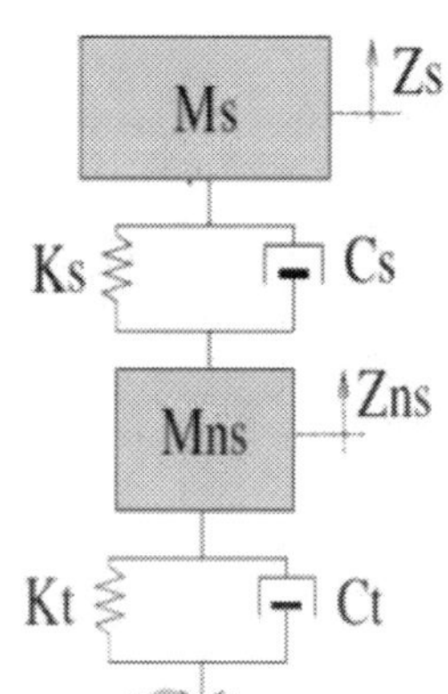

Figure 6. 2 DOF mass-spring-damper system

In Figure 6, Ms represents the mass of the vehicle while K_s and C_s resemble the spring constant and damping constant for its suspension system, respectively. Similarly, M_{ns} represents the combined mass of the piezoelectric cylinders within the module while K_t and C_t resemble its spring constant and damping constant, respectively.

The force exerted due to the vertical acceleration of the vehicle suspension system is the same force responsible for stressing the piezoelectric material within the module. The free body diagram of the two masses in the system yields the following two equations:

$$M_s \ddot{Z}_s = K_s(Z_{ns} - Z_s) + C_s(\dot{Z}_{ns} - \dot{Z}_s) \quad (1)$$

$$M_{ns} \ddot{Z}_{ns} = -K_t Z_{ns} - C_t \dot{Z}_{ns} - M_s \ddot{Z}_s \quad (2)$$

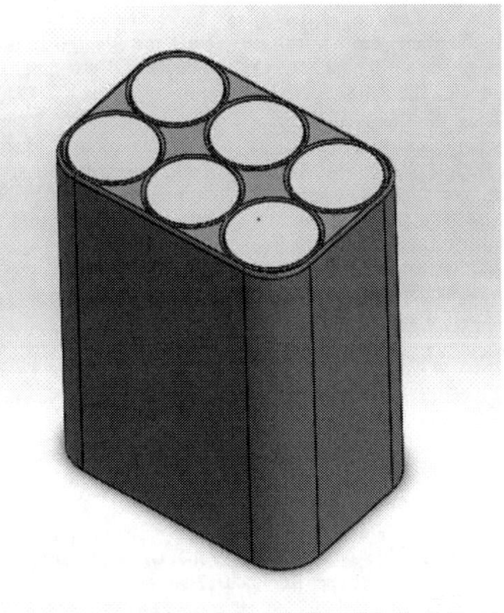

Figure 7. Piezoelectric energy harvester module

Thus, the acting force on the piezoelectric module depends on the vertical acceleration of the vehicle during motion. The module design is shown in Figure 7.

V. STRESS ANALYSIS OF HARVESTER

Stress analysis of the module was essential in determining the mechanical feasibility of the proposed design [21]. The acting force on the upper plate of the module was fixed as per the value discussed in the previous section. The stress analysis of the piezoelectric cylinders is as shown in Figure 8. From this dynamic analysis, it is shown that the stress exerted on the piezoelectric cylinder is approximately 0.8 MPa, which is less than the modulus of rupture for the PZT-5H material. Hence, the piezoelectric cylinders can be expected to operate as expected according to the calculations presented in the previous section.

Figure 9 represents the displacement plot for the piezoelectric cylinders under applied stress. Hence, the maximum displacement occurs at the upper layer of the piezoelectric cylinder with a value of approximately 2.4e-2 mm (as expected). The stress analysis of the steel block with the upper pressuring plate is as shown in Figure 10. The maximum stress experienced by the steel block is within the elastic limit of the material. Thus, the validity of the design is verified.

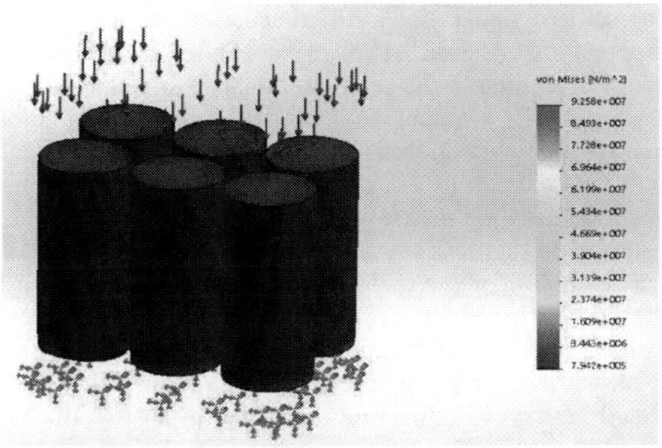

Figure 8. Stress analysis for piezoelectric cylinders

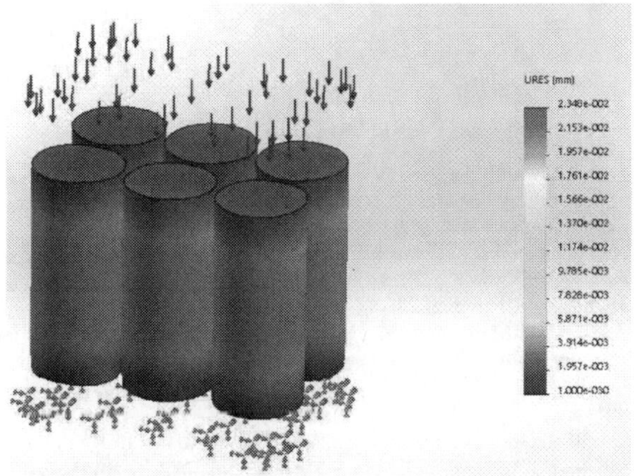

Figure 9. Displacement plot for piezoelectric cylinders

Figure 10. Stress plot for steel block with upper plate

VI. CONCLUSION

The material selections for the steel block and the piezoelectric cylinders are justified according to the method of application desired. The piezoelectric cylinders are designed according to the value of the input force (weight of the vehicle). For a value of maximum possible input force (weight of the vehicle), the corresponding power and voltage outputs are successfully calculated using Matlab. The average power over the time interval [0, 200] seconds, as a result of this design is theoretically obtained to be close to 233W, which is larger than that of the previous attempts. The design of the energy harvester is successfully validated via stress analysis in SolidWorks. The actual calculation for input force is successfully illustrated in Section 4 of this study. The expected price of the proposed energy generator is approximately $550 and the expected life of the proposed device is about 5 years. Future work will focus on a proposition of installation method of converter in real situation, which can hold much more load.

REFERENCES

[1] J. Szargut, A. Ziebik, and W. Stanek, "Depletion of the non-renewable natural exergy resources as a measure of the ecological cost", Energy Conversion and Management, Vol. 43, pp. 119-1163, 2002.

[2] N. Papamanolis N, "An overview of solar energy applications in buildings in Greece", International Journal of Sustainable Energy, Vol. 35, no. 8, pp. 814-823, 2016.

[3] A. Jamar, Z. Majid, W. Azmi, M. Norhafana, and A. Razak, "A review of water heating system for solar energy applications", International Communications in Heat and Mass Transfer, Vol. 76, pp. 178-187, 2016.

[4] C. Abbey and G. Joos, "Supercapacitor Energy Storage for Wind Energy Applications", IEEE Transactions on Industry Applications, vol. 43, no. 3. pp. 769 – 776, 2007.

[5] L. Mishnaevsky, "Composite materials for wind energy applications: micromechanical modelling and future directions", Computational Mechanics, vol. 50, no. 2, pp. 195-207, 2012.

[6] R. Pravalie, C. Patriche, and G. Bandoc, "Spatial assessment of solar energy potential at global scale. A geographical approach", Journal of Cleaner Production, vol. 209, pp. 692-721, 2019.

[7] C. Li, B. Li, X. Yang, and M. Meng, "Finite element analysis of a novel piezoelectric arch energy harvester", 2015 IEEE International Conference on Information and Automation, Lijiang, China, pp. 2749-2754, 2015.

[8] C. Yang, Y. Song, M. Woo, J. Eom, J. Song, J. Kim, T. Lee, J. Choi, and T. Sung, "Feasibility study of impact-based piezoelectric road energy harvester for wireless sensor networks in smart highways", Sensors and Actuators A: Physical, vol. 261, pp. 317-324, 2017.

[9] S. Gareh, B. Kok, C. Uttraphan, K. Thong, and A. Borhana, "Evaluation of piezoelectric energy harvester outcomes in road traffic applications", in IET Clean Energy and Technology Conference, Kuala Lumpur, Malaysia, pp. 1-5, 2016.

[10] Y. Song, C. Yang, S. Hong, S. Hwang, J. Kim, J. Choi, S. Ryu, and T. Sung, "Road energy harvester designed as a macro-power source using the piezoelectric effect". International Journal of Hydrogen Energy, vol. 41, pp. 12563-12568, 2016.

[11] H. Yang, L. Wang, Y. Hou, and M. Guo, "Development in stacked-array-type piezoelectric energy harvester in asphalt pavement", Journal of Materials in Civil Engineering, vol. 29, no. 11, p. 04017224, 2017.

[12] Z. Zhang, H. Xiang, and Z. Shi, "Theoretical Modelling on Piezoelectric Energy Harvesting from Bridges Considering Roadway Surface Irregularities", In Transportation Research Congress 2016: Innovations in Transportation Research Infrastructure, Reston, VA: American Society of Civil Engineers, pp. 673-684, 2016.

[13] Y. Song, C. Yang, S. Hwang, J. Kim, and T. Sung, "Design of Road Energy Harvester with Multiple Piezoelectric Cantileve Beams and a Single Tip Mass", in 5th International Conference on Renewable Energy Research and Applications, Birmingham, UK, pp. 12563-12568, 2016

[14] F. Jiménez, M. Rodriguez, D. Alnoso, and J. Frutos, "Virtual instrument to obtain an optimal linear model for piezoelectric elements involved in road traffic energy harvesting", Computer Standards and Interfaces, vol. 51, pp. 1-13, 2017.

[15] V. Vivekananthan, N. Alluri, Y. Purusothaman, A. Chandrasekhar, and S. Kim, "A flexible, planar energy harvesting device for scavenging road side waste mechanical energy via the synergistic piezoelectric response of K0.5Na0.5NbO3-BaTiO3/PVDF composite films", Nanoscale, The Royal Society of Chemistry, pp. 15122-15130, 2017.

[16] Z. Zhang, X. Zhang, Y. Rasim, C. Wang, B. Du, and Y. Yuan, "Design, modelling and practical tests on a high-voltage kinetic energy harvesting (EH) system for a renewable road tunnel based on linear alternators", Applied Energy, vol. 164, pp. 152-161, 2016.

[17] M. Abdelkareem, L. Xu, M. Ali, A. Elagouz, J. Mi, S. Guo, Y. Liu, and L. Zuo, "Vibration energy harvesting in automotive suspension system: A detailed review", Applied Energy, vol. 229, pp. 672-699, 2018.

[18] T. Ching, D. Tsai, and C. Hsiao, "Developing a mechanical roadway system for waste energy capture of vehicles and electric generation", Applied Energy, vol. 92, pp. 1-8, 2012.

[19] S. Platt, S. Farritor, and H. Haider, "On Low-Frequency Electric Power generation with PZT ceramics", ASME Transactions on Mechatronics, vol. 10, no. 2, pp. 240-252, 2005.

[20] M. Hooker, "Properties of PZT-Based Piezoelectric Ceramics Between-150 and 250°C", National Aeronautics and Space Administration, CR-1998-208707 report, 1998.

[21] D. Zhang and B Wei, "Interactions and optimizations analysis between stiffness and workspace of 3-UPU robotic mechanism", Measurement Science Review 17.2, pp. 83-92, 2017.

VLC Connected Cooperative Driving

Manuel Augusto Vieira, Manuela Vieira, Paula Louro,
ADETC/ISEL/IPL,
R. Conselheiro Emídio Navarro, 1959-007
Lisboa, Portugal
CTS-UNINOVA
Quinta da Torre, Monte da Caparica, 2829-516,
Caparica, Portugal

e-mail: mv@isel.ipl.pt, mv@isel.pt, plouro@deetc.isel.pt

Pedro Vieira
ADETC/ISEL/IPL,
R. Conselheiro Emídio Navarro, 1959-007
Lisboa, Portugal
Instituto das Telecomunicações
Instituto Superior Técnico, 1049-001,
Lisboa, Portugal
e-mail: pvieira@isel.pt

***Abstract*—Using a new concept of request/response in a two-way-to-way traffic light controlled crossroad, the redesign of the trajectories can be accomplished by the application of methods for navigation, guidance and combination of expert knowledge of vehicle road traffic control. In this work, the bi-directional communication between the Vehicles (V2V), between vehicles and Infrastructures (V2I)) is performed through Visible Light Communication (VLC), using the street lamps and the traffic signaling to broadcast the information. Data is encoded, modulated and converted into light signals emitted by the transmitters. Tetra-chromatic white sources are used, providing a different data channel for each chip. As receivers and decoders, SiC Wavelength Division Multiplexer (WDM) devices, with light filtering properties, are considered. A Vehicle-to-Everything (V2X) traffic scenario is proposed, and bidirectional communication between the infrastructure and the vehicles is tested, using the VLC request/response concept. A phasing traffic flow is developed as a proof of concept. The experimental results confirm the cooperative VLC architecture. A significant increase in traffic throughput with the least dependency on infrastructure is achieved.**

Keywords- Vehicular Communication; Light Fidelity, Visible Light Communication, white LEDs, SiC photodetectors, OOK modulation scheme, Traffic control.

I. INTRODUCTION

Connected Autonomous Vehicles (CAVs) [1][2][3]. To increase the efficiency of traffic management and control, many efforts have been made. Two technical challenges were considered: trajectory redesign and real-time traffic planning. Our goal is to increase the safety and throughput of traffic intersections using VLC connected cooperative driving.

For vehicular communications, two emerging technological trends in the vehicular industry are reshaping the physical world, which are corresponding to the self-driving and remote driving technologies [4][5]. To enable both driving technologies, massive Vehicle-to-Everything (V2X) communications will be studied and incorporated in 6G [6]. V2X communication technologies give new possibilities to autonomous cars, since they create the opportunity for constant cooperation among different vehicles and between vehicles and intelligent road infrastructure, thus making tasks like route planning and accident avoidance much easier. Communication between fixed locations and vehicles is essential to transfer information in real time. Here, the communication is performed through VLC [7][8] using the street lamps and the traffic signaling to broadcast the information.

The proposed system is composed of several transmitters, the street lights and the traffic signals, which transmit map information and traffic messages required to the moving vehicles. Data is encoded, modulated and converted into light signals emitted by the transmitters. Then, this information is transferred to receivers installed in the vehicles. Tetra-chromatic white sources are used providing a different data channel for each chip. The receiver modules include a photodetector based on a tandem a-SiC:H/a-Si:H pin/pin light controlled filter [9][10][11].

In this work, a two-way communication between vehicles and the traffic lights is implemented, using VLC. The redesign of the trajectory, inside a complex intersection, is presented. Street lamps and traffic lights broadcast the information. The On-vehicle VLC receivers decode the messages and perform V2V distance measurements. An I2X traffic scenario is proposed and characterized. A phasing traffic flow is developed as a Proof-of-Concept (PoC). The arrival of vehicles is controlled and scheduled to cross the intersection at times that minimize delays. Delays between left-turns and forward movements are also allocated. The simulated results confirm that the redesign of the intersection and its management through the cooperative request/response VLC architecture allows to increase the safety and to decrease the trip delay.

In this paper, a traffic scenario for a light controlled crossroad is proposed, along with the transmitter to receiver setup. The paper is organized as follow. After the introduction (Section I), in Section II, the performance of a cooperative driving system is analyzed. To achieve cooperative vehicular communications (I2X), streams of messages containing the ID physical address of the emitters are used, transmitting a codeword that is received and decoded by the SiC pin/pin devices. As a PoC, in Section

III, a traffic scenario with bidirectional cooperative communication between the infrastructures and the vehicles is presented and tested. Finally, in Section IV, conclusions are addressed.

II. VEHICULAR COMMUNICATION

Vehicular communication using visible light is analysed using redesign concepts were the request/response idea between the vehicles and the infrastructures is implemented.

A. Redesign Concepts

The redesign of the traffic-actuated controller uses a vehicle request/respond message information.

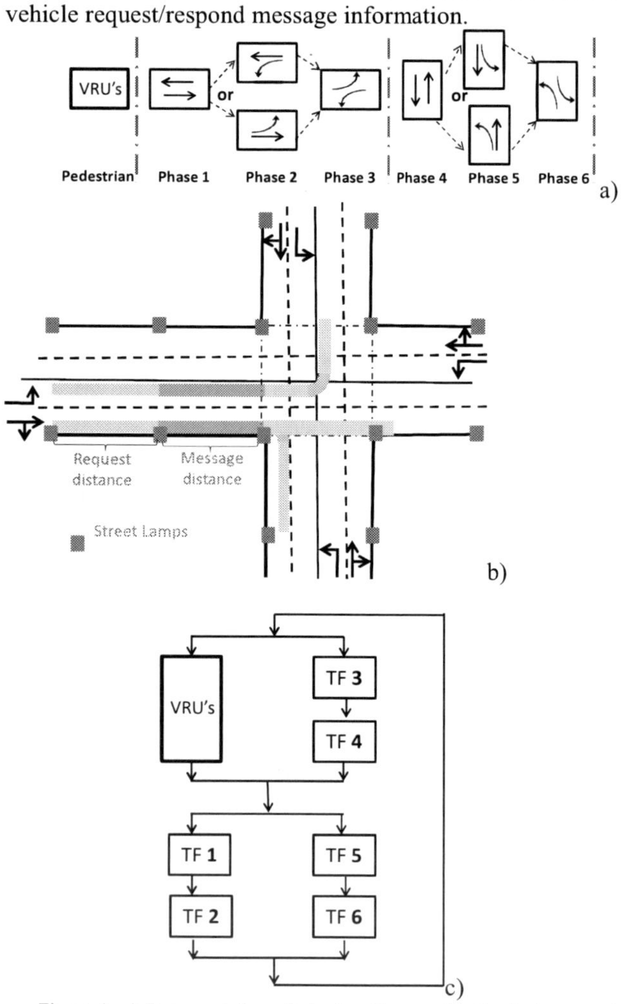

Figure 1. a) Representation of phasing diagram. b) Physical area and channelization. c) Timing function configuration.

This information generates phase durations appropriate to accommodate the demand on each cycle. Examples of the representation of a redesigned phasing diagram, a functional area with two-way-two-way intersection and a timing function configuration are presented in Figure 1. In Figure 1a, a phasing diagram is displayed. Each Timing Function (TF) controls only one movement. Since two movements can proceed simultaneously without conflict as shown in Figure 1b, hence two of the timing functions will always have simultaneous control, as exemplified in Figure 1c. The problem that the traffic-actuated intersection manager has to solve is to allocate the reservations among a set of drivers in a way that a specific objective is maximized. Signal timing involves the determination of the appropriate cycle length and apportionment of time among competing movements and phases. The timing apportionment is constrained by minimum "green" times that must be imposed to provide pedestrians to cross and to ensure that motorist expectancy is not violated.

The use of both navigation and lane control signs to communicate lane restrictions is demanding. Downstream from that location (request distance in Figure 1b), lane restrictions should be obeyed. Vehicles may receive their intentions (*e.g.*, whether they will turn left or continue straight and turn right) or specifically the need to interact with a trafic controler at a nearby crossroad (message distance in Figure 1b). In the sequence, a traffic message coming from a transmitter nearby the crossroad will inform the drivers of the location of their destination (*i.e.*, the intended intersection exit leg).

B. Virtual V2X scenario .

To build the I2V, it is proposed a simplified cluster of unit square cells in an orthogonal topology that fills all the service area. To realize both the communication and the street illumination, white light tetra-chromatic sources are used providing a different data channel for each chip. At each node, only one chip of the LED is modulated for data transmission, the Red (R: 626 nm), the Green (G: 530 nm), the Blue (B: 470 nm) or the Violet (V) while the others provide constant current for white perception. Thus, each transmitter, $X_{i,j}$, carries its own color, X, (RGBV) as well as its horizontal and vertical ID position in the surrounding network (*i,j*). In the PoC, was assumed that the crossroad is located in the interception of line 2 with column 3, and the emitters at the nodes along the roadside (Figure 2).

The VLC photosensitive receiver is a double pin/pin photodetector based on a tandem heterostructure, p-i'(a - SiC:H)-n/p-i(a-Si:H)-n. [12][13]. To receive the I2V information from several transmitters, the receiver must be located at the overlap of the circles that set the transmission range of each transmitter. The nine possible overlaps are displayed in Figure 2 for each unit square cell. When a probe vehicle enters the streetlight´s capture range, the receiver replies to the light signal, and assigns a unique ID and the traffic message [14].

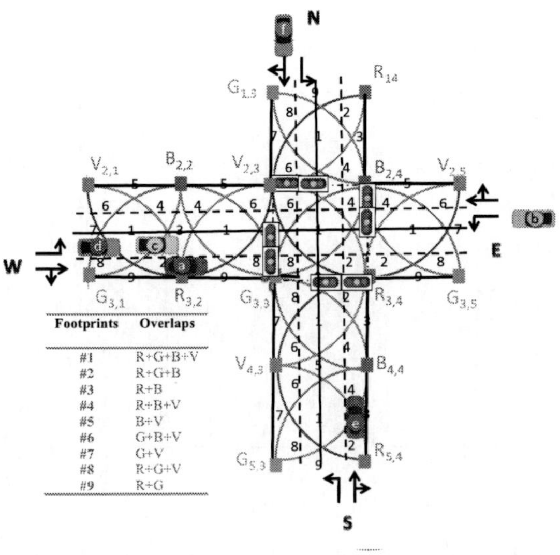

Figure 2 .V2X lighting plan model and generated joint footprints in a crossroad (LED array=RGBV color spots).

Four traffic flows were considered: One from West (W) with three vehicles ("a", "c", "d") approaching the crossroad, Vehicle *a* with straight movement and Vehicle *c* and Vehicle *d* with left turn only. In the second flow, Vehicle *b* from East (E), approaches the interception with left turn only. In the third flow, Vehicle *e*, oncoming from South (S), has e right-turn approach. Finally, in the fourth flow, Vehicle *f*, coming from North, goes straight. Using the I2V communication, each street lamp (transmitter) sends a message, which is received and processed by a SiC receiver, located at the vehicle's rooftop. Using the headlights as transmitters, the information is resent to a leader vehicle (V2V) or, depending on the predefined occupied lane, a "request" message to go forward or turn right (right lane) or to turn left (left lane) is sent directly to a crossroad receiver (V2I), at the traffic light, interconnected to a local manager that feeds one or more signal heads. For crossroad coordination, a emitting local controller located at the light signal, sends a "response" message to the intersection approaching vehicles. In the following, bidirectional communication is stablished (V2I2V).

To build the V2V system, the follower sends the message that is received by the leader and can be retransmitted to the next car or to the infrastructure [15]. The leader vehicle infers the drive distance and the relative speed between them [16]. This information can be directed to the next car (V2V) or to an infrastructure (V2I).

For the intersection manager crossing coordination, the vehicle and the intersection manager exchange information through two specific types of messages, "request" (V2I) and "response" (I2V). Inside the request distance, an approach "request" is sent, using as emitter the headlights. To receive the "requests", two different receivers are located at the same traffic light, facing the cross roads (local controller of the traffic light). The "request" contains all the information that is necessary for a vehicle's space-time reservation for its intersection crossing. Intersection manager uses this information to convert it in a sequence of timed rectangular spaces that each assigned vehicle needs to occupy the intersection. An intersection manager's acknowledge is sent from the traffic signal over the facing receiver to the in car application of the head vehicle. The response includes both the infrastructure and the vehicle identifications and the "confirmed vehicle" message. Once the response is received (message distance in Figure 1b), the vehicle is required to follow the occupancy trajectories (footprint regions, Figure 2) provided by the intersection manager. If a request has any potential risk of collision with all other vehicles that have already been approved to cross the intersection, the control manager only sends back to the vehicle (V2I) the "response" after the risk of conflict is exceeded.

C. *Coding/decoding Techniques*

To encode the messages, an on-off keying (OOK) modulation scheme was used. The codification of the optical signals is synchronized and includes the information related to the ID position of the transmitters and the message to broadcast. We have considered a 32 bits codification as described in Figure 3.

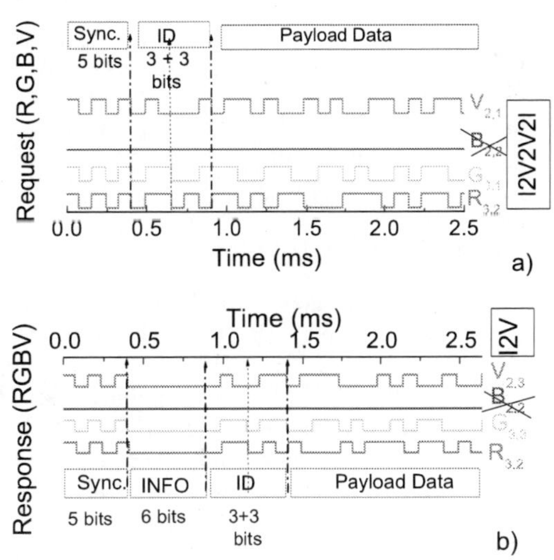

Figure 3 Frame structure representations. a) Codification used to drive the headlights of a vehicle in a request message from footprint #8. $R_{3,2}$, $G_{3,1}$, and $V_{2,1}$ are the transmitted node packet, in a time slot .b) Encoded message response of the controller to the request message of the vehicle in positio #8 ($R_{3,2}$, $G_{3,1}$, and $V_{2,1}$).

Each frame is divided into three or four blocks depending on the kind of transmitter: street lamps, headlamps (Figure 3a) or traffic light (Figure 3b). We assigned the first block to the synchronization (SYNC) in a [10101] pattern and the last one to the message to transmit (Payload Data). A stop bit is used at the end of each frame. Thus, $R_{3,2}$, $G_{3,1}$, and V_{21} are the transmitted node packets, in a time slot by the headlamps. In Figure 3b, the second block (INFO) in a pattern [000000] means that a response message is being sent by the controller manager. Here, the signal controller responds to the request of the vehicle located in position # 8 ($R_{3,2}$, $G_{3,3}$, and V_{23}) at the request time. This response is received in the unit cell adjacent to the crossroad (message distance, Figure 1b) that shares a common node ($R_{3,2}$) with the request distance (see Figure 2).

In Figure 4, a MUX signal due to the joint transmission of four R, G, B and V optical signals, in a data frame, is displayed. The bit sequence (on the top of the figure) was chosen to allow all the *on/off* sixteen possible combinations of the four input channels (2^4).

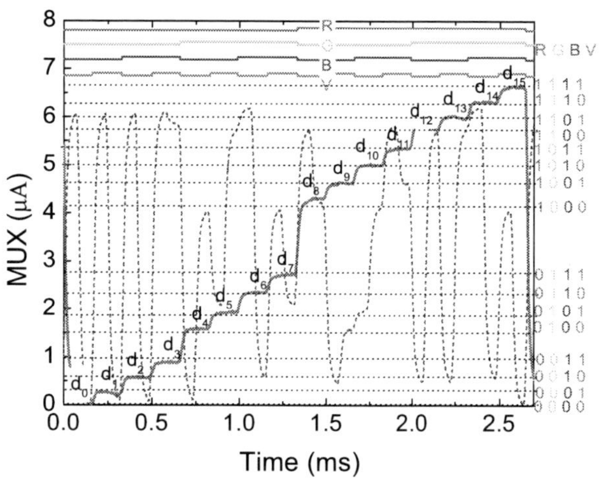

Figure 4. MUX signal of the calibrated cell. On the top the transmitted channels packets [R, G, B, V] are depicted. A received MUX signal is also superimposed to exemplify the decoding algorithm.

Results show that the code signal presents as much separated levels as the *on/off* possible combinations of the input channels, allowing decoding the transmitted information [9]. All the levels (d_0-d_{15}) are pointed out at the correspondent levels, and displayed as horizontal dotted lines. In the right hand side, the match between MUX levels and the 4 bits binary code assigned to each level is shown. For demonstration of the decoding technique, the signal transmitted in Figure 3a and received, in the same frame of time, is also added (dotted curve). Hence, the signal can be decoded by assigning each output level (d_0-d_{15}) to a 4- digit binary code [X_R, X_G, X_B, X_V], with X=1 if the channel is *on* and X=0 if it is *off*.

III. VEHICULAR COMMUNICATION

Vehicular communication based on LED assisted navigation is analyzed and the proof of concept presented.

A. Led assisted navigation, position and travel direction

In Figure 5, for a I2V communication, the normalized MUX signals acquired by a receiver at the crossroad, in positions #1, #2, #4, #6 or #8, confirms the decoding process.

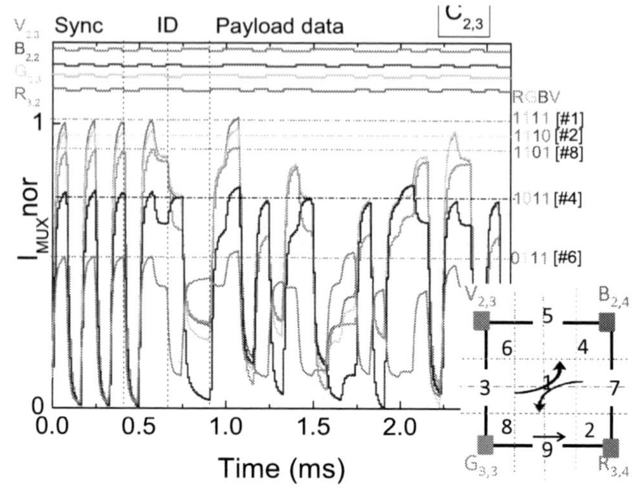

Figure 5. Normalized MUX signals acquired by a receiver at the crossroad, in positions #1, #2, #4, #6 or #8 On the top the transmitted channels packets [R, G, B, V] are decoded.

On the right hand side of the figure, the match between MUX levels and the 4 bits binary code ascribed to each higher level is shown. Decoding, when the four channels overlap (#1), is set on the top of the figure to direct into the packet sent by each node. After decoding the MUX signals, and taking into account, the frame structure (Figure 3), the position of the receiver in the unit cell and its ID in the network is revealed [17]. The footprint position comes directly from the synchronism block, where all the received channels are, simultaneously, *on* or *off* and is pointed out in the right hand of Figure 5. For instance, in #4 the maximum amplitude detected corresponds to the binary word [1011], meaning that it has received the joint transmission from the red, blue and violet channels. Each decoded message carries, also, the transmitter's node address. So, the next block of six bits gives it ID. In position #4 the network location of the transmitters are $R_{3,4}$ [011;100], $B_{2,4}$ [010;100] and $V_{2,3}$ [010;011]. The last block is reserved for the traffic message (Payload data). The stop bit (0) is used always at the end of each frame.

To compute the point-to-point along a path, we need the data along the path. Taking into account Figure 1 and Figure 5, in this example, Vehicle *a* enters the crossroad in position #8 and it goes straight to position #2 (Phase1, TF1), while vehicle *c* turn left, moving across position 1 (Phase2, TF2). In Phase3, TF3, Vehicle *b,* coming from East and Vehicle *d* coming from West, both turn left. The speed of Vehicle *b* was reduced, maintaining a safe distance between Vehicle *b* and Vehicle *a.* Results show that, as the receiver moves between generated point regions, the received information pattern changes. The vehicle speed can be calculated by measuring the actual travelled distance overtime, using the ID's transmitters tracking. Two measurements are required: distance and elapsed time. The distance is fixed while the elapsed time will be obtained through the instants where the number of received channels changes. Between two consecutive data sets, there is a navigation data bit transition (channel is missing or added). It was observed that when the receiver moves from #8 to # 2 (Figure 7) one ID channels was lost ($B_{2,4}$) and one are added ($V_{2,3}$). Here, the 4-bynary bit code has changed from [1101] to [1110] while Vehicle *c* and *d* change theirs from [1111] to [0011] and Vehicle *b* to [1100]. The spacing between reference points is fixed while the correspondent time integrated by the receiver varies and depends on the vehicle's speed. The receivers compute the geographical position in the successive instants (path) and infer the vehicle's speed. In the following, this data will be transmitted to another leader vehicle through the V2V communication or to control manager at the traffic light through V2I.

B. Cooperative system and phasing diagram

To model the worst-case scenario, vehicles approaching the intersection from different flows are assumed to have a conflicting trajectory (Figure 2). Two instants are considered for each vehicle, the request time (t) and the response time (t'). All the requests contain vehicle positions and approach speeds. If a follower exists (Vehicle *d*), the request message from its leader includes the position and speed previously received by V2V. This information alerts the controller to a later request message (V2I), confirmed by the follow vehicle. In the PoC we have assumed that $t_a<t_c<t_d$, and $t_a<t_b<t_c$.

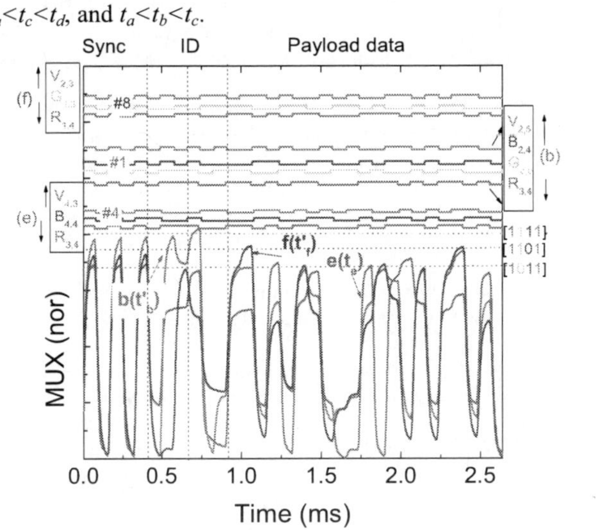

Figure 6. MUX signals and the assigned decoded messages (at the top of the figure) from vehicles *b*, *e* and *f* at different request and response times (I2V).

As an example, in Figure 6, the I2V MUX signals received and decode (on the top of the figure) by the receivers of the vehicles *b*, *e* and *f* are also displayed at request (t_e) and (t'_b and t'_f) response times. In the right side, the received channels for each vehicle are identified by its 4-digit binary codes and associated positions in the unit cell After decoding we have assigned position #4 ($R_{3,4}\,G_{4,4}\,V_{4,3}$) for Vehicle *e*, position #1 ($R_{3,4}\,G_{3,5}\,B_{2,4}\,V_{2,5}$) for Vehicle *b* and position #8 ($R_{1,4}\,G_{1,3}\,V_{2,3}$) to Vehicle *f*, respectively at theirs request and response times t_e , t'_b and t'_f . Here, $t'_e<t'_f$.

C. Traffic Signal Phasing in a V2X Communication

A phasing diagram and a timing function configuration were presented in Figure 1, for functional areas with two-way-two-way intersection. A traffic scenario was simulated (Figure 2) using the new concept of VLC request/response messages. A brief look into the process of timing traffic signals is given in Figure 7.

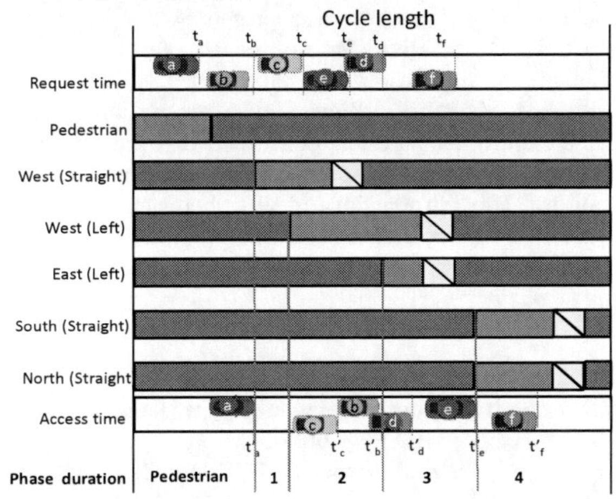

Figure 7 Requested phasing of traffic flows: pedestrian phase, Phase 1 (W straight flow), Phase 2 (W straight and left flows), Phase 3(W and E left flows), Phase 4 (N and S straight flows). $t_{[x]}$ is the request time from the Vehicle *x* and $t'_{[X]}$ the correspondent response time from the manage controller.

Redesign traffic-actuated controller uses *a*, *b*, *c*, *d*, *e* and *f* vehicles requesting and responding message information to generate phase durations appropriate to accommodate the demand on each cycle. Each driving vehicle is assigned an individualized time to request (*t*) and access (*t'*) the intersection. The exclusive pedestrian stage, "Walk" interval begins at the end of Phase 5 (see Figure 1).

A first-come-first-serve approach could be realized by accelerating or decelerating the vehicles such that they arrive at the intersection when gaps in the conflicting traffic flows and pedestrians have been created. However, a one-by-one service policy at high vehicle arrival rates is not efficient. From the capacity point of view, it is more efficient if Vehicle *c* is given access at t'_c before Vehicle *b*, at t'_b to the intersection and Vehicle *d* is given access at t'_d before Vehicle *e*, at t'_e then, forming a west left turn of set of vehicles (platoon) before giving way to the fourth phase (north and south conflicting flows), as stated in Figure 7.

The speed of Vehicle *e* was reduced, keeping a safe distance between Vehicle *e* and Vehicle *d*.

IV. CONCLUSIONS

This paper presents a new concept of request/response for the redesign and management of a trajectory in a two-way-two-way traffic lights controlled crossroad, using VLC between connected cars. The connected vehicles receive information from the network (I2V), interact with each other (V2V) and also with the infrastructure (V2I), using the request redesign distance concept. In parallel, a control manager coordinates the crossroad and interacts with the vehicles (I2V) using the response redesign distance concept. A simulated traffic scenario was presented and a generic model of cooperative transmission for vehicular communication services was established. As a PoC, a phasing of traffic flows is suggested. The simulated/experimental results confirmed that the proposed cooperative VLC architecture is suitable for the intended applications. The introduction of VLC between connected vehicles and the surrounding infrastructure allows the direct monitoring of relative speed thresholds and inter-vehicle spacing.

ACKNOWLEDGEMENTS

This work was sponsored by FCT within the Research Unit CTS reference UID/EEA/00066/2019 .
Are also acknowledge the projects: IPL/IDI&CA/2019/Bid-VLC/ISEL, and IPL/IDI&CA/2019/Geo-Loc/ISEL

REFEEENCES

[1] D. Elliott, W. Keen, and L. Miao, "Recent advances in connected and automated vehicles" Journal of Traffic and Transportation Engineering, Vol. 6, Issue 2, pp. 109-131(April 2019).

[2] N. J. Bajpai, "Emerging vehicle technologies & the search for urban mobility solutions, Urban, Planning and Transport Research, 4:1, pp.83-100, DOI: 10.1080/21650020.2016.1185964(2016).

[3] R. Azimi, G. Bhatia, R. Rajkumar, and P. Mudalige, "V2V-Intersection Management at Roundabouts," SAE Int. J. Passeng. Cars - Mech. Syst. 6(2) pp.681-690, 2013, https://doi.org/10.4271/2013-01-0722 (2013).

[4] N. Cheng, et al., "Big data driven vehicular networks," IEEE Network, vol. 32, no. 6, pp. 160–167, (Nov. 2018).

[5] P. Singh, G. Singh, and A. Singh, "Implementing Visible Light Communication in intelligent traffic management to resolve traffic logjams,"-Int. J. Comput. Eng. Res., 2015 - academia.edu (2015).

[6] S. Yousefi, E. Altman, R. El-Azouzi, and M. Fathy, "Analytical Model for Connectivity in Vehicular Ad Hoc Networks," IEEE Transactions on Vehicular Technology, 57, pp.3341-3356 (2008).

[7] D. O'Brien, at al., "Indoor Visible Light Communications: challenges and prospects," Proc. SPIE 7091, 709106 (2008),.

[8] P. H. Pathak, F. Xiaotao, H. Pengfei, and M. Prasant,"Visible Light Communication, Networking and Sensing: Potential and Challenges," September 2015, IEEE Communications Surveys & Tutorials 17(4): Fourthquarter 2015, 2047 – 2077 (2015).

[9] M. Vieira, P. Louro, M. Fernandes, M. A. Vieira, A. Fantoni, and J. Costa, "Three Transducers Embedded into One Single SiC Photodetector: LSP Direct Image Sensor, Optical Amplifier and Demux Device," Advances in Photodiodes InTech, Chap.19, pp. 403-425 (2011).

[10] M. A. Vieira, P. Louro, M. Vieira, A. Fantoni, and A. Steiger-Garção, "Light-activated amplification in Si-C tandem devices: A capacitive active filter model," IEEE Sensor Journal, 12(6), pp. 1755-1762 (2012).

[11] M. A. Vieira, M. Vieira, P. Vieira, and P. Louro, "Optical signal processing for a smart vehicle lighting system using a-SiCH technology," Proc. SPIE 10231, Optical Sensors 2017, 102311L (2017);

[12] .M. A. Vieira, M. Vieira, V. Silva, P. Louro, and J. Costa, "Optical signal processing for data error detection and correction using a-SiCH technology," Phys. Status Solidi C 12 (12), pp. 1393–1400 (2015).

[13] .M. A. Vieira, M. Vieira, P. Louro, and P. Vieira, "Bi-directional communication between infrastructures and vehicles through visible light," Proc. SPIE 11207, Fourth International Conference on Applications of Optics and Photonics, 112070C (3 October 2019); doi: 10.1117/12.2526500 (2019).

[14] .M. A. Vieira, M. Vieira, P. Vieira, and P. Louro, "Vehicle-to-Vehicle and Infrastructure-to-Vehicle Communication in the Visible Range," Sensors & Transducers, 218 (12), pp.40-48 (2017)

[15].M. A. Vieira, M. Vieira, P. Louro, and P. Vieira, "Smart Vehicle Lighting System in the Visible Range: Vehicle-to-Vehicle Communication," The Eighth International Conference on Sensor Device Technologies and Applications. SENSORDEVICES 2017. - Rome, Italy. Copyright (c) IARIA ISBN: 978-1-61208-581-4, pp. 57-62 (2017).

[16] .M. A. Vieira; M. Vieira; P. Louro, and P. Vieira, "Cooperative vehicular communication systems based on visible light communication," Opt. Eng. 57(7), 076101 (2018).

[17] M. A. Vieira, M. Vieira, P. Louro, V. Silva, and P. Vieira, "Optical signal processing for indoor positioning using a-SiCH technology," Opt. Eng. 55 (10), 107105 (2016), doi: 10.1117/1.OE.55.10.107105 .

SAW-based Differential Sensor Exploiting Metallocorroles Properties For The Selective Measurement Of Carbon Monoxide

M. Vanotti[1], S. Poisson[1], V. Soumann[1], V. Quesneau[2], S. Brandès[2], N. Desbois[2], J. Yang[2], L. André[2], C.P. Gros[2], V. Blondeau-Patissier[1].

[1] Femto-ST institue, Time and frequency department, 25030 Besançon Cedex, France.
[2] Institut de Chimie Moléculaire de l'Université de Bourgogne (ICMUB, UMR CNRS 6302), Université Bourgogne Franche-Comté, 21078 Dijon Cedex, France.

emails : meddy.vanotti@femto-st.fr*, sacha.poisson@femto-st.fr, valerie.soumann@femto-st.fr, valentin.quesneau@u-bourgogne.fr, stephane.brandes@u-bourgogne.fr, nicolas.desbois@u-bourgogne.fr, jian.yang@u-bourgogne.fr, laurie.andre@u-bourgogne.fr, claude.gros@u-bourgogne.fr, virginie.blondeau@femto-st.fr.

Abstract— **During the last decades, the potential impact of indoor air quality on human health has stimulated an interest in hazardous compounds survey, such as carbon monoxide (CO). The detection of these compounds has consequently become a vital need. To address this issue, we propose a Surface Acoustic Wave (SAW) device functionalized with metallocorroles used for the selective detection of CO. Here, we insist on the necessity to detect CO in the presence of interferents, such as O_2 that is obviously present in the air, carbon dioxide (CO_2) present in significant quantity in urban area (400 ppm) and humidity (H_2O) which is a well-known interferent in the case of SAW-based gas sensors. Here, we report on the interest of a differential configuration of the sensor that takes advantage of accurate organic layers, to improve the stability of the sensor's signal and lower the sensitivity to interferents. As an introduction, we provide the context of this study and introduce the two main components of our sensor, which are the SAW device and the metallocorroles.**

Keywords- Gas sensor; Carbon monoxide; SAW; metallocorroles.

I. INTRODUCTION

Indoor air quality monitoring has become a subject of increasing importance since a few decades [1]. Among gases (such as CO, CO_2, NOx, etc) produced by combustion or delivered (such as formaldehyde, benzene, ethylene glycol) by furniture, detection of carbon monoxide is of great importance due to its characteristic: this colorless, tasteless and odorless gas is impossible to detect by human beings. Moreover, the LC_{Lo} is about 5 000 ppm in 5 minutes [2]. The French Institute for Health Surveillance (INVS) reports that accidental domestic poisoning by the CO affects about 1000 households [3], and is responsible for about 100 deaths in France each year. So, both individuals and industrials interests on that topic have led to the development of new solutions to measure carbon monoxide concentration in the air [3][4].

In this paper, a new type of carbon monoxide sensor relying on nitrogen-based macrocyclic molecules that show a great affinity towards this gas is studied. In this paper, we firstly present experimental data to attest the efficiency of cobalt corroles to trap CO molecules with high selectivity, and secondly, we establish the capability of a Surface Acoustic Wave (SAW) device to probe the mechanical properties of the corroles layer to reveal the adsorption of the target gas. Among the technologies available, we chose the SAW devices for their ability to deliver real time response, low power consumption, high sensitivity to gravimetric perturbation, stability and eligibility in wireless sensor [5][6][7]. Their intrinsic lack of selectivity represents the major disadvantage of this technology. But we intend to overcome that issue by the association with highly selective cobalt corroles. Indeed, the robustness of SAW devices in delay line configuration allows for the deposition of a selective layer compatible with its normal operation [8][9]. Finally, we propose a differential configuration for the sensor to overcome the sensitivity to outer parameters and interferent gases. In that purpose, a reference device based on copper corroles was implemented as part of the sensor. Measurements of carbon monoxide concentration in the 100-7000 ppm range in the presence of major interferents, such as O_2, CO_2 and H_2O (humidity) were achieved. Based on the experimental results, we have shown the capability of cobalt corroles as sensing material as well as the interest of copper corroles as part of a reference device to improve the stability of the phase signal. The advantage of the differential configuration in terms of sensitivity and repeatability of the measurements is discussed as a conclusion.

In Section II, we describe the configuration and manufacturing of the SAW device as well as the gas sorption properties of both copper and cobalt corroles used for the functionalization of our sensor. In Section III, we show CO measurements, in presence of major interferents, that emphasize the advantage of the differential configuration. In the conclusion, based on the presented data, we highlight the validity of our approach for the development of a selective CO sensor.

II. MATERIALS AND METHODS

In this section, the design and fabrication of the SAW device are briefly described as well as the surface functionalization process. The sorption properties of metallocorroles are also exposed emphasizing their interest for the functionalization of the sensor's surface.

A. *Surface Acoustic Wave sensor*

In designing our sensor, we chose a double delay line configuration allowing for differential measurement. Fig. 1 shows the geometry of the sensor composed of these two delay lines. Both lines are composed of two Inter-Digitated Transducers (IDT) for both generation and detection of the acoustic wave at the input and output of the delay line. The IDTs are made of aluminum deposited on YXl36 quartz and shaped by mean of a lift-off process using negative photoresist. In order to allow the Love-mode acoustic wave to propagate at the surface of the device, a silica guiding layer is deposited by mean of a PECVD technique on top of the IDTs. Both IDTs consist of 50 splitted finger pairs with a grating period of 10 μm yielding an acoustic wavelength equal to 40 μm. The aperture of the delay lines represents 75 wavelengths and the propagation path length is 5 mm. As the wave velocity approaches 5100 $m.s^{-1}$, the frequency operation is in the vicinity of 125 MHz.

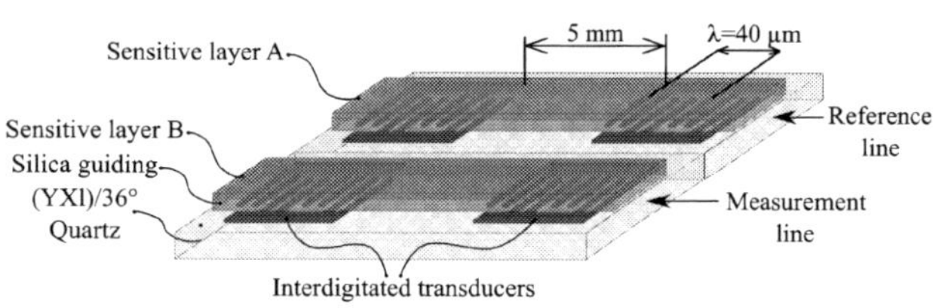

Figure 1. SAW device used for the manufacturing of the gas sensors.

The first line is coated with cobalt corroles, described in the next section, which allows for the selective trapping of carbon monoxide. The second line is coated with copper corroles, which does not show affinity to carbon monoxide. The first will be used to measure the target gas concentration and the second will be used as a reference for this measurement. The deposition of the metallocorroles is achieved by mean of a spray-coating technique. To ensure the reproducibility of the deposition process, the amount of corroles deposited on the SAW's surface is monitored by mean of the gravimetric sensitivity of the SAW sensor.

B. *Metallocorroles as functionalization layer*

The metallocorrole [5,10,15-tris(2,6-dichlorophenyl) corrolato]cobalt(III), named here cobalt corrole, was synthesized as already described in our previous work [10]. The reactivity of the complex was studied by adsorption measurements in static and dynamic conditions. The gas adsorption isotherms for CO, O_2 and CO_2 recorded at 298 K are shown in Fig. 2a. Solid lines represent the fitting curves using a triple-site Langmuir model for CO and a single one for O_2 and N_2. The isotherms show that the cobalt corrole presents a high CO uptake and low adsorption capacities for N_2 and O_2. For these two last gases, the uptake values are respectively equal to 1.9 $cm^3.g^{-1}$ and 4.8 $cm^3.g^{-1}$, respectively. The cobalt corrole shows a CO sorption volume equal to 21.9 $cm^3.g^{-1}$ (2.7% (w/w)) at 1 atm and the isotherm can be described by a combination of two different processes. The first one is assigned to an adsorption phenomenon with a high affinity in the low-pressure range (0-0.05 atm) thanks to the coordination of one carbon monoxide molecule on the cobalt center. These outcomes make cobalt corroles an suitable compound for the functionalization of the measurement line.

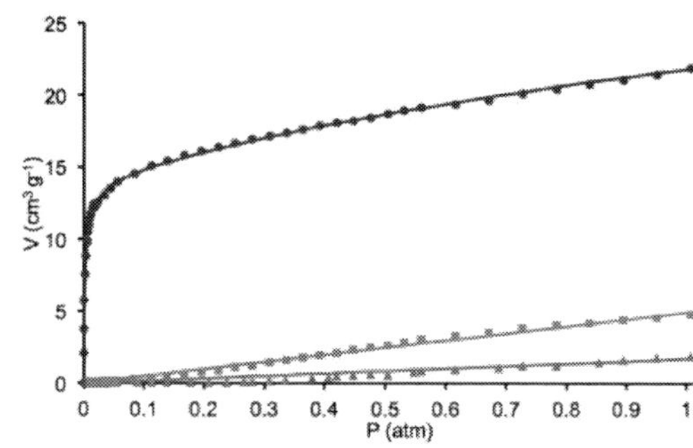

(a)

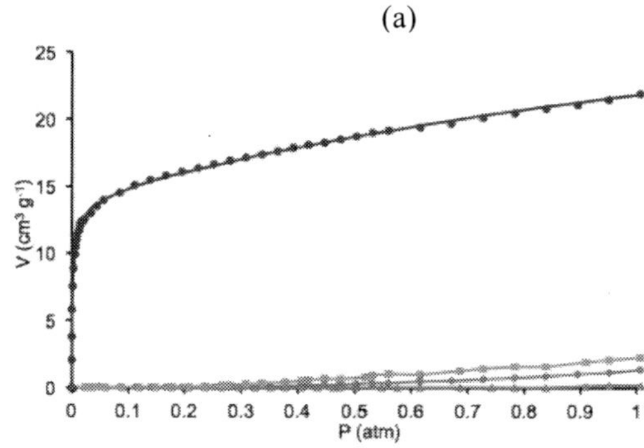

(b)

Figure 2. a) Adsorption isotherms of CO (blue), O2 (pink) and N2 (red) for cobalt corrole recorded at 298 K; b) Adsorption isotherms of CO (blue) for cobalt corrole compared to CO (green), O2 (pink) and N2 (red) for copper corrole recorded at 298 K.

In view to design a differential configuration of the sensor, the use of an accurate organic layer with no affinity for CO is required as a reference sample using a two delay lines system (vide infra) in order to reduce the outer parameters as well as interfering compounds. As a result, the copper complex [5,10,15-tris(2,6-dichlorophenyl)corrolato] copper(III) was chosen for the reference line, since this complex shows no sorption properties of CO (Fig. 2b).

III. RESULTS AND DISCUSSION

Fig. 3 shows the signal on the measurement line functionalized with cobalt corroles (red curve) and the reference line covered with copper corroles (blue curve). One can notice a drift of the phase attributed to outer parameters. The black curve represents the differential signal obtained by subtracting the phase of the reference to the phase of the measurement line. This differential signal (green curve) shows the compensation of the phase drift that results in a stable basic level of the signal.

Fig. 4 shows a series of measurements of CO concentrations in various conditions with (Diff) and without (Raw) the use of the differential system. We notice a dramatic reduction of the measurements dispersion when using the differential system. A statistical characterization of these data reveals that the standard deviation induced by CO_2 at 20 000 ppm is reduced by a factor 4.5 compared to an ideal case in pure nitrogen. In the case of oxygen at 20%, which is one of the main interferents, the deviation is greatly reduced by a factor 30. These results emphasize the interest of a differential configuration of the sensor to improve the repeatability of the measurements. It also strengthens our will to synthesize organic compounds for the development of a well-designed reference line.

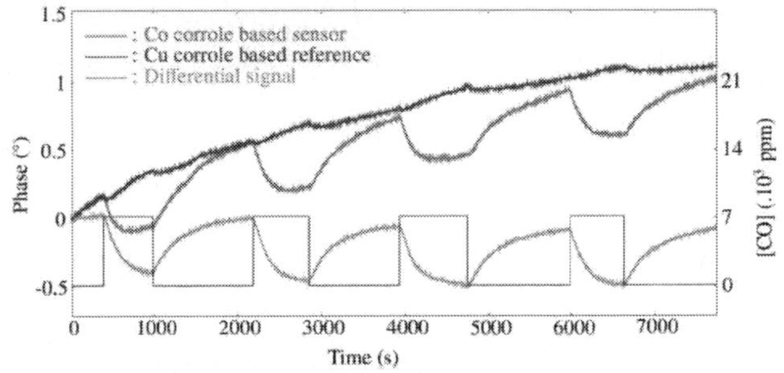

Figure 3. Comparison between phase signals from the measurement line (in red), the reference line (in blue) and the differential signal (in green).

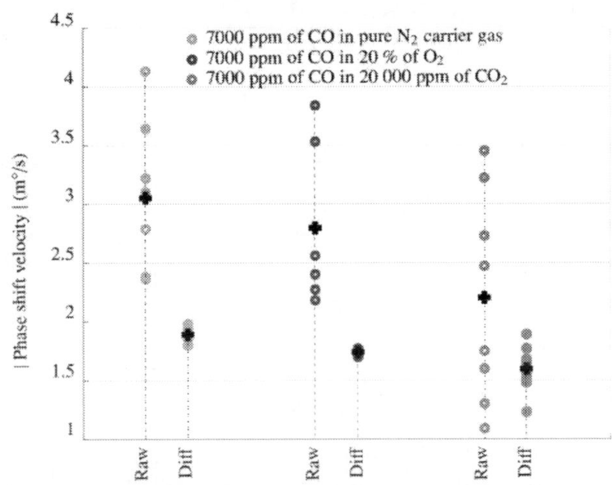

Figure 4. Influence of the differential acquisition on the repeatability of the measurements of 7000 ppm of CO in various carrier gases. Raw data represent the signal from the measurement line and the Diff data the differential signal. The mean value is represented by the cross.

The impact of O_2 and CO_2 at high concentration has been determined. As expected from previous works [11], a linear correlation between CO concentration, from 100 ppm to 7000 ppm, and the phase shift velocity undergone by the sensor is observed. Experimental results, presented in Fig. 5, show that this linear behavior stands regardless of the composition of the carrier gas for both measurement line and differential sensor. From there, the sensitivity of the sensors could be determined. In pure nitrogen, the measurement line sensitivity is 263±124 n°/s/ppm. The uncertainty on the sensitivity drops dramatically in the case of the differential sensor for which the sensitivity is 238±6.5 n°/s/ppm. It appears that in the presence of 20% of oxygen the uncertainty remains equivalent for both sensor configurations. In the presence of CO_2 at 20 000 ppm the measurement line sensitivity is 166±29 n°/s/ppm while the differential sensor exhibits a selectivity of 225±3 n°/s/ppm. The same characterization was made in the presence of water in the carrier gas and a spectacular difference between the raw measurements without reference and the differential acquisition has been observed. As shown in Fig. 5, the uncertainty on the sensor sensitivity is divided by 50 with the use of a differential acquisition.

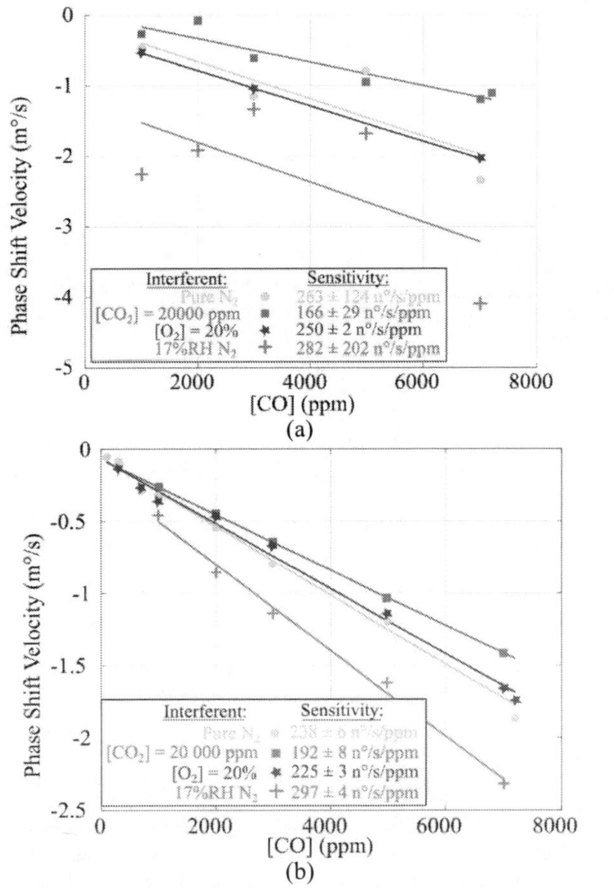

Figure 5. a) Measurement line sensitivity in presence of oxygen (blue), carbon dioxide (red) and humidity (pink) on the carrier gas. b) Differential sensor's sensitivity in the presence of the same interferent.

The effect of the other pollutant gas, such as H_2 or H_2S, on the sensor selectivity will draw our attention in further works. Even if the quartz substrate used for the manufacturing of the sensor is a temperature compensated AT-cut, a sensitivity to temperature may rise from the functionalization of the device. The effect of temperature on the sensor stability will, consequently, provide a focus of work.

IV. CONCLUSION

In this research, we developed an original sensor for carbon monoxide monitoring based on a SAW device and metallocorroles. This approach takes advantage of the intrinsic high sensitivity to gravimetric phenomena of SAW sensors, combined with CO selective sorption capabilities of the cobalt corroles. Copper corroles have been exploited for the development of a dedicated reference line. We have shown that the use of a proper reference line as part of a differential sensor provides improvement in the repeatability of the measurements and allows for the diminution of the uncertainty in the sensor sensitivity. These results pave the way for the detection of other gases with acoustic waves devices associated with dedicated functionalization compounds for the development of a multi-gas monitoring system.

REFERENCES

[1] J. A. Raub, M. Mathieu-Nolf, N. B. Hampson, and S. R. Thom, « Carbon monoxide poisoning - a public health perspective », *Toxicology*, vol. 145, n° 1, pp. 1-14, avr. 2000, doi: 10.1016/S0300-483X(99)00217-6.

[2] H. Chojer, P. T. B. S. Branco, F. G. Martins, M. C. M. Alvim-Ferraz, and S. I. V. Sousa, « Development of low-cost indoor air quality monitoring devices: Recent advancements », *Science of The Total Environment*, vol. 727, pp. 138385, juill. 2020, doi: 10.1016/j.scitotenv.2020.138385.

[3] A. Cincinelli and T. Martellini, « Indoor Air Quality and Health », *International Journal of Environmental Research and Public Health*, vol. 14, n° 11, pp.1286, nov. 2017, doi: 10.3390/ijerph14111286.

[4] N. Docquier and S. Candel, « Combustion control and sensors: a review », *Progress in Energy and Combustion Science*, vol. 28, n° 2, pp. 107-150, janv. 2002, doi: 10.1016/S0360-1285(01)00009-0.

[5] Z. Awang, « Gas Sensors: A Review », *Sensors & Transducers*, vol. 168, n° 4, pp. 61-75, 2014.

[6] W. Buff, « SAW sensors for direct and remote measurement », in *2002 IEEE Ultrasonics Symposium, 2002. Proceedings*, oct. 2002, vol. 1, pp. 435-443.

[7] B. Liu *et al.*, « Surface acoustic wave devices for sensor applications », *J. Semicond.*, vol. 37, n° 2, pp. 21001, févr. 2016, doi: 10.1088/1674-4926/37/2/021001.

[8] M. Vanotti, V. Blondeau-Patissier, V. Moutarlier, and S. Ballandras, « Analysis of palladium and yttrium–palladium alloy layers used for hydrogen detection with SAW device », *Sensors and Actuators B: Chemical*, vol. 217, pp. 30-35, oct. 2015, doi: 10.1016/j.snb.2015.02.049.

[9] P. Zheng *et al.*, « Langasite SAW device with gas-sensitive layer », in *2010 IEEE International Ultrasonics Symposium*, pp. 1462-1465, oct. 2010.

[10] V. Quesneau *et al.*, « Cobalt Corroles with Bis-Ammonia or Mono-DMSO Axial Ligands. Electrochemical, Spectroscopic

Characterizations and Ligand Binding Properties », *Eur. J. Inorg. Chem.*, vol. 2018, n° 38, pp. 4265-4277, oct. 2018, doi: 10.1002/ejic.201800897.

[11] M. Vanotti *et al.*, « Surface Acoustic Wave Sensors for the Detection of Hazardous Compounds in Indoor Air », *Proceedings*, vol. 1, n° 4, pp. 444, 2017.

Geolocation and Wayfinding in Complex Buildings Using Visible Light Communication

Manuela Vieira, Manuel Augusto Vieira, Paula Louro, Alessandro Fantoni
ADETC/ISEL/IPL,
R. Conselheiro Emídio Navarro, 1959-007
Lisboa, Portugal
CTS-UNINOVA
Quinta da Torre, Monte da Caparica, 2829-516,
Caparica, Portugal

e-mail: mv@isel.ipl.pt, mv@isel.pt, plouro@deetc.isel.pt,
afantoni@deetc.isel.ipl.pt

Pedro Vieira
ADETC/ISEL/IPL,
R. Conselheiro Emídio Navarro, 1959-007
Lisboa, Portugal
Instituto das Telecomunicações
Instituto Superior Técnico, 1049-001,
Lisboa, Portugal
e-mail: pvieira@isel.pt

***Abstract*— This paper investigates the applicability of an intuitive wayfinding system in complex buildings using Visible Light Communication (VLC). Data from the sender is encoded, modulated and converted into light signals emitted by the transmitters. Tetra-chromatic white sources, located in ceiling landmarks, are used providing a different data channel for each chip. At the mobile receivers, the modulated light signals, containing the ID and the 3D geographical position of the transmitter and wayfinding information, is received by SiC photodetector with light filtering and demultiplexing properties. The effect of the location of the Access Points (APs) is evaluated and a model for the cellular networks is analyzed using orthogonal topologies. A 3D localization design, demonstrated by a prototype implementation, is presented. Uplink transmission is also implemented and the 3D best route to navigate calculated. The results showed that the system allows determining the position of a mobile target inside the network, to infer the travel direction along the time and to interact with information received optimizing the route towards the destination.**

Keywords- Visible Light Communication; Indoor navigation; Bidirectional Communication; Wayfinding; Optical sensors;Multiplexing/demultiplexing techniques.

I. INTRODUCTION

Optical wireless communication has been widely studied during the last years in short-range applications. Therefore, communications within personal working/living spaces are highly demanded. Multi-device connectivity can tell users, from any device, where they are, where they need to be and what they need to do when they get there. In the future accurate indoor positioning might not be viable by sole utilizing RF communications. Research has shown that compared to outdoors, people tend to lose orientation a lot easier within complex buildings [1] [2]. Fine-grained indoor localization can be useful enabling several applications [3] [4].

To support people's wayfinding activities in unfamiliar indoor environments, a method able to generate ceiling landmark route instructions using VLC is proposed. VLC is a data transmission technology [5] [6]. It can be easily used in indoor environments using the existing LED lighting infrastructure with few modifications [7] [8]. This means that the LEDs are twofold by providing illumination as well as communication. Research is still needed to design LED arrangements that can optimize communication performance while meeting the illumination constraints.

Each luminaire for downlink transmission become a single cell in which the optical access point (AP) is located in the ceiling. Data from the sender (the map information and the path messages necessary to wayfinding) is encoded, modulated and converted into light signals emitted by the transmitters. Tetra-chromatic white sources are used providing a different data channel for each chip. The use of white polychromatic LEDs in the ceiling offers also, the possibility of Wavelength Division Multiplexing (WDM) which enhances the transmission data rate. To receive the mapped information generated from the ceiling light in visual light form, the users are equipped with a receiver module that displays this fabricated information in the mobile terminal. Receiver modules includes a photodetector based on a tandem a-SiC:H/a-Si:H pin/pin light controlled filter [9] [10] [11] that multiplexes the different optical channels, performs different filtering processes (amplification, switching, and wavelength conversion) and finally decodes the encoded signals, recovering the transmitted information. This kind of receiver has proved to be adequate when used in large indoor environments with a 2D building model [12]. However, vertical positioning is also important [13] [14]. 3D tracking is difficult by the need for additional coverage for passages between floors (e.g., stairs, elevators).

In this paper, a dynamic LED-assisted positioning and navigation VLC system is proposed. A 3D model for the building is established. The transmitted information, indoor position, motion direction, as well as bi-directional communication are determined. The proposed LED aided system involves wireless communication, smart sensoring and optical sources network, building up a transdisciplinary approach framed in cyber-physical systems.

The paper is organized as follows. After the introduction (Section I), in Section II, a VLC scenario for large environments is established and the dynamic navigation system explained. In Section III, the protocol communication is presented and the encoding techniques used analyzed. In Section IV, the wayfinding evaluation is discussed. Finally, in Section V, conclusions and future trends are addressed.

II. DYNAMIC NAVIGATION SYSTEM

When we are looking for the shortest route to a place, we want to be guided on a direct, shortest path to our destination. A destination can be targeted by user request to the Central Manager (CM).

The dynamic navigation system is composed of several transmitters, which send the map information and path messages required to wayfinding. Mobile optical receivers, using joint transmission, extracts theirs location to perform positioning and, concomitantly, the transmitted data from each transmitter. To synchronize the signals from multiple LEDs, the transmitters use different ID's, such that the signal is constructively at the receiver. Bidirectional communication between the emitters and the receivers is available in strategic optical access point (Li-Fi zone).

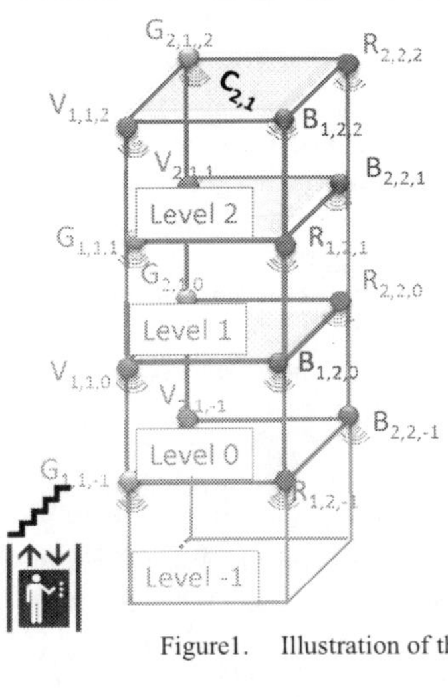

Footprint	Overlap
#1	R+G+B+V
#2	R+G+B
#3	R+B
#4	R+B+V
#5	B+V
#6	G+B+V
#7	G+V
#8	R+G+V
#9	R+G

Figure1. Illustration of the 3D virtual floorplan.

The indoor environment chosen is a shopping center with several floors. The 3D virtual floorplan with the information about the number of floors and the nodes localization is draft in Figure 1.

The ground floor is level *0*, and the user can go both below and above from there. Each unit cell can be referred as $C_{i,j,k}$ were *i, j, k* are respectively the line, the row and the level of the top left node of each unit cell. To exemplify, Cell $C_{2,1}$ is depicted in the figure for levels -1, 0, 1 and 2. Therefore, each node, $X_{i,j,k}$ carries its own color, *X*, (RGBV), as well as its horizontal (line and row) and vertical (level) ID position in the network (*i,j,k*). For data transmission commercially available polychromatic white LEDs were used.

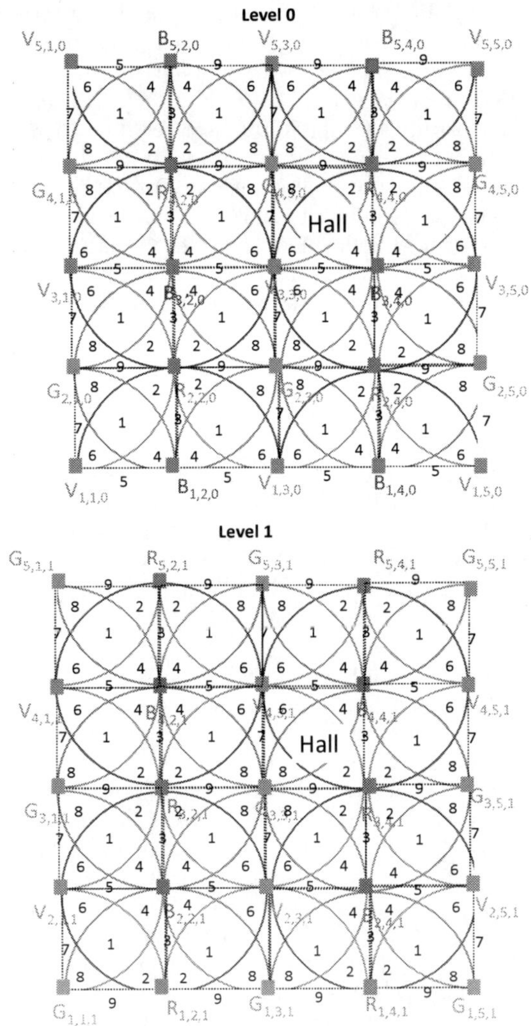

Figure 2 . Illustration of the proposed scenario. Ceiling plans for the LED array layout in a 3D building, for even and odd floors. The footprint regions assigned to the overlaps are pointed out in Figure 1.

In Figure 2, the ceiling plans for the LED array layout in a 3D building, for even and odd floors is shown (R,G,B,V are the modulated color spots for data transmission in each level). A multi-layer orthogonal geometry with lines and rows for each floor was considered for a square unit cell framed with four tetra-chromatic LEDs. Only one chip, in each node, is modulated, the Red (R; 626 nm), the Green (G;530 nm), the Blue (B; 470 nm) and the Violet (V; 390 nm)], the other have a *dc* driving current for white perception [15]. To receive the information from several transmitters, the receiver must be positioned where the circles from each transmitter overlaps, producing at the receiver, a multiplexed (MUX) signal that, after demultiplexing, acts twofold as a positioning system and a data transmitter. The overlap regions, the footprints, are also pointed out in Figure 1. Nine reference points, for each unit cell, are identified and give a fine grained resolution in the localization of the mobile device across each cell. The user positions is represented as P (x, y, z) by providing the horizontal positions (x, y) and the correct floor number z. By integrating floor number information into the previous 2D system [16], the overall performance of the system will not be significantly affected as this time the 2D positions are more important and the floor detection accuracy is high enough to handle automatic floor plan changes. Also, there needs to be stairs or an elevator to enable a connection between the floors.

The VLC photosensitive sensor, in the receiver module, is a double pin/pin photodetector based on a tandem heterostructure, p-i'(a -SiC:H)-n/p-i(a-Si:H)-n sandwiched between two transparent contacts [3]. The device is an active filter able to identify the wavelengths and intensities of the impinging optical signals. Its quick response enables the possibility of high speed communications [17]. Bi-directional communication between VLC emitters and receivers is available at a VLC ready handheld device through a CM interconnected with a billboard receiver located in a Li-Fi zone.

Different users are considered. Depending on the time available, they can find a friend, shop, have a meal or rest. When arriving, they notify the controller manager (CM) of their location (*x,y,z*), asking for help to find the best way for their needs. A code identifies each user. If a user wishes to find a friend both need previously to combine a common code for the schedule meeting. The first arriving initiates the alert notification to be triggered when the other is in his floor vicinity and generates a buddy list for the meeting. The buddy finder service uses the location information from the network's VLC location from both users to determine their proximity and sends a response message with the location and path of the meeting point.

III. COMMUNICATION PROTOCOL.

An on-off keying modulation scheme was used to code the information. To create a communication protocol and overcome the technology constraints, a 64 bits data frame was designed. In Figure 3, it is displayed the representation of one original encoded message, in a time slot. Here, the transmitted node packet ($R_{4,4,0}$; $G_{4,3,0}$; $B_{3,4,0}$; $V_{3,3,0}$) from cell $C_{4,3,0}$ (ground floor Hall; Figure 2) are displayed.

Several control fields are used depending on the type of transmitter. The synchronism (Sync) is the first and the next are used for the identification of the ceiling. A stop bit is always used at the end of each frame. For the luminaires, the cell ID (x,y,z) begin the second block while for the CM transmitter a pattern [000] precedes this identification.

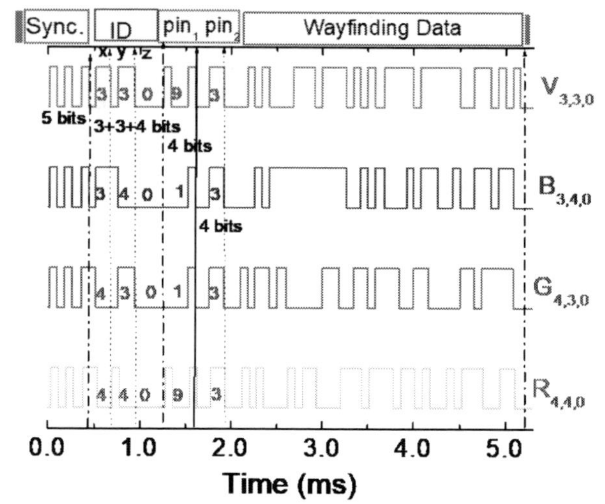

Figure 3 .Data frame structure. Representation of one original encoded message, in a time slot: $R_{4,4,0}$; $G_{4,3,0}$; $B_{3,4,0}$ and $V_{3,3,0}$ are the transmitted node packet from the unit cell $C_{4,3,0}$ in the network.

Those sequences are followed by a new block (pin_1) with the password of the user if a request is needed, if not this block is set at zero and the user only receives its own location. The last block is used to transmit the wayfinding message and may include, in the beginning, the code of the request meeting (pin_2).

The same synchronization header [10101], in an ON-OFF pattern, is imposed simultaneously to all emitters. Each color signal (RGBV) carries its own ID-BIT. Cell's IDs are encoded using a binary representation for the decimal number. At the beginning of the binary code of the *z* coordinate an extra bit was added to represent the flor's sign: setting that bit to *0* is for a positive number, and setting it to *1* for a negative number, the remaining 3 bits indicate the absolute value of the *z* coordinate. The last bits, in the frame, are reserved for the message send by the $X_{i,j,k}$ node (payload data). When bidirectional communication is required, the user has to register by choosing a user name with 4 decimal numbers, each one associated to a colour channel. Here, each channel (RGBV) needs a binary 4-digid code. The decimal numbers assigned to each ID block are pointed out in the Figure 3. Results show that $R_{4,4,0}$, $G_{4,3,0}$, $B_{3,4,0}$ and $V_{3,3,0}$ are the transmitted node packets, in a time slot, from an AP ($C_{4,3,0}$) located in level 0. In this location, an identified user *9119* [1001, 0001, 0001, 1001] receives his response message [wayfinding needs] from the infrastructure.

In Figure 4, a MUX signal received by the user located in footprint #6 bellow AP $C_{4,3,1}$, and the decoded information (in the top of the figure) are shown. The data acquisition was obtained with the presence of environment light. For demonstration of the decoding technique, the signal received; in the same frame of time due to the joint transmission of four calibrated R, G, B and V optical signals is superimposed. The bit sequence for the calibrated cell was chosen to allow all the *on/off* sixteen possible combinations of the four RGBV input channels (2^4). Results show that the code signal presents as much separated levels as the *on/off* possible combinations of the input channels, allowing decoding the transmitted information. All the ordered levels (d_0-d_{15}) are pointed out at the correspondent levels, and are displayed as horizontal dotted lines. In the right hand side the match between MUX levels and the RGBV 4 bits binary code assigned to each level is shown. Here, *0* means that the channel is *off* and *1* that it is *on*. Comparing the calibrated levels (d_0-d_{15}) with the different assigned 4-digit binary code, the decoding is straightforward.

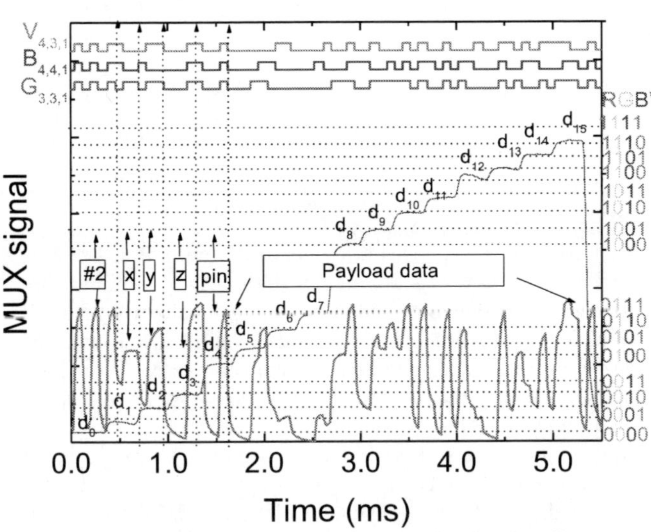

Figure 4 MUX/DEMUX signals received in the first floor in cell $C_{4,3,1}$ footprint #6. On the top the received information is decoded. The MUX signal of the calibrated cell in the same frame of time is superimposed

After decoding the MUX signals, and taking into account, the frame structure (Figure 3), the position of the receiver and its ID in the network is revealed [15]. The footprint position comes directly from the synchronism block, where all the received channels are, simultaneously, *on* or *off*. In the received MUX signal, the maximum amplitude detected corresponds to the binary word [0111], meaning that it has only received the overlap transmission from the green (G), blue (B) and the violet (V) channels (footprint #6). The next block of ten bits gives de ID of the received nodes. In footprint #6, the network location of the received signal are $G_{3,3,1}$ [011;011:0001], $B_{4,4,1}$ [100;100;0001] and $V_{4,3,1}$ [100;001;0001]. The next 4 bits identifies the user code [1001, 1001, 1001, 1001] and finally the last block is reserved for the transmission of the wayfinding message (Payload data). The stop bit (0) is used always at the end of each frame.

IV. WAYFINDING EVALUATION

The evaluation of the system is performed and the experimental results discussed bellow

A. *Fine grained positioning and travel direction*

To compute the point-to-point along a path, we need the data along the path. As a proof of concept, in the lab, a navigation data bit transition was tested by moving the receiver along a known pattern path. In Figure 5, the MUX signal acquired by a user, as well as the decoded information, is displayed in different instants. The visualized cells, paths and the reference points (footprints) are also shown. The user enters the floor 1 (see Figures 1 and 2) by line #7 ($C_{4,1,1}$), it goes to position #1(t_0) and it can chooses the supermarket at $C_{5,2,1}$ or the kinder garden at $C_{3,2,1}$ zones, being directed by the CM into one of the two indicated directions ($C_{4,2,1}$ # 5, $C_{4,2,1}$; # 9) where he arrives at t_3 passing through footprints #3 (t_1) and #1(t_2) from the next cell.

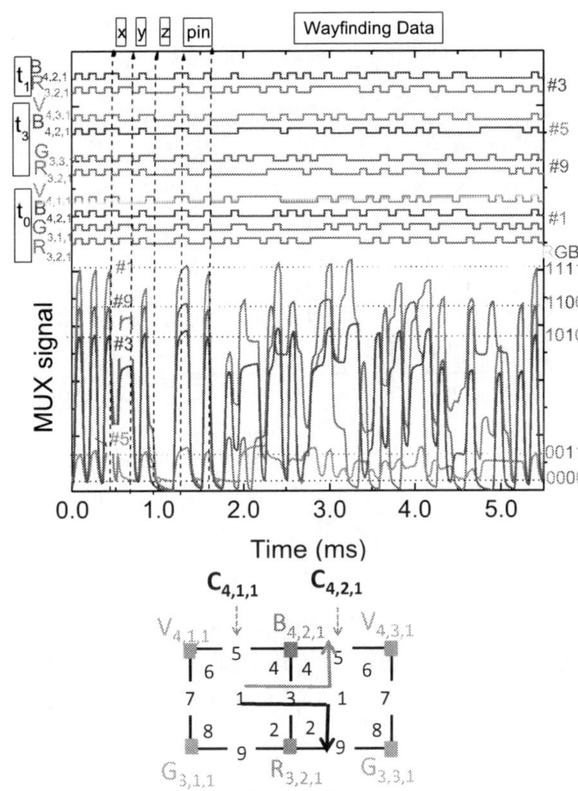

Figure 5 Fine-grained indoor localization and navigation in successive instants. On the top the transmitted channels packets are decoded [R, G, B, V] in the successive instants.

Results show that the location and path of a mobile receiver was obtained based on the dynamic LED-based navigation system. As the receiver moves between generated point regions, the received information pattern changes. Between two consecutive data sets, there is always a navigation data bit transition (channels are missing or added). For instance, when the receiver moves in the reverse direction, from $C_{4,1,1}$ #3 to $C_{4,1,1}$ # 1 two different ID channels are added ($G_{3,1,1}$ and $V_{4,1,1}$). Here, the 4-bynary bit code has changed from [1010] to [1111]. In the forward direction ($C_{4,2,1}$), the added channels have the same colour but different ID ($G_{3,3,1}$ and $V_{4,3,1}$). So, just by tracking the path in successive instant the direction of the receiver is known. Going forward corresponds to crossing lines #3 and #7, turning left cross of line #5 and turning right to line #9. Main results show that fine grained localization is achieved by detecting the wavelengths of the received channels in each region. The location and path of a mobile receiver was obtained based on the dynamic LED-based navigation system. In an orthogonal layout, the square topology is the best. It allows crossroads and the client can walk easily in the horizontal, vertical or both directions.

B. *Bi-directional Communication: Buddy services.*

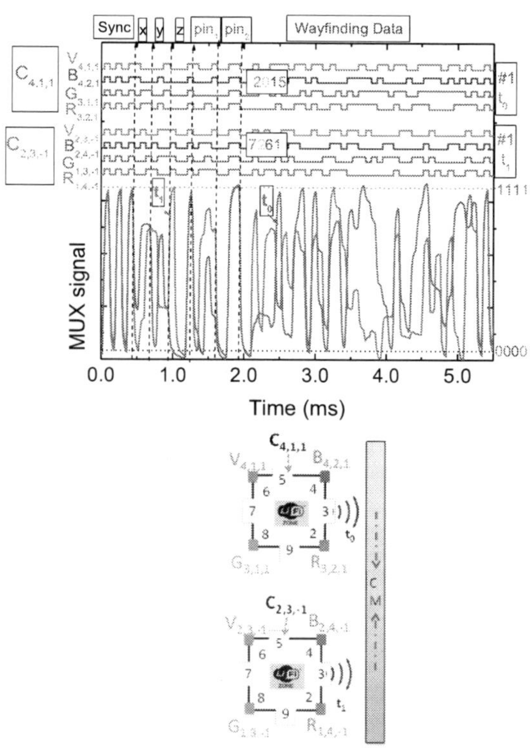

Figure 6 . MUX/DEMUX signals assigned to a "request". MUX signal received by the CM receiver from two users ("2015" and "7261") at different locations (C4,1,1; #1 and C2,3,-1; #1) in successive instants (t0 and t1). On the top the transmitted channels packets are decoded [Xi,j].

Bi-directional communication is available at ready handheld device through a control manager (CM) interconnected with a billboard receiver located at each unit cells in a Li-Fi zone ($C_{i,j,k}$, #1). In Figure 6, the MUX synchronized signals from two identify users are displayed. In the right side, the match between the MUX signal and the 4-binary code is pointed out. On the top the decoded channels packets are shown [R, G, B, V]. Taking into account Figure 2, results show that in a time slot, two identified users ("2015" and "7261"; pin_1) have successively (t_0, t_1) request to the buddy wayfinding services, the right track (wayfinding data) for their previously scheduled meeting, pin_2 [0011/3;]. At the right hand of the figure the scenario is illustrated. In the proposed scenario, user "2015" initiates the alert notification ($C_{4,1,1}$; t_0) to be triggered in his floor vicinity (level 1) and initializes the buddy list that includes all the users who have the same meeting code (pin_2:[0011]; 3). User "7261" arrives later ($C_{2,3,-1}$; t_1), identifies himself and uses the same code in the buddy wayfinding services to track the best way to the scheduled meeting. For route coordination the CM sends a personalized "response" message at the requested position ($C_{2,3-1}$). In this message the buddy finder service uses the location information from both to determine their proximity and sends a response message to user "7261" with the best route to the meeting.

V. CONCLUSIONS

This paper proposes a generating method of ceiling landmark route instructions using VLC. Each luminaire for downlink transmission becomes a single cell in which the optical access point is located in the ceiling. Data from the sender is encoded, modulated and converted into light signals emitted by the transmitters. The mobile users are scattered within the overlap discs of each cell. For lighting, data transmission and positioning, white LEDs were used. A SiC optical MUX/DEMUX mobile receiver decodes the data and, based on the synchronism and ID of the joint transmitters, it infers its path location, timing and user flows.

A 3D building model for large indoor environments was presented, and a VLC scenario in a three level building was established. The communication protocol was presented. Bi-directional communication between the infrastructure and the mobile receiver was analysed. Global results show that the location of a mobile receiver, concomitant with data transmission is achieved. The dynamic LED-aided VLC navigation system enables to determine the position of a mobile target inside the network, to infer the travel direction along the time and to interact with received information.

The VLC system, when applied to large building, can help to find the shortest path to a place, guiding the users on a direct, shortest path to their destinations. Research is still necessary to optimize the coverage; effects as synchronization, shadowing and ambient light could be minimized through MIMO techniques. Also, the design concerning the LED arrangements has to be improved in future, to optimize the communication performance while meeting the illumination constraints.

Minding the benefits of VLC, it is expected that this type of communication will have an important role in positioning applications. Moving towards real implementation, the performances of such systems still need to improve. As a future goal, we plan to finalize the embedded application, for experimenting in several network layouts. Effects as synchronization, shadowing and ambient light noise will be minimized by distributing lighting sources (MIMO techniques) to optimize the coverage.

ACKNOWLEDGEMENTS

This work was sponsored by FCT – Fundação para a Ciência e a Tecnologia, within the Research Unit CTS – Center of Technology and systems, reference UID/EEA/00066/2019 and projects reference by: IPL/IDI&CA/2019/Bi-VLC and IPL/IDI&CA/2020/Geo-Loc/ISEL.

REFERENCES

[1] H. H. Liu, and Y. N. Yang, "WiFi-based indoor positioning for multi-floor environment," *TENCON 2011 - 2011 IEEE Region 10 Conference*, Bali, 2011, pp. 597-601, doi: 10.1109/TENCON.2011.6129175.

[2] Y. Wang, H. Li, X. Luo, Q. Sun, and J. Liu, "A 3D Fingerprinting Positioning Method Based on Cellular Networks," International Journal of Distributed Sensor Networks, 2014. doi:10.1155/2014/248981.

[3] M. Vieira, M. A. Vieira, P. Louro, P. Vieira., and A. Fantoni, "Fine-grained indoor localization: optical sensing and detection," Proc. SPIE 10680, Optical Sensing and Detection V, 106800H, 9 May 2018.

[4] A. Jovicic, J. Li, and T. Richardson, "Visible light communication: opportunities, challenges and the path to market," Communications Magazine, IEEE, vol. 51, no. 12, pp. 26–32, 2013.

[5] E. Ozgur, E. Dinc, and O. B. Akan, "Communicate to illuminate: State-of-the-art and research challenges for visible light communications," Physical Communication 17, pp. 72–85, (2015).

[6] C. Yang, and H. R. Shao, "WiFi-based indoor positioning," IEEE Commun. Mag., vol. 53, no. 3, pp. 150–157, Mar. 2015.

[7] D. Tsonev et al. "A 3-Gb/s single-LED OFDM-based wireless VLC link using a Gallium Nitride μLED," IEEE Photon. Technol. Lett. 26(7), pp. 637–640 (2014).

[8] S. O'Brienet al. "Indoor visible light communications: challenges and prospects," Proc. SPIE 7091, 709106, 2008.

[9] M. A. Vieira, M. Vieira, , P. Vieira, and P. Louro, "Optical signal processing for a smart vehicle lighting system using a-SiCH technology," Proc. SPIE 10231, Optical Sensors 2017, 102311L, 2017.

[10] M. Vieira, P. Louro, M. Fernandes, M. A. Vieira, A. Fantoni and J. Costa, "Three Transducers Embedded into One Single SiC Photodetector: LSP Direct Image Sensor, Optical Amplifier and Demux Device," Advances in Photodiodes InTech, Chap.19, pp.403-425, 2011.

[11] M. A. Vieira, P. Louro, M. Vieira, A Fantoni, and A. Steiger-Garção, "Light-activated amplification in Si-C tandem devices: A capacitive active filter model," IEEE sensor journal, 12, NO. 6, pp. 1755-1762, 2012.

[12] M. A. Vieira, M. Vieira, P. Louro, V. Silva, and P. Vieira, "Optical signal processing for indoor positioning using a-SiCH technology," Opt. Eng. 55 (10), 107105 (2016), doi: 10.1117/1.OE.55.10.107105, 2016.

[13] N. Csanyi, and C. Toth, "Point positioning accuracy of airborn LIDAR systems: A rigorous analysis," Stilla U et al (Eds) PIA07. International Archives of Photogrammetry, Remote Sensing and Spatial Information Sciences, 36 (3/W49B).

[14] B. Hung, A. King, A. Bruce A. and W. Chen "Conceptual Issues Regarding the Development of Underground Railway Laser Scanning Systems." ISPRS Int. J. Geo-Inf. 2015, 4, pp. 185-198; doi:10.3390/ijgi4010185.

[15] M. Vieira, M. A. Vieira, P. Louro, P. Vieira and A Fantoni, "Light-emitting diodes aided indoor localization using visible light communication technology," Opt. Eng. vol. 57, no. 8, pp. 087105, 2018. https://doi.org/10.1117/1.OE.57.8.087105

[16] M. Vieira, M. A. Vieira, P. Louro, and P. Vieira, "Positioning and advertising in large indoor environments using visible light communication," Opt. Eng. Vol. 58 no. 6, pp. 066102-1-066102-8, 2019, doi: 10.1117/1.OE.58.6.066102.

[17] M. A. Vieira, M. Vieira, V. Silva, P. Louro, and J. Costa, "Optical signal processing for data error detection and correction using a-SiCH technology," Phys. Status Solidi C, vol. 12, no.12, pp.1393–1400, 2015.

Tuning of Magnetic Properties of Magnetic Microwires by Post-Processing

Paula Corte-León, Valentina Zhukova, Mihail Ipatov,
Dept. Advanced Polymers and Materials: Physics, Chemistry and Technology, Faculty of Chemistry, Univ. Basque Country, UPV/EHU, 20018 San Sebastian, Spain
e-mail: paula.corte@ehu.eus, valentina.zhukova@ehu.es, mihail.ipatov@ehu.eus

Juan Maria Blanco,
Department Applied Physics I, Univ. Basque Country, EIG, UPV/EHU, 20018, San Sebastian, Spain
e-mail: juanmaria.blanco@ehu.es

Arcady Zhukov
Dept. Advanced Polymers and Materials: Physics, Chemistry and Technology, Faculty of Chemistry, Univ. Basque Country, UPV/EHU, 20018 San Sebastian and Ikerbasque, Bilbao Spain
e-mail: arkadi.joukov@ehu.es

***Abstract*—The influence of post-processing conditions on the magnetic properties of amorphous and nanocrystalline microwires has been analyzed, paying attention on the effect of magnetoelastic and magnetocrystalline anisotropies on the hysteresis loops of Fe-, Ni- and Co-rich microwires. We demonstrated that the selection of appropriate chemical composition and geometry of as-prepared microwires and appropriate post-processing consisting of annealing or glass-coated removal allow tuning of magnetic properties of glass-coated microwires. Magnetic hardening of the microwires can be achieved by the devitrification of Fe-Pt-Si microwires.**

Keywords- magnetic microwires; magnetic softness; hysteresis loops; internal stresses; magnetic anisotropy.

I. INTRODUCTION

A family of amorphous and nanocrystalline materials prepared using rapid melt quenching is one of the most promising families of soft magnetic materials with a number of advantages, such as excellent magnetic softness, fast and inexpensive manufacturing process, dimensionality suitable for various sensor applications, and good mechanical properties [1]-[6]. Such excellent physical properties have been reported in amorphous materials with either planar (ribbons) [1]-[3] or cylindrical (wires) geometry [4]-[6].

Amorphous and nanocrystalline wires can present quite peculiar magnetic properties, such as spontaneous magnetic bistability associated with single and large Barkhausen jump [7]-[9] or Giant Magneto-Impedance, GMI, effect [10]-[13]. In spite that both large Barkhausen and GMI effect have been also observed in crystalline wires [14][15], as well as in properly heat treated amorphous ribbons [3][12]. However, fast single domain wall, DW, propagation and high GMI effect have been observed in amorphous magnetic wires even without any post-processing [7]-[13].

These features of amorphous and nanocrystalline microwires can be attributed to the combination of cylindrical geometry together with the specific magnetoelastic anisotropy. The latter is linked with the internal stresses distribution characteristic of rapid melt quenching, allowing to obtain a core-shell domain structure either with a high circumferential magnetic permeability (in negative magnetostrictive Co-rich compositions), or with the presence of an axially magnetized single inner domain responsible for the observation of a single and the large Barkhausen jump and the associated single DW propagation [16][17].

The main interest in GMI effect is justified by extremely high impedance sensitivity to an external magnetic field (up to 10 %/A/m) reported for magnetic microwires [18]-[20]. Several sensor applications, such as magnetic compass and acceleration sensors integrated in Complementary Metal-Oxide-Semiconductor (CMOS) circuits, reduced-sized magnetometer suitable for magnetic field mapping, detection of a biomagnetic field with the pico-Tesla sensitivity, magnetoelastic and temperature sensors have been developed [10][12][20]-[22].

On the other hand, magnetically bistable microwires are suitable various applications. Single and controllable DW propagation is suitable for magnetic logic, magnetic memory and electronic surveillance [23]-[26]. The former application is based on use of magnetic tags containing several microwires with well-defined coercivities (characteristic for magnetically bistable microwire) [26]. This application requires a variety of coercivity, H_c, values that can be achieved by the H_c tunability (either by compositional H_c dependence or influence of heat treatments on H_c -values). Accordingly, microwires with rectangular hysteresis loops and plurality of coercivities are requested in electronic surveillance applications.

The additional advantages of glass-coated microwires are excellent corrosion and mechanical properties, biocompatibility, fast and simple fabrication method and reduced dimensionality [4][5][27]-[30]. Such features allow to extend the applications possibilities.

As reported elsewhere, magnetic properties of amorphous microwires are affected by the fabrication conditions (like quenching rate or glass-coating thickness), chemical composition of the metallic alloy and post-processing conditions [9][12][15]. Accordingly, we will analyze the influence of various factors on the magnetic properties of glass-coated microwires and provide the guideline for selection of appropriate post-processing for optimization of properties of magnetic microwires.

In section 2, we present the description of the experimental techniques, while in section 3 we describe the results on effect of fabrication and post-processing conditions on hysteresis loops of the microwires.

II. Experimental Details

We prepared and analyzed amorphous glass-coated microwires based on Fe-, Co- and Ni- alloys with minor metalloid additions (Si, B, C) necessary for preparation of amorphous alloys [9][15]. The employed Taylor-Ulitovsky technique is described earlier elsewhere [15].

We studied as-prepared and annealed samples. The annealing temperature, T_{ann}, was between 200 °C to 700 °C for annealing time, t_{ann}, up to 256 min. Typically, the crystallization of amorphous microwires was reported for $T_{ann} \geq 490$ °C [31].

Hysteresis loops of single microwires have been measured using the fluxmetric method previously described in details elsewhere [32]. In order to compare the samples with different compositions and subjected to different post-processing, we represent the hysteresis loops as the normalized magnetization, M/M_0, versus magnetic field, H, where M is the magnetic moment at a given magnetic field and M_0 is the magnetic moment of the sample at the maximum magnetic field amplitude, H_m.

In the case of magnetically hard microwires, the hysteresis loops have been measured using vibrating sample magnetometer by Physical Properties Measurements System by Quantum design.

The magnetostriction coefficient, λ_s, of the studied microwire, was evaluated by the Small Angle Magnetization Rotation (SAMR) method recently adapted for microwire [33].

III. Experimental Results and Discussion

The magnetostriction coefficient, λ_s, sign and value affects the hysteresis loops of amorphous microwires (see Figure 1). The character of hysteresis loops of amorphous microwires with positive and negative λ_s-values is quite different: microwires with positive λ_s-values present rectangular hysteresis loops, while hysteresis loops of microwires with negative λ_s-values are almost non-hysteretic with low coercitivity, H_c, values. Such influence must be attributed to the fact that the magnetoelastic anisotropy is the main source of magnetic anisotropy in amorphous materials [33].

The rectangular hysteresis loop observed in Fe-rich microwires with positive λ_s-values was interpreted in terms of axial magnetic anisotropy intrinsically related to a peculiar domain structure consisting of inner axially magnetized single domain and the outer domain shell with radial magnetization orientation [17].

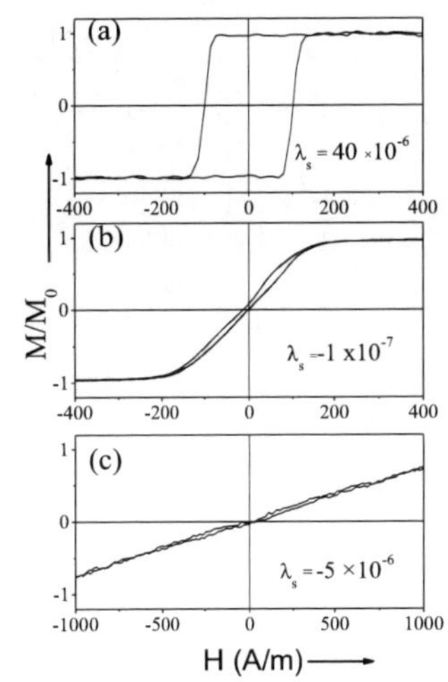

Figure 1. Hysteresis loops of magnetic microwires $Fe_{75}B_9Si_{12}C_4$ with positive (a) $Co_{67.1}Fe_{3.8}Ni_{1.4}Si_{14.5}B_{11.5}Mo_{1.7}$ with vanishing (b) and $Co_{77.5}Si_{15}B_{7.5}$ with negative (c) λ_s values.

The remagnetization of such microwires is running by the single and large Barkhausen jump within the inner domain [8][17]. Perfectly rectangular hysteresis loop character is related to an extremely fast magnetization switching by single domain wall propagation. Such microwires with rectangular hysteresis loops are suitable for the electronic surveillance applications. However, plurality of H_c-values is required for such applications. One of the possibilities to tune the H_c-values is the control of the internal stresses.

There are several factors responsible for the internal stresses value and distribution: (i) the difference in the thermal expansion coefficients of metallic alloy nucleus solidifying simultaneously with the glass coating surrounding it; (ii) the quenching stresses itself related to the rapid solidification of the metallic alloy nucleus from the surface inside the wire axis; and (iii) the drawing stresses [34]-[37].

Most theoretical evaluations of the internal stresses value and distribution show that the largest internal stresses are associated with the difference in the thermal expansion coefficients of the metallic alloy and the glass coating [34]-[37]. Accordingly, we must assume that the internal stresses value inside the metallic nucleus can be tuned by the ρ -ratio between the metallic nucleus diameter, d, and the total microwire diameter, D ($\rho = d/D$) [34]-[37].

Provided below hysteresis loops of $Fe_{70}B_{15}Si_{10}C_5$ microwires with different ρ–ratio experimentally confirm such assumption (see Figure 2). The difference of the hysteresis loops of microwires with the same chemical composition must be related to different internal stresses, σ_i, values. Indeed, the magnetoelastic anisotropy, K_{me}, is given by [8][9][34][38]:

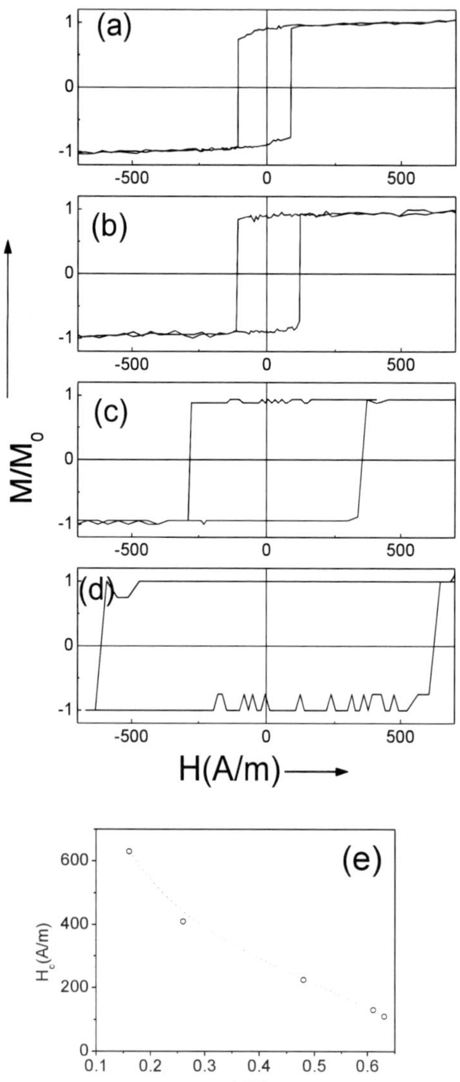

Figure 2. Hysteresis loops of $Fe_{70}B_{15}Si_{10}C_5$ amorphous microwires with different metallic nucleus diameter d and total diameters D: with $\rho = 0.63$; $d = 15$ μm (a); $\rho = 0.48$; $d = 10.8$ μm (b); $\rho = 0.26$; $d = 6$ μm (c); $\rho = 0.16$; $d = 3$ μm (d) and $H_c(\rho)$ dependence of the same microwires(e).

$$K_{me}=3/2\ \lambda_s\sigma_i \qquad (1)$$

Naturally, controllable glass-coating removal is the other route to tune hysteresis loops of glass-coated microwires.

The chemical etching of the glass-coating of $Co_{68.5}Si_{14.5}B_{14.5}Y_{2.5}$ microwire with higher negative λ_s-values allows transformation of linear hysteresis loop into rectangular (see Figure 3). As previously reported, after etching in 10% HF for 50 min, the glass-coating thickness decreases from 8.5 to 4 μm [39]. Accordingly, chemical etching of the glass-coating makes Co-rich microwires suitable for the electronic surveillance applications. Such remarkable influence of chemical etching must be associated with the relaxation of the internal stresses related

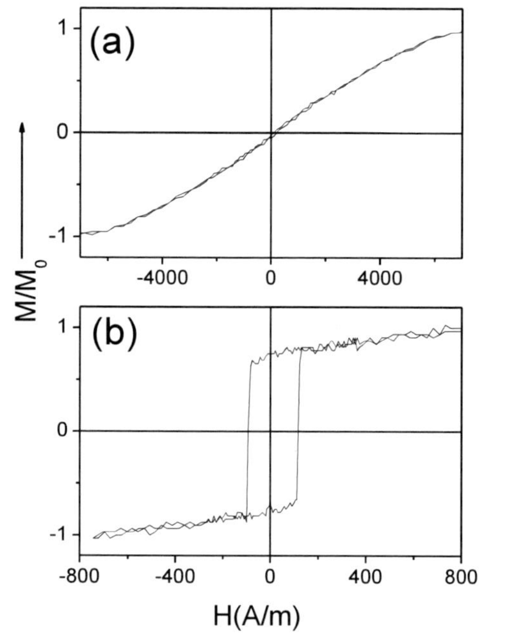

Figure 3. Hysteresis loops of as-prepared (a), and subjected to chemical etching for 50 min (b) $Co_{68.5}Si_{14.5}B_{14.5}Y_{2.5}$ microwires, adapted from [38].

to different thermal expansion coefficients of glass coating and metallic alloy. Accordingly, one can assume that the annealing allowing internal stresses relaxation must be the other route for adapting of glass-coated microwires for the electronic surveillance applications. Furthermore, such processing allows to keep the flexible and insulating glass coating.

In the case of $Fe_{70}B_{15}Si_{10}C_5$ amorphous microwires, annealing allows a slight coercivity decrease, however the shape of the hysteresis loops remains the same (see Figure 4).

More remarkable and complex annealing influence is observed in Fe-Ni based microwires. As-prepared $Fe_{62}Ni_{15.5}Si_{7.5}B_{15}$ microwires present rectangular hysteresis loops (see Figure 5a) as expected for microwires with

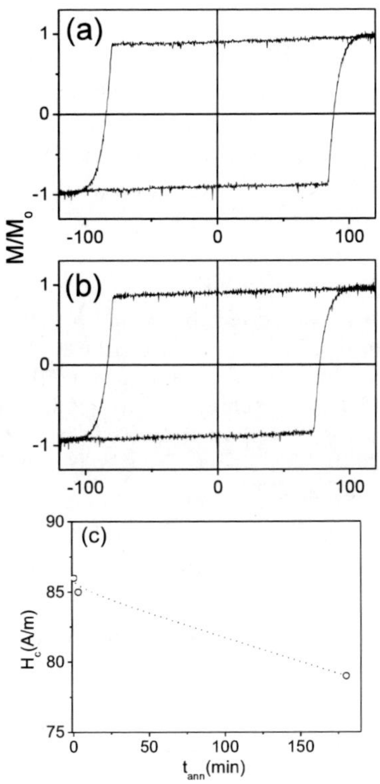

Figure 4. Hysteresis loops of as-prepared (a), and annealed at T_{ann} = 400 °C for 180 min (b) $Fe_{75}B_9Si_{12}C_4$ microwires and dependence of coercivity on annealing time (c).

positive λ_s-values (about 27 × 10^{-6}). After annealing of $Fe_{62}Ni_{15.5}Si_{7.5}B_{15}$ microwires, a remarkable increase in coercivity, H_c, is generally observed (see Figures 5b–f). The hysteresis loop character remains unchanged: all hysteresis loops present rectangular shape.

One of the origins of a rather different effect of annealing on coercivity of Fe and Fe-Ni based microwires can be a domain wall stabilization due to directional ordering of atomic pairs being considered [41]–[44]. However, local nano-sized precipitations and clustering observed in annealed Fe-Ni based microwires by the atom probe tomography can be the other origin of remarkable magnetic hardening and complex $H_c(t_{ann})$ dependence [42]. Furthermore, atom pair ordering and hence DW stabilization is reported for Fe-Ni and Fe-Co amorphous alloys [41]–[44]. Such DW stabilization is considered as the main origin of the H_c rising upon annealing observed in amorphous materials containing two or more ferromagnetic elements [43][44]. Accordingly, annealing of Fe-Ni based microwires allows considerable variation of coercivity in Fe-Ni based microwire with rectangular hysteresis loops.

Even more remarkable hardening upon conventional annealing has been reported in a variety of Co-rich microwires with vanishing λ_s-values [31][32]. Thus,

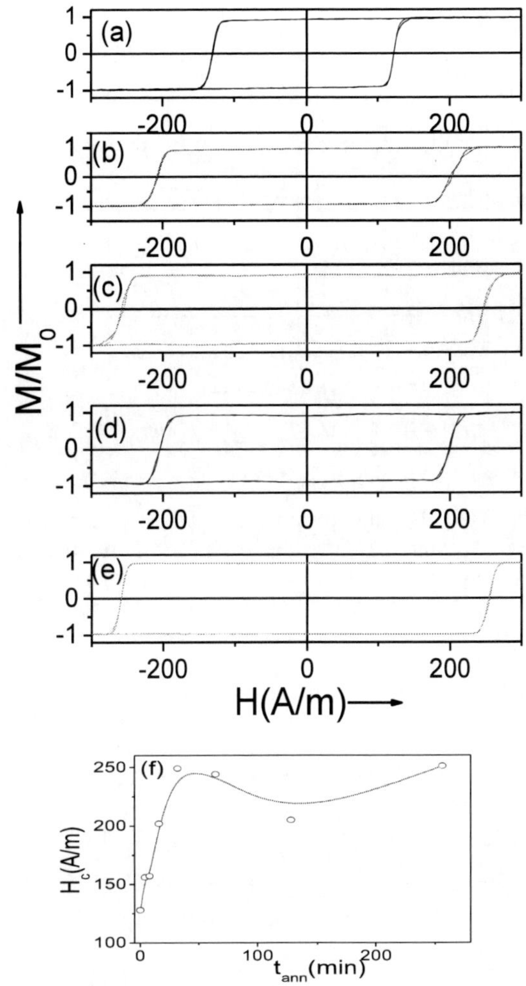

Figure 5. Hysteresis loops of as-prepared (a) and annealed at T_{ann} = 410 °C for 16 min (b) 32 min (c), 128 min (d), and 256 min (e) $Fe_{62}Ni_{15.5}Si_{7.5}B_{15}$ microwires and $H_c(t_{ann})$ dependence of the same microwire.

transformation of linear hysteresis loop with low coercivity ($H_c \approx$ 4 A/m) into rectangular with $H_c \approx$ 90 A/m and considerable magnetic hardening are observed in $Fe_{3.6}Co_{69.2}Ni_1B_{12.5}Si_{11}Mo_{1.5}C_{1.2}$ microwire upon annealing without stress (see Figure 6).

Observed annealing influence must be attributed to the internal stresses relaxation and rising of the inner axially magnetized inner core diameter. Similar evolution of hysteresis loops upon annealing is confirmed in various Co-based microwires with low and negative λ_s-values [9][45]. Consequently, similarly to glass-coating removal, annealing of Co-rich microwires allows for obtaining magnetically bistable Co-rich microwires.

On the other hand, magnetically hard and semi-hard wires are desirable for various applications like the electronic article surveillance, compass needles, motors, tachometers, magnetic tips for magnetic force microscopy,

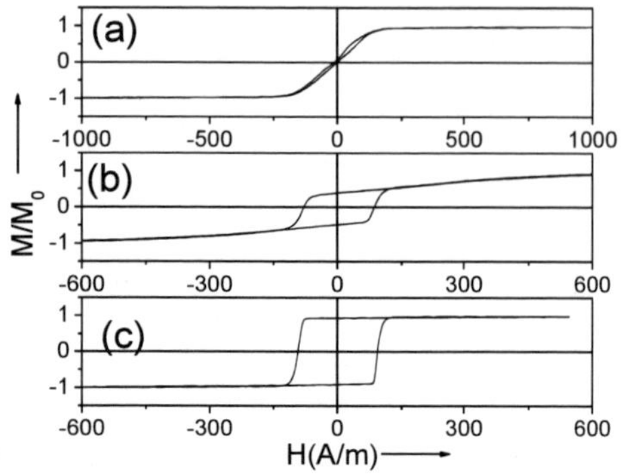

Figure 6. Hysteresis loop of as-prepared (a) and annealed at T_{ann} = 250 °C (b) and T_{ann} = 300 °C (c) $Fe_{3.6}Co_{69.2}Ni_1B_{12.5}Si_{11}Mo_{1.5}C_{1.2}$ microwires.

or dentistry [46]. For this purpose, $Fe_{50}Pt_{40}Si_{10}$ microwires have been prepared. As-prepared $Fe_{50}Pt_{40}Si_{10}$ microwires present amorphous structure. Magnetic hardening in $Fe_{50}Pt_{40}Si_{10}$ microwires has been observed after annealing (see Figure 7). In this case, after devitrification of amorphous $Fe_{50}Pt_{40}Si_{10}$ microwire, $H_c \approx 40$ kA/m is observed. Such magnetic hardening has been attributed to the formation of L10-type superstructure after crystallization of as-prepared amorphous precursor. As can be appreciated, magnetic hardening is observed in a wide temperatures range.

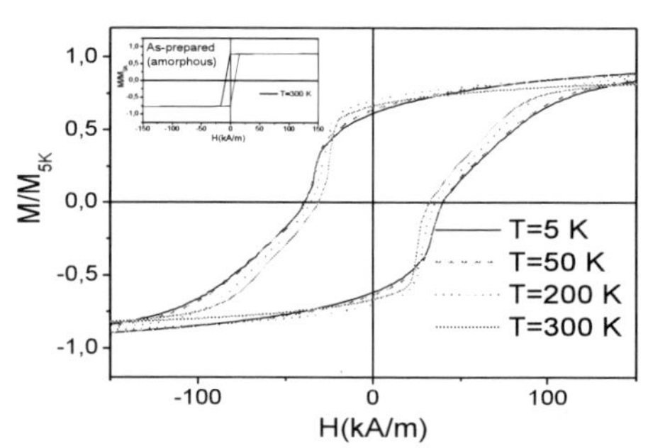

Figure 7. Hysteresis loops of annealed at 500 °C for 1 h $Fe_{50}Pt_{40}Si_{10}$ microwires measured at different temperatures. Hysteresis loops of as-prepared are provided in the inset Adapted from Ref. [46].

IV. CONCLUSIONS

We showed that the magnetic properties of amorphous magnetic microwires can be tuned either in as-prepared state or by controlling the magnetoelastic anisotropy through the magnetostriction coefficient value and by the internal stresses values related to the fabrication conditions and geometry of microwires. Furthermore, appropriate post-processing (including either conventional heat treatment, heat treatment in the presence of applied stress or magnetic field, or glass-coating removal) allows further tuning of magnetic properties of magnetic microwires. We showed that the microwires with coercivities from 1 A/m to 40 kA/m can be prepared. Future work will focus on the influence of external stimuli (temperature, stresses) on the magnetic properties of magnetic microwires.

ACKNOWLEDGMENT

This work was supported by Spanish MCIU under PGC2018-099530-B-C31 (MCIU/AEI/FEDER, UE) and by the Government of the Basque Country under PIBA 2018-44 and Elkartek (RTM 4.0) projects. The authors thank for technical and human support provided by SGIker of UPV/EHU (Medidas Magnéticas Gipuzkoa) and European funding (ERDF and ESF).

REFERENCES

[1] J. Durand, "Magnetic Properties of Metallic Glasses" in Topics in Applied Physics, vol. 53, 1983, Glassy Metals II. Atomic Structure and Dynamics, Electronic Structure, Magnetic Properties, Editors: H. Beck and H. -J. Giintherodt, Springer-Verlag, Berlin, Heidelberg, New York, Tokyo.

[2] G. Herzer, "Amorphous and Nanocrystalline Materials", in: Encyclopedia of Materials: Science and Technology, pp. 149–157, Elsevier Science Ltd., 2001, ISBN: 0-08-0431526.

[3] A. P. Zhukov, "The remagnetization process of bistable amorphous alloys", Mater. Des., vol. 5, pp. 299-305, 1993.

[4] M. Hagiwara, A. Inoue, and T. Masumoto, "Mechanical properties of Fe–Si–B amorphous wires produced by in-rotating-water spinning method", Metall. Trans. A, vol. 13, pp. 373-382, 1982.

[5] T. Goto, M. Nagano, and N. Wehara, "Mechanical properties of amorphous $Fe_{80}P_{16}C_3B_1$ filament produced by glass-coated melt spinning", Trans. JIM, vol. 18, pp. 759-764, 1997.

[6] D. C. Jiles, "Recent advances and future directions in magnetic materials", *Acta Mater.*, vol. 51, pp. 5907-5939, 2003.

[7] K. Mohri, F.B. Humphrey, K. Kawashima, K. Kimura, and M. Muzutani, "Large Barkhausen and Matteucci effects in FeCoSiB, FeCrSiB, and FeNiSiB amorphous wires", IEEE Trans.Magn., vol. 26, pp. 1789-1781, 1990.

[8] V. Zhukova J. M. Blanco, V. Rodionova, M. Ipatov, and A. Zhukov, "Domain wall propagation in micrometric wires: Limits of single domain wall regime", J. Appl. Phys., vol. 111, p. 07E311, 2012.

[9] A. Zhukov, J. M. Blanco, V. Rodionova, M. Ipatov, and A. Zhukov, "Manipulation of magnetic properties of glass-coated microwires by annealing", J. Magn. Magn. Mater., vol. 383, pp. 232–236, 2015

[10] A. F. Cobeño, A. Zhukov, J. M. Blanco, V. Larin, and J. Gonzalez, "Magnetoelastic sensor based on GMI of amorphous microwire", Sens. Actuat. A-Phys., vol. 91, pp. 95-98, 2001.

[11] A. Zhukov, M. Ipatov, and V. Zhukova, "Advances in Giant Magnetoimpedance of Materials", in Handbook of Magnetic Materials, ed. K. H. J. Buschow, vol. 24, ch. 2, 2015, pp. 139-236.

[12] K. Mohri, T. Uchiyama, L. P. Shen, C. M. Cai, and L. V. Panina, "Amorphous wire and CMOS IC-based sensitive micro-magnetic sensors (MI sensor and SI sensor) for intelligent

measurements and controls", J. Magn. Magn. Mater., vol. 249, pp.351-356, 2001.
[13] A. Zhukov et al., "Giant magnetoimpedance in rapidly quenched materials," J. Alloy Compd., vol. 814, p.152225, 2020.
[14] E.P. Harrison, G. L. Turney, H. Rowe, "Electrical Properties of Wires of High Permeability", Nature, vol. 135, p. 961, 1935.
[15] A. Zhukov et al., "Correlation of Crystalline Structure with Magnetic and Transport Properties of Glass-Coated Microwires", Crystals, vol. 7, p.41, 2017.
[16] M. Takajo, J. Yamasaki, and F.B. Humphrey, "Domain structure of chemically thinned Fe-Si-B amorphous wires", IEEE Trans. Magn, vol. 35, pp. 3904–3906, 1999.
[17] V. Zhukova, J. M. Blanco, A. Chizhik, M. Ipatov, and A. Zhukov, "AC-current-induced magnetization switching in amorphous microwires", Front. Phys. vol. 13(2), p.137501, 2018.
[18] K.R. Pirota, L. Kraus, H. Chiriac, and M. Knobel, "Magnetic properties and GMI in a CoFeSiB glass-covered microwire", J. Magn. Magn. Mater., vol. 21, p. L243-L247, 2000.
[19] P. Corte-León et al., "Engineering of magnetic properties of Co-rich microwires by joule heating", Intermetallics, vol. 105, pp.92-98, 2019.
[20] A. Zhukov, V. Zhukova, J.M. Blanco, and J. Gonzalez "Recent research on magnetic properties of glass-coated microwires", J. Magn. Magn., Mater. vol. 294, pp.182-192, 2005.
[21] Y. Honkura, and S. Honkura, "The Development of ASIC Type GSR Sensor Driven by GHz Pulse Current", Sensors, vol. 20, p. 1023, 2020.
[22] T. Uchiyama, K. Mohri, and S. Nakayama, "Measurement of Spontaneous Oscillatory Magnetic Field of Guinea-Pig Smooth Muscle Preparation Using Pico-Tesla Resolution Amorphous Wire Magneto-Impedance Sensor." IEEE Trans. Magn. Vol. 47, pp. 3070–3073, 2011.
[23] S. Parkin and S.-H Yang, "Memory on the racetrack", Nature Nanotechnology, vol. 10, pp.195-198, 2015.
[24] D.A. Allwood et al., "Magnetic Domain-Wall Logic", Science, vol. *309*, pp. 1688–1692, 2005.
[25] A. Zhukov, J.González, J.M. Blanco, M.Vázquez, and V. Larin, "Microwires coated by glass: a new family of soft and hard magnetic materials", J. Mater. Res., vol. 15, pp. 2107-2113, 2000.
[26] S. Gudoshnikov et al., "Evaluation of use of magnetically bistable microwires for magnetic labels", Phys. Status Solidi A, vol. 208(3), pp.526–529, 2011.
[27] D. Kozejova et al., "Biomedical applications of glass-coated microwires", J. Magn. Magn. Mater., 470 (2019) 2-5.
[28] A. Talaat et al., "Ferromagnetic glass-coated microwires with good heating properties for magnetic hyperthermia", Sci. Rep. vol. 6, p.39300, 2016.
[29] O. Mitxelena-Iribarren et al., "Glass-coated ferromagnetic microwire-induced magnetic hyperthermia for in vitro cancer cell treatment", Materials Science & Engineering C, vol. 106, p. 110261, 2020.
[30] V. Zhukova et al., "Correlation between magnetic and mechanical properties of devitrified glass-coated $Fe_{71.8}Cu_1Nb_{3.1}Si_{15}B_{9.1}$ microwires", J. Magn. Magn. Mater. vol. 249(P1-II), pp. 79-84, 2002.
[31] L. Gonzalez-Legarreta et al., "Route of magnetoimpedance and domain walls dynamics optimization in Co-based microwires", J. Alloys Compound. Vol. 830, p.154576, 2020.
[32] L. Gonzalez-Legarreta et al., "Optimization of magnetic properties and GMI effect of Thin Co-rich Microwires for GMI Microsensors", Sensors, vol. 20, p.1588, 2020.
[33] M. Churyukanova et al., "Magnetostriction investigation of soft magnetic microwires" Phys. Status Solidi A, Vol. 213, Issue 2, pp. 363–367, 2016.
[34] H. Chiriac, T. A. Ovari, and Gh. Pop, "Internal stress distribution in glass-covered amorphous magnetic wires", Phys. Rev. B, vol. 42, p. 10105, 1995.
[35] A. Zhukov et al., "Ferromagnetic resonance and structure of Fe-based glass-coated microwires", J. Magn. Magn. Mater., vol. 203, pp. 238-240, 1999.
[36] S. A. Baranov, V. S. Larin, and A. V. Torcunov, "Technology, preparation and properties of the cast glass-coated magnetic microwires", Crystals, vol. 7, p. 136, 2017.
[37] H. Chiriac, T. -A- Ovari, and A. Zhukov, "Magnetoelastic anisotropy of amorphous microwires", J. Magn. Magn. Mater., vol. 254-255, pp. 469-471, 2003.
[38] V. Zhukova e.al, "Optimization of Magnetic Properties of Magnetic Microwires by Post-Processing", Processes, vol. 8, p. 1006, 2020.
[39] C.F. Catalan et al. "Effect of glass coating on magnetic properties of amorphous microwires", Rapidly Quenched & Metastable Materials. Mater. Sci. Eng. A, Supplement pp.438–441, 1997.
[40] V. Zhukova et al., "Engineering of magnetic properties and domain wall dynamics in Fe-Ni-based amorphous microwires by annealing", Aip Adv., vol. 10, p. 015130, 2020.
[42] A. Zhukov et al., "Effect of annealing on magnetic properties and magnetostriction coefficient of Fe–Ni-based amorphous microwires", J. Alloys Compd. Vol. 651, pp. 718–723, 2015.
[43] F. Luborsky and J. Walter, "Magnetic anneal anisotropy in amorphous alloys". IEEE Trans. Magn. Vol. 13, pp. 953–956, 1977.
[44] J. Haimovich, Y. Jagielinski, and T. Egami, "Magnetic and structural effects of anelastic deformation of an amorphous alloy", J. Appl. Phys. vol. 57, pp. 3581–3583, 1985.
[45] A. Zhukov et al., "Engineering of magnetic properties and GMI effect in Co-rich amorphous microwires", J. Alloys Compd. Vol. *664*, pp. 235–241, 2016.
[46] A. Zhukov et al.,"Magnetic hardening of Fe-Pt and Fe-Pt-M (M=B, Si) microwires", J. Alloys Compd. Vol. 735, pp. 1071–1078, 2018.

Surface Acoustic Waves Sensors Based Lithium Niobate And Quartz For Particulates matter Measurments

Fatima-Ezzahraa Dbibih
Time and frequency Department
FEMTO-ST Institute
Besançon, France
e-mail: fe.dbibih@femto-st.fr

Jean-Marc Cote
Time and frequency Department
FEMTO-ST Institute
Besançon, France
e-mail: jeanmarc.cote@femto-st.fr

Valérie Soumann
Time frequency Department
FEMTO-ST Institute
Besançon, France
e-mail: valerie.soumann@femto-st.fr

Virginie Blondeau-Patissier
Time and frequency Department
FEMTO-ST Institute
Besançon, France
e-mail: virginie.blondeau@femto-st.fr

***Abstract*—This abstract presents a comparison between three types of surface acoustic wave (SAW) sensors for measurement of particulate matter PM10 and PM2.5 and surface cleaning of sensors after saturation. The first SAW sensor is a Love wave device based on SiO_2/AT-quartz cut substrate, the second one is a Rayleigh wave sensor based Lithium Niobate ($LiNbO_3$) 128° YX $LiNbO_3$ and the last one is a Pseudo wave sensor on SiO_2/41° YX $LiNbO_3$. The SAW sensors are used in combination with a 3 Lpm cascade impactor to classify particulates by size before being measured. The sensitivity was investigated using two type of aerosols PM2.5 and PM10 in the [0-200] μg/m^3 concentration range. The sensors based on AT-Quartz show higher sensitivity for particulates matter measurements.**

Keywords-PM2.5; PM10; SAW sensors; Lithium Niobate; Quartz.

I. INTRODUCTION

Particulate matter (PM) causes over 7 million premature deaths per year worldwide according to World Health organization [1]. PM can cause health effects like dangerous pneumonia diseases [2] and environmental damage. Over the last years, PM measurement has become a very important axis of research. Since the existing monitoring systems are of a considerable size and too expensive, miniaturization of monitoring systems has become one of the hot spot in actual research. The equipment of measurements has to be instantly reactive by performing measurements in real time. In our team, we have developed a system that combines a miniaturized cascade impactor features elastic surface acoustic wave sensor SAW [3]. This system takes advantage of a 3 Lpm cascade impactor as filtration system to separate PM10 and PM2.5 and integrated SAW sensors for real time measurement. The purpose of this study is to compare the sensitivity of three types of SAW sensor based on different piezoelectric substrates. The first sensor exploits Love waves on an AT-cut Quartz substrate, these having already been studied in previous works [3] but whose k^2 value is not sufficient to allow a potential cleaning of the surface. The second one is based on Rayleigh waves on a 128° YX $LiNbO_3$ substrates and the third one is a Pseudo Surface Acoustic Wave (PSAW) on 41°YX $LiNbO_3$. A layer of silica with a thickness of 1.5 μm is deposited on the top of the PSAW and Love SAW sensors as a guiding layer with shear velocity lower than the substrates (3764 m/s). Lately, PSAW devices have become attractive in several sensing applications such as liquid sensing [4] and biosensing [5]. PSAW can be generated on 36°YX $LiTaO_3$ and 41°YX $LiNbO_3$. The PSAW SAW crystals have a high electromechanical coupling factor and better temperature stability. The SAW sensors characteristics beside test conditions will be discussed in the section 2. The sensitivity results obtained will be presented in the last section.

II. EXPERIMENTAL

SAW sensors consisting of delay lines are fabricated using a conventional photolithography process. The input and output interdigital transducers (IDT) consist of double finger pairs with a periodicity p of 10 μm and wavelength λ of 40 μm. The region lying between the two IDTs constitutes the sensing area. Prior to conducting the measurements of the sensor's responses, the electrical characterization was performed to measure the insertion loss and the phase response vs frequency. This step allows the validation of sensors before testing. The working frequency of delay lines are described in Table 1 for the three types of sensors.

TABLE I. CARACTERISTICS OF SAW SENSORS

Substrate	*Type of wave*	*Working frequency (MHz)*	*Velocity (m/s)*	*Electomechan-ical coupling factor (k^2) (%)*
AT-Quartz	Love wave	125	5100	0.14
128° YX $LiNbO_3$	Rayleigh wave	100	3950	5.5
41° YX $LiNbO_3$	PSAW wave	115	4450	17.2

SAW sensors were exposed to PM2.5 and PM10 particles by an experimental set-up bench consisting of 1 m^3 chamber, the particle's generator AGK 2000 (Palas® Model AGK 2000) and the optical reference system FIDAS® 100. For the generation of PM, sodium chloride (NaCl) was used, while PM10 is derived from silicon carbide (SiC). The concentration of these two types of particles evolving between 0 and 200 μg/m³. When the particles fall on the sensor surface, the propagation of the acoustic waves is perturbed. Accordingly, the particle's concentration can be determined by measuring the phase velocity shift of the wave from the phase signal with a dedicated electronic open loop interrogation [4].

III. RESULTS AND DISCUSSION

Figure 1 and 2 present plots of phase variation dϕ/dt of sensors based AT-Quartz (in red), 128° YX $LiNbO_3$ (in black) and 41° YX $LiNbO_3$ (in blue) with the concentration of PM2.5 and PM10, respectively, measured with the optical system FIDAS®.

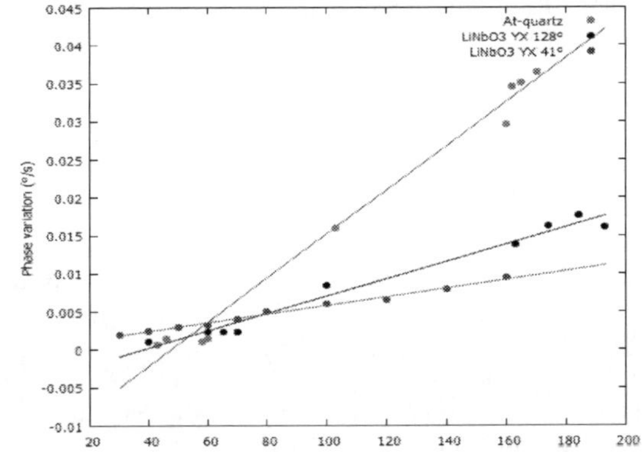

Figure 1. Phase derivative of SAW sensors based on AT-Quartz substrate (red) 128° YX $LiNbO_3$ substrate (black) and 41° YX $LiNbO_3$ substrate as a function of PM2.5 concentration.

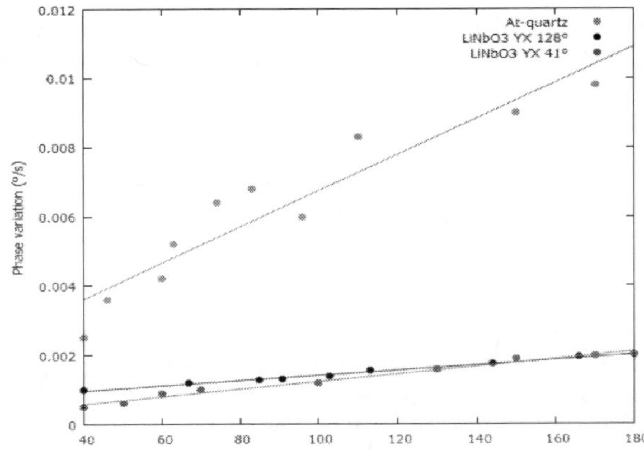

Figure 2. Phase derivative of SAW sensors based on AT-Quartz substrate (red) 128° YX $LiNbO_3$ substrate (black) and 41° YX $LiNbO_3$ substrate as a function of PM10 concentration.

According to these results, Love wave sensors based on AT quartz cut shows the best sensitivity for both PM2.5 and PM10. In the second range, Rayleigh wave based 128° YX $LiNbO_3$ shows higher sensitivity than PSAW wave sensors for both type of particles PM10 and PM 2.5. The sensors sensitivity is estimated by applying a linear fit of the plotted data. The sensitivity of sensor based on Quartz is 3.10^{-4} °s^{-1}μ$g^{-1}m^3$ for PM 2.5 and 5.10^{-5} °s^{-1}μ$g^{-1}m^3$ for PM 10. The sensitivity is approximately 3 times lower for the 128° YX $LiNbO_3$ based sensors (1.10-4s^{-1}μ$g^{-1}m^3$ for PM 2.5 and 1.10-5 ° s^{-1}μ$g^{-1}m^3$ for PM 10) and 5 times for the 41° YX $LiNbO_3$ (6.10^{-5} s^{-1}μ$g^{-1}m^3$ for PM2.5 and 1.10^{-4} ° s^{-1}μ$g^{-1}m^3$). The dispersion of response points observed in the case of PM10 measurement can be explained by the fact that most adhesion forces depend linearly on the diameter of the particles [5]. As a result, smaller particles settle more on the sensor surface, unlike larger particles, which are rebounded. Work is underway to develop a layer to overcome this phenomenon. Although the sensitivities of the sensors made from these last two substrates are less good than for quartz, they nevertheless seem interesting and sufficient to allow both a measurement of the particles targeted in environment while allowing the cleaning of the sensors to be tested once they will be used and fouled.

ACKNOWLEDGMENT

This work has been supported by the French RENATECH network and its FEMTO-ST technological facility.

REFERENCES

[1] 'Air pollution'. https://www.who.int/news-room/fact-sheets/detail/ambient-(outdoor)-air-quality-and-health (accessed Oct. 24, 2019).

[2] H. Lin *and al.*, 'Particle size and chemical constituents of ambient particulate pollution associated with cardiovascular mortality in Guangzhou, China', *Environmental Pollution*, vol. 208, pp. 758–766, Jan. 2016, doi: 10.1016/j.envpol.2015.10.056.

[3] L. Djoumi, M. Vanotti, and V. Blondeau-Patissier, 'Real Time Cascade Impactor Based On Surface Acoustic Wave Delay Lines for PM10 and PM2.5 Mass Concentration Measurement', *Sensors (Basel)*, vol. 18, pp. 255-266, Jan. 2018, doi: 10.3390/s18010255.

[4] J. Hechner and W. Soluch, 'Pseudo surface acoustic wave dual delay line on 41°YX $LiNbO_3$ for liquid sensors', *Sensors and Actuators B: Chemical*, vol. 111–112, pp. 436–440, Nov. 2005, doi: 10.1016/j.snb.2005.03.042.

[5] E. Berkenpas, P. Millard, and M. Pereira da Cunha, 'Detection of Escherichia coli O157:H7 with langasite pure shear horizontal surface acoustic wave sensors', *Biosensors and Bioelectronics*, vol. 21, no. 12, pp. 2255–2262, Jun. 2006, doi: 10.1016/j.bios.2005.11.005.

Simultaneous Localization and Communication Methods Using Short-Time and Narrow-Band Acoustic Signals

Masanari Nakamura
Hokkaido University
Sapporo 060-0814, Japan
Email: masanari@ist.hokudai.ac.jp

Hiromichi Hashizume
National Institute of Informatics
Tokyo 101-8430, Japan
Email: has@nii.ac.jp

Masanori Sugimoto
Hokkaido University
Sapporo 060-0814, Japan
Email: sugi@ist.hokudai.ac.jp

***Abstract*—In this paper, we describe simultaneous localization and communication methods using acoustic signals transmitted simultaneously from multiple speakers. In the case where short-time and narrow-band acoustic signals are used, the interference of signals could cause a systematic error of localization and communication depending on the modulation value. To reduce this systematic error, a noninterference region was constituted in the received signal, and localization and demodulation were processed using this region. Through simulation and real-environment experiments, it was confirmed that the proposed method can reduce the systematic error.**

***Keywords*–indoor localization; TDoA; acoustic signal; acoustic communication; DPSK.**

I. INTRODUCTION

Mobile devices, such as smartphones, tablets, and smart glasses are widely used nowadays. Complementing these is the location data of mobile devices, which are employed in various services. Outside a building, mobile devices can precisely locate themselves via the Global Navigation Satellite System (GNSS). However, inside a building, the GNSS could make large errors due to shielding. To circumvent this, alternative methods for indoor environments have been widely researched [1].

In this paper, we describe the indoor localization method using acoustic signals. Acoustic signals simultaneously transmitted by speakers installed in an indoor environment are captured by a microphone. The location of the microphone is estimated by using the Time Difference of Arrival (TDoA) of these signals. As a microphone is embedded in mobile devices, this system can localize mobile devices without any additional hardware.

With regard to localization performance, the precision of localization mainly depends on the transmitted signal. In general, the wider the bandwidth of the signal, the more precise is the TDoA estimation. However, from the viewpoint of scalability, it is desirable to have as narrow a bandwidth as possible. Similarly, the longer the length of the signal, the more precise is the TDoA estimation due to the signal-to-noise ratio (SNR). However, from the viewpoint of the update rate, it is desirable that the length of the signal be as short as possible.

Herein, if signals for localization can contain some information, it simultaneously enables acoustic communication. Therefore, acoustic signals can be used more efficiently and could expand the range of applications. For indoor acoustic communication, some methods have been proposed [2][3]. As errors due to multipath propagation occur, using Differential Phase-Shift Keying (DPSK) is desirable as it can cancel these errors. However, if short-time and narrow-band acoustic signals are used, the communication performance deteriorates due to interference between the signals transmitted simultaneously by different speakers. In addition, when the acoustic signals are modulated, the estimated TDoA have systematic errors depending on the modulated values.

In this paper, we propose simultaneous localization and communication methods that can reduce the above systematic error using short-time and narrow-band signals. In the received signal of our proposed method, there is a region where each signal is orthogonal to each other. As the TDoA estimation and demodulation are processed using this region, our proposed method reduces the systematic error due to interference.

To concisely discuss the influence of signal interference on localization and communication, we evaluated the azimuth estimation performance by the TDoA of two speakers as one-dimensional localization.

The remainder of this paper is structured as follows. Section II shows the details of the issues dealt with herein and the related research. Section III describes the proposed method. In Section IV, comparative evaluations of the conventional and proposed methods, performed under simulation and real environments are discussed. Section V presents the experimental results and discussions. Conclusions are provided in Section VI.

II. RELATED WORK

Herein, we describe the problem while performing azimuth estimation using two speakers and communication by DPSK simultaneously using short-time and narrow-band signals. To describe these processes of transmitting and receiving acoustic signals, we use the chirp signals as an example. The i-th signals simultaneously transmitted from the left and right speakers are

$$s_R^i(t) = \begin{cases} \sin(2\pi(f_1 t + \frac{1}{2}\alpha_{12}t^2) + \phi_i^R) & 0 \le t \le T \\ 0 & otherwise \end{cases} \quad (1)$$

$$s_L^i(t) = \begin{cases} \sin(2\pi(f_3 t + \frac{1}{2}\alpha_{34}t^2) + \phi_i^L) & 0 \le t \le T \\ 0 & otherwise \end{cases} \quad (2)$$

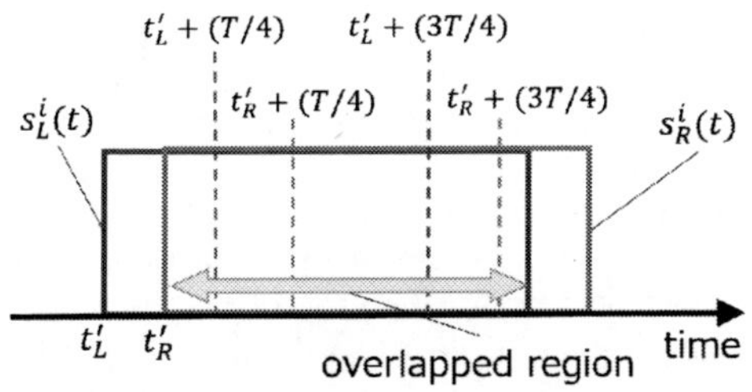

Figure 1. Illustration of the received signals.

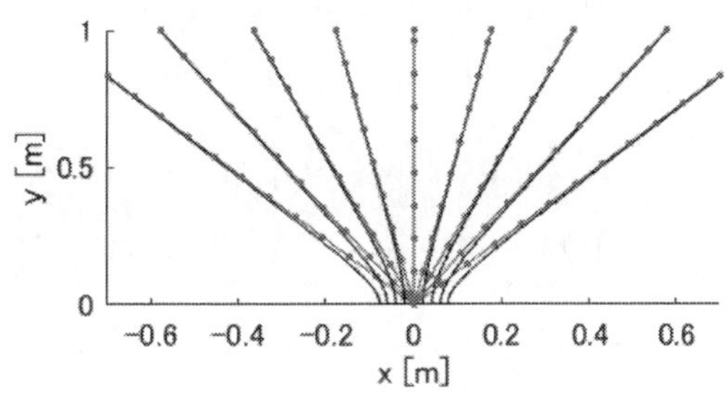

Figure 2. Hyperbola of TDoA (black lines) and its asymptote (red lines).

where ϕ_i^R and ϕ_i^L are DPSK modulation values and $\alpha_{12} = (f_2 - f_1)/T$, $\alpha_{34} = (f_4 - f_3)/T$. We call these signals a symbol. The received signal can be expressed as

$$r^i(t) = a_R s_R^i(t - t_R) + a_L s_L^i(t - t_L) \tag{3}$$

where t_R and t_L represent the reception times of the left and right signals of the speaker. The analytic signals corresponding to the above signals are

$$e_R(t) = \begin{cases} \exp(j2\pi(f_1 t + \frac{1}{2}\alpha_{12}t^2)) & 0 \le t \le T \\ 0 & otherwise \end{cases} \tag{4}$$

$$e_L(t) = \begin{cases} \exp(j2\pi(f_3 t + \frac{1}{2}\alpha_{34}t^2)) & 0 \le t \le T \\ 0 & otherwise \end{cases} \tag{5}$$

The received signal is processed using the matched filter with analytic signals as follows:

$$\begin{aligned} c_R^i(t) &= \int_t^{t+T} r^i(\tau) e_R(\tau - t) d\tau \\ &= \int_t^{t+T} a_R s_R^i(\tau - t_R) e_R(\tau - t) d\tau \\ &+ \int_t^{t+T} a_L s_L^i(\tau - t_L) e_R(\tau - t) d\tau \end{aligned} \tag{6}$$

The reception time of speaker R is estimated as follows:

$$t_R = \arg\max_t |c_R^i(t)| \tag{7}$$

If the second term $\int_t^{t+T} s_L^i(\tau - t_L) e_R(\tau - t) d\tau$ in (6) is not zero, the time that has the maximum value of $|c_R^i(t)|$ could not match the true reception time, and some error occurs in the estimated value of the reception time. As the phases of each term in (6) depend on ϕ_i^R and ϕ_i^L in (1) and (2), the error in reception time could change depending on the DPSK modulation value. To calculate TDoA, a similar process is applied to estimate the reception time of speaker L's signal t_L; subsequently, an error of the same type occurs in t_L estimation.

When the following the Orthogonal Frequency Division Multiplexing (OFDM) signals are used instead of chirp signals, the above systematic error would occur. This is because $s_R^i(t)$ and $s_L^i(t)$ are not orthogonal except where the microphone is located at the same distance from the speakers R and L.

$$s_R^i(t) = \begin{cases} \sum_{k=1}^K \sin(2\pi f_k^R t + \psi_k^R + \phi_i^R) & 0 \le t \le T \\ 0 & otherwise \end{cases} \tag{8}$$

$$s_L^i(t) = \begin{cases} \sum_{k=1}^K \sin(2\pi f_k^L t + \psi_k^L + \phi_i^L) & 0 \le t \le T \\ 0 & otherwise \end{cases} \tag{9}$$

In (8), (9), ψ_K^R and ψ_k^L are the initial phases that determine the waveform of the OFDM signal.

The second term in (6) that represents interference decreases as the length and bandwidth of the signal increase. Therefore, in conventional methods, such as chirp signal-based [4][5], OFDM-based [6][7][8], and CDMA-based methods [9][10][11][12], and random signal methods [13][14], interference was avoided by setting the length and bandwidth of signals to sufficiently large values.

In this paper, we propose a method that can reduce the above systematic errors with short-time and narrow-band signals. Our proposed method is an extension of the localization method FDM-PAM [15][16][17] to enable simultaneous communication.

III. Proposed Method

In this section, we propose simultaneous localization and communication methods that can reduce the systematic error using short-time and narrow-band signals.

A. Transmission Signal

In our proposed method, the speakers R and L transmit the following signals simultaneously,

$$s_R^i(t) = \begin{cases} \sin(2\pi f_1 t + \phi_i^R) + \sin(2\pi f_2 t + \phi_i^R + \pi) & 0 \le t \le T \\ 0 & otherwise \end{cases} \tag{10}$$

$$s_L^i(t) = \begin{cases} \sin(2\pi f_3 t + \phi_i^L) + \sin(2\pi f_4 t + \phi_i^L + \pi) & 0 \le t \le T \\ 0 & otherwise \end{cases} \tag{11}$$

where frequency f_n is set to $f_n = f_1 + ((n-1)/(T/2))$.

B. TDoA Estimation and Demodulation

The process of TDoA estimation for the i-th symbol is described below. The signals transmitted from the left and right speakers are received by the microphone as follows:

$$r^i(t) = a_R s_R^i(t - t_R) + a_L s_L^i(t - t_L) \tag{12}$$

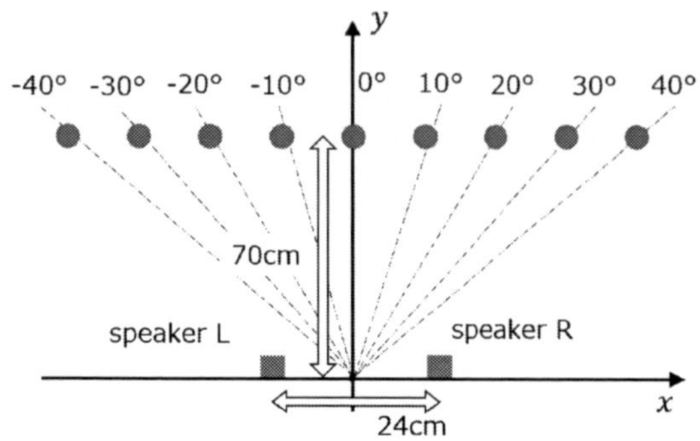

Figure 3. Speaker and microphone arrangement.

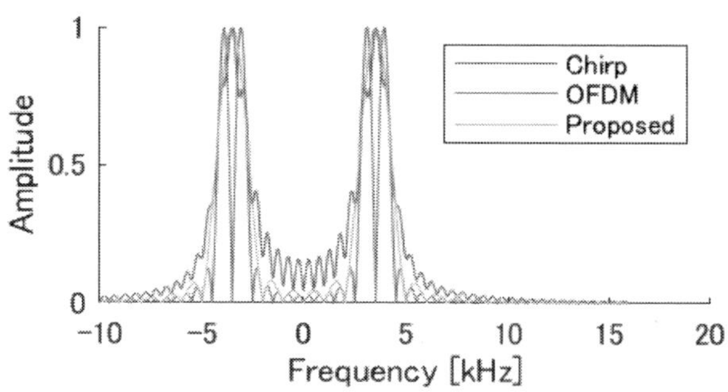

Figure 4. Frequency spectrum of the signal transmitted by speaker R.

The received signal is processed using the matched filter with analytic signals as follows:

$$e_R(t) = \begin{cases} \exp(j2\pi f_1 t) + \exp(j(2\pi f_2 t + \pi)) & 0 \leq t \leq T \\ 0 & otherwise \end{cases} \tag{13}$$

$$e_L(t) = \begin{cases} \exp(j2\pi f_3 t) + \exp(j(2\pi f_4 t + \pi)) & 0 \leq t \leq T \\ 0 & otherwise \end{cases} \tag{14}$$

Calculate the temporary reception time t'_R,t'_L as follows.

$$t'_R = \arg\max_t |c^i_R(t)| \tag{15}$$

$$t'_L = \arg\max_t |c^i_L(t)| \tag{16}$$

where c^i_R and c^i_L are

$$c^i_R(t) = \int_t^{t+T} r^i(\tau) e_R(\tau - t) d\tau \tag{17}$$

$$c^i_L(t) = \int_t^{t+T} r^i(\tau) e_L(\tau - t) d\tau. \tag{18}$$

Figure 1 indicates an illustration of received signal. Here, suppose the absolute value of TDoA $|\Delta t| = |t_L - t_R|$ is less than $T/4$. From the definition of f_n and the appendix, if the signal of length $T/2$ is cut out of the overlapped region of the received signal (Figure 1), sine waves that compose the cut-out signal are mutually orthogonal. As shown in Figure 1, the signal of length $T/2$ is obtained by cutting out a region from $t'_L + (T/4)$ to $t'_L + (3T/4)$ or from $t'_R + (T/4)$ to $t'_R + (3T/4)$.

In the following, t_{max} is the reference time of cutting out. To avoid the error due to the influence of (17), (18), t_{max} is set to t'_R or t'_L as follows. $|c^i_R(t'_R)|$ is larger than or equal to $|c^i_L(t'_L)|$, t_{max} is set to t'_R. If $|c^i_R(t'_R)|$ is less than $|c^i_L(t'_L)|$, t_{max} is set to t'_L. In this section, we take $t_{max} = t'_R$ as an example. The same is obviously true for the case of $t'_{max} = t_L$.

The cut-out signal $r^i_c(t)$ is represented as follows:

$$\begin{aligned} r^i_c(t) &= a_R \sin(2\pi f_1(t + t_{max} + \frac{T}{4}) + \phi^R_i) \\ &+ a_R \sin(2\pi f_2(t + t_{max} + \frac{T}{4}) + \phi^R_i) \\ &+ a_L \sin(2\pi f_3(t + t_{max} + \frac{T}{4} + \Delta t) + \phi^L_i) \\ &+ a_L \sin(2\pi f_4(t + t_{max} + \frac{T}{4} + \Delta t) + \phi^L_i) \end{aligned} \tag{19}$$

where $r^i_c(t) = 0$ for $t < 0, t > T/2$. To obtain the phase value of each sine wave of (19), the inner product of $r^i_c(t)$ and complex sine wave is calculated as follows:

$$c^i_n = \int_0^{T/2} r^i_c(t) \exp(-j2\pi f_n t) dt \tag{20}$$

c^i_1, c^i_2, c^i_3 and c^i_4 can be represented as follows (see Appendix for details):

$$c^i_1 = \frac{a_R T}{4j} \exp(j(2\pi f_1(t_{max} + \frac{T}{4}) + \phi^R_i)) \tag{21}$$

$$c^i_2 = \frac{a_R T}{4j} \exp(j(2\pi f_2(t_{max} + \frac{T}{4}) + \phi^R_i)) \tag{22}$$

$$c^i_3 = \frac{a_L T}{4j} \exp(j(2\pi f_3(t_{max} + \frac{T}{4} + \Delta t) + \phi^L_i)) \tag{23}$$

$$c^i_4 = \frac{a_L T}{4j} \exp(j(2\pi f_4(t_{max} + \frac{T}{4} + \Delta t) + \phi^L_i)). \tag{24}$$

The phase values of jc^i_1, jc^i_2, jc^i_3, jc^i_4 can be calculated as follows:

$$\phi^i_1 = 2\pi f_1(t_{max} + \frac{T}{4}) + \phi^R_i \tag{25}$$

$$\phi^i_2 = 2\pi f_2(t_{max} + \frac{T}{4}) + \phi^R_i \tag{26}$$

$$\phi^i_3 = 2\pi f_3(t_{max} + \frac{T}{4} + \Delta t) + \phi^L_i \tag{27}$$

$$\phi^i_4 = 2\pi f_4(t_{max} + \frac{T}{4} + \Delta t) + \phi^L_i \tag{28}$$

The phase differences of each speaker's signal are

$$\begin{aligned} \phi^i_2 - \phi^i_1 &= 2\pi(f_2 - f_1)(t_{max} + \frac{T}{4}) + (\phi^R_i - \phi^R_i) \\ &= 2\pi \frac{1}{T/2}(t_{max} + \frac{T}{4}) \end{aligned} \tag{29}$$

$$\begin{aligned} \phi^i_4 - \phi^i_3 &= 2\pi(f_4 - f_3)(t_{max} + \frac{T}{4} + \Delta t) + (\phi^L_i - \phi^L_i) \\ &= 2\pi \frac{1}{T/2}(t_{max} + \frac{T}{4} + \Delta t). \end{aligned} \tag{30}$$

from the definition of f_n. Therefore, TDoA Δt can be calculated as follows:

$$\Delta t = \frac{(\phi^i_4 - \phi^i_3) - (\phi^i_2 - \phi^i_1)}{2\pi}(T/2) \tag{31}$$

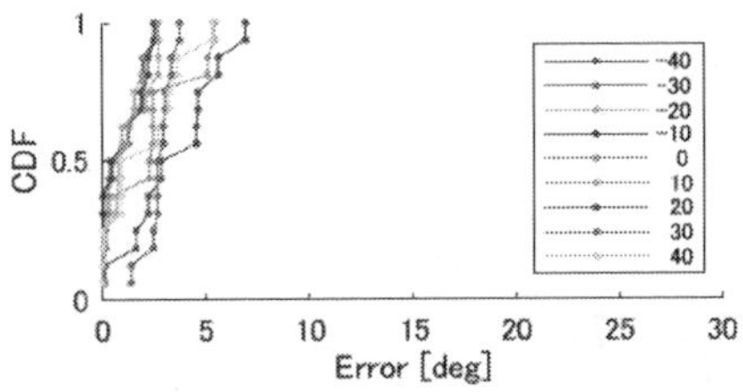

(a) Azimuth estimation: chirp method.

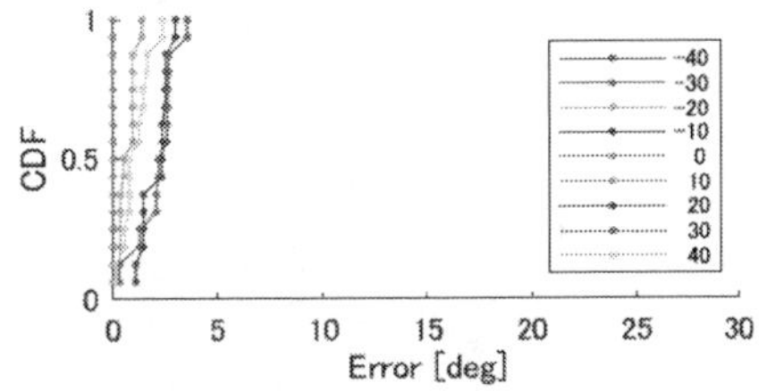

(b) Azimuth estimation: OFDM method.

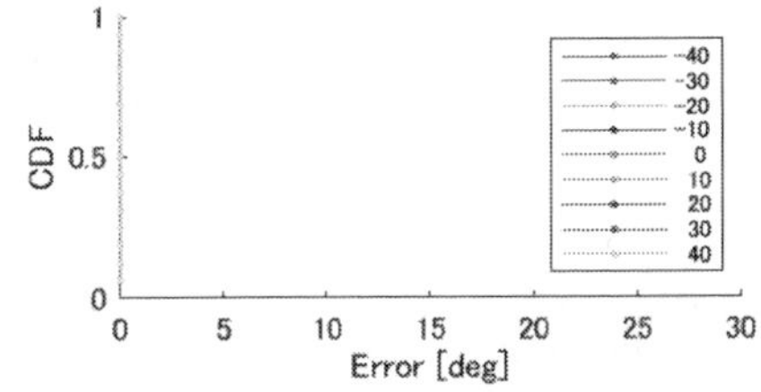

(c) Azimuth estimation: proposed method.

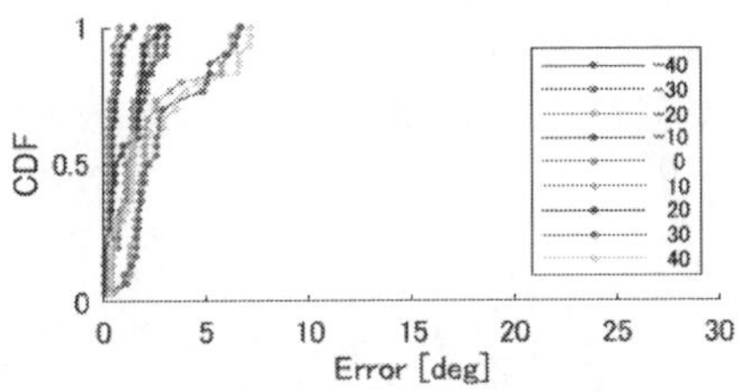

(d) Demodulation: chirp method.

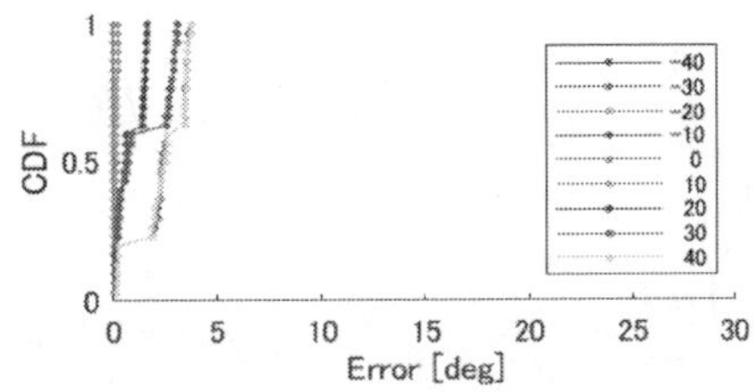

(e) Demodulation: OFDM method.

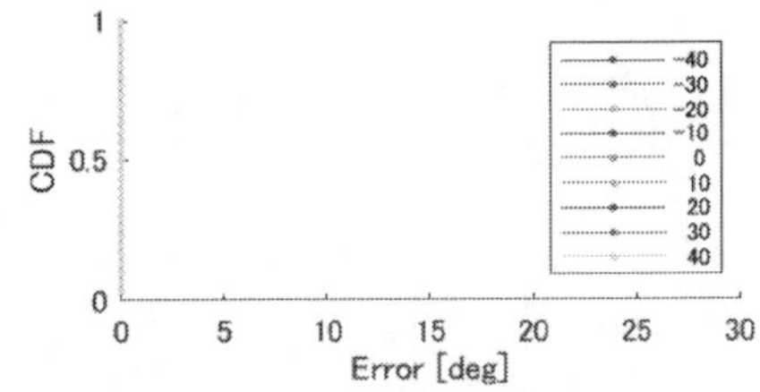

(f) Demodulation: proposed method.

Figure 5. Simulation results (Legends indicate the azimuth θ of the microphone's location).

TABLE I. ENCODED VALUES.

i	1	2	3	4	5	6	7	8	9	10	11	12	13	14	15	16
ϕ_i^R	0	$\frac{\pi}{4}$	$\frac{\pi}{2}$	$\frac{3\pi}{4}$	0	$\frac{\pi}{4}$	$\frac{\pi}{2}$	$\frac{3\pi}{4}$	0	$\frac{\pi}{4}$	$\frac{\pi}{2}$	$\frac{3\pi}{4}$	0	$\frac{\pi}{4}$	$\frac{\pi}{2}$	$\frac{3\pi}{4}$
ϕ_i^L	0	$\frac{\pi}{4}$	$\frac{\pi}{2}$	$\frac{3\pi}{4}$	$\frac{\pi}{4}$	$\frac{\pi}{2}$	$\frac{3\pi}{4}$	0	$\frac{\pi}{2}$	$\frac{3\pi}{4}$	0	$\frac{\pi}{4}$	$\frac{3\pi}{4}$	0	$\frac{\pi}{4}$	$\frac{\pi}{2}$

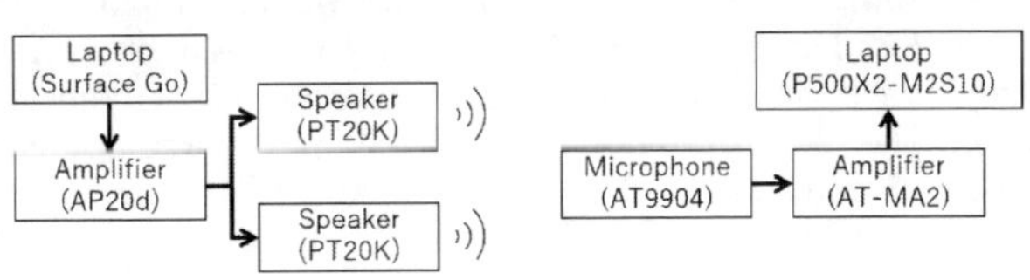

Figure 6. Experimental setup for the real environment.

In (29) and (30), the modulation values ϕ_i^R and ϕ_i^L are canceled out. Therefore, our proposed method can obtain TDoA without systematic error due to modulation values.

In our proposed method, signals are demodulated by using phase difference between successive symbols [18]. As the reference time of demodulation, we utilized the first symbol's t_{max}.

C. Azimuth Estimation

In this section, we describe the process of converting TDoA Δt to azimuth. The relation between TDoA Δt and the locations of speakers and a microphone is as follows:

$$c\Delta t = \sqrt{(\boldsymbol{x}_L - \boldsymbol{x})^T(\boldsymbol{x}_L - \boldsymbol{x})} - \sqrt{(\boldsymbol{x}_R - \boldsymbol{x})^T(\boldsymbol{x}_R - \boldsymbol{x})} \tag{32}$$

where $\boldsymbol{x}_R$, $\boldsymbol{x}_L$, $\boldsymbol{x}$ denote the 2D locations of the speakers R, L, and the microphone. c denotes the speed of sound.

Equation (32) indicates a hyperbola. The hyperbola asymptotically approaches a straight line passing through the origin.

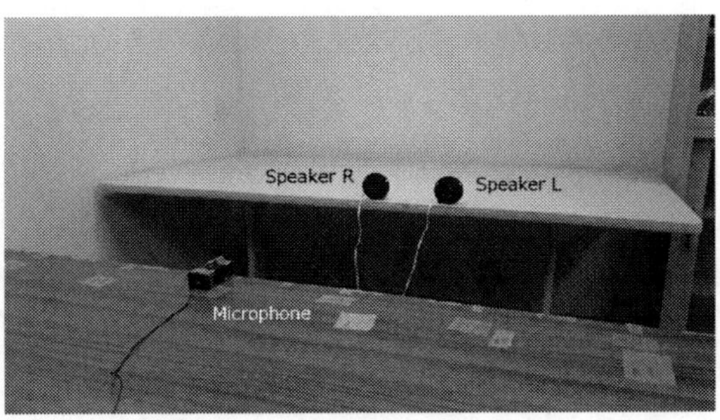

Figure 7. Experimental environment.

Hence, the azimuth can be calculated using this straight line. Figure 2 shows the hyperbola of TDoA and its asymptote. In Figure 2 the length of baseline is set to 24 cm. In this paper, the front direction of the speakers is set to 0 degree and the right direction is set to positive, as shown in Figure 3. The azimuth θ can be calculated by using TDoA Δt as follows:

$$\theta = \tan^{-1}\left(\frac{c\Delta t}{\sqrt{B^2 - c^2\Delta t^2}}\right) \tag{33}$$

where B is the length of the baseline.

IV. EXPERIMENTS

In this section, we conduct simulation and real-environment experiments.

A. Simulation Experiments

1) Experimental Setting: To evaluate the influence of interference and modulation, we conduct the following simulation experiment. Chirp signals and OFDM signals are used for comparison with our proposed method. The chirp signals are given by (1) and (2), and its parameters are $f_1 = 2.5$ kHz, $f_2 = 4.5$ kHz, $f_3 = 4.5$ kHz, $f_4 = 6.5$ kHz, and $T = 2$ ms. The OFDM signals are given by (8), (9), and its parameters

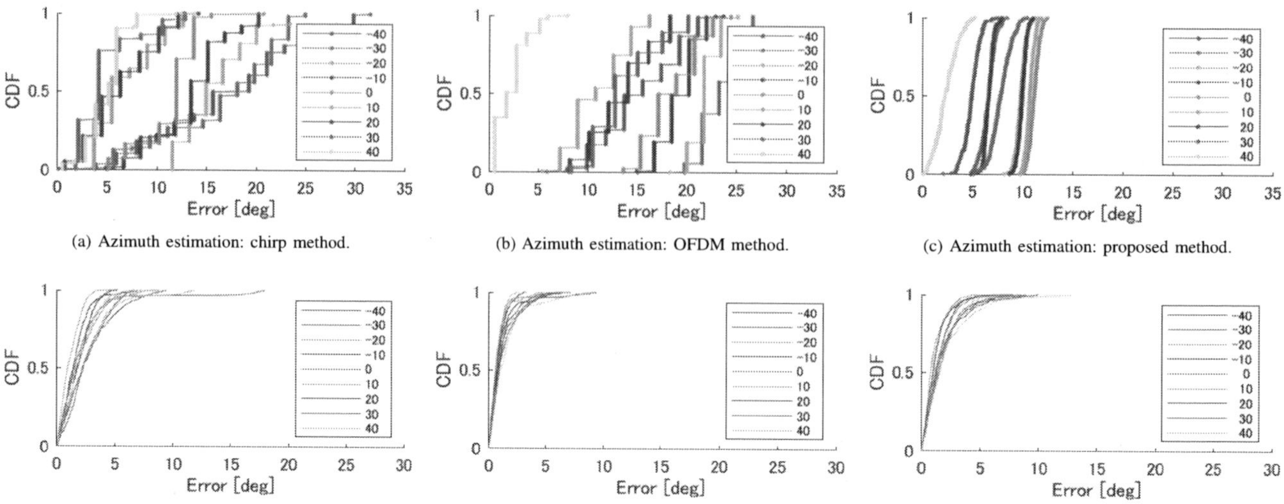

(a) Azimuth estimation: chirp method.
(b) Azimuth estimation: OFDM method.
(c) Azimuth estimation: proposed method.
(d) Demodulation: chirp method.
(e) Demodulation: OFDM method.
(f) Demodulation: proposed method.

Figure 8. Measurement results of the proposed method (Legends indicate the azimuth θ of the microphone's location).

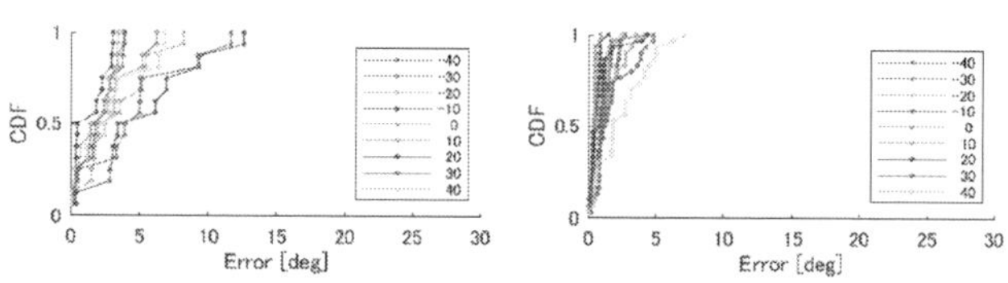

(a) Azimuth estimation: chirp method.
(b) Demodulation: chirp method.

Figure 9. Simulation results that reflect the amplitude of received signals.

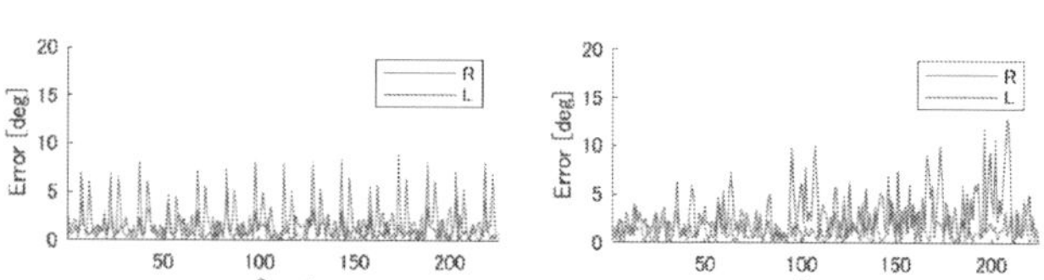

(a) Chirp method.
(b) Proposed method.

Figure 10. Demodulation error of each symbol (Legends indicate speaker).

are $f_1 = 3$ kHz, $f_2 = 4$ kHz, $f_3 = 5$ kHz, $f_4 = 6$ kHz, $\psi_1^R = \psi_1^L = 0$, $\psi_2^R = \psi_2^L = \pi$ and $T = 2$ ms. To evaluate the validity of these method as a comparator, we compare the frequency spectrum of these method. In Figure 4, although the frequency spectrum of each method does not match, the bandwidths are almost the same. Thus, the chirp and OFDM signals are considered to be appropriate as a comparator. We call the localization with these signals as the chirp method and OFDM method, respectively. The reception times of these methods are estimated by the matched filter. The parameters of the proposed method are $f_1 = 3$ kHz, $f_2 = 4$ kHz, $f_3 = 5$ kHz, $f_4 = 6$ kHz, and $T = 2$ ms. To avoid the effects of aliasing, the sampling rate was set to 960 kHz. Figure 3 shows the location of the speakers and a microphone. The microphone's locations were 9 points, which correspond to the azimuths of -40 degrees to 40 degrees in steps of 10 degrees shown in Figure 3. In this simulation, the amplitudes of the received signals were set to the same value for all locations. The number of symbol values of ϕ_i^R and ϕ_i^L was set to 4. To cover all combinations of ϕ_i^R and ϕ_i^L, the values of symbol sequence were set as shown in Table I.

2) Results: Figure 5 shows the azimuth estimation error and demodulation error of DPSK for each location. Figures 5a and 5d show that a systematic error occurs in the chirp method due to interference between the signals transmitted by speakers R and L at all locations. Figures 5b and 5e show that a systematic error occurs in the OFDM method due to interference without the location where the azimuth θ equals 0 degree. This is because TDoA is zero at $\theta = 0$ degree. Figures 5c and 5f shows that our proposed method has no systematic error due to interference at all locations.

B. Real Environmental Experiments

1) Experimental Settings: To confirm the effectiveness of our proposed method, we conducted experiments in a real environment. The signals and locations of the speakers and a microphone are the same as in the simulation experiments. In the real-environment experiments, the symbol sequence having the encoded values in Table I were measured 15 times at each location. Therefore, the number of localizations was $15 \times 16 = 240$ and the number of demodulation values was $15 \times 15 = 225$. The transmission interval of symbols was set to 100 ms.

The configuration of the measurement system is shown in Figure 6. For the transmission system, we used a tablet PC (Microsoft Surface Go) as a signal generator, an amplifier (Fostex AP20d), and speakers (Fostex PT20K). For the receiving system, we used a microphone (Audiotechnica AT9904), an amplifier (Audiotechnica AT-MA2), and a laptop (Mouse Computer m-Book P500X2-M2S10) as the recorder. The sampling rate was set to 48 kHz. Figure 7 shows the experimental environment.

2) Results: Figure 8 shows the azimuth estimation and demodulation error of each location. With regard to azimuth estimation, our proposed method shows the best estimation performance from Figures 8a, 8b, and 8c. The standard deviation of azimuth estimation by the chirp, OFDM, and proposed methods were within 7.36, 3.93, and 1.15 degrees, respectively. As for DPSK, the demodulation performance of each method were similar in Figures 8d, 8e, and 8f. The standard deviation of demodulation by the chirp, OFDM, and proposed methods were within 3.73, 2.27, and, 2.95 degrees, respectively.

V. DISCUSSION

In this section, we discuss the cause for systematic and random errors in real-environment experiments.

A. Systematic error of azimuth estimation

According to Figures 5 and 8, there are clear differences between simulation and real-environment experiments, and the received noises are not enough to explain these differences. In this section, we discuss the causes for this mismatch. In our proposed method, although systematic errors depending on the modulation value do not occur, there are some systematic errors at each location. We consider that these errors are caused by multipath signals reflected from the walls or ceilings in the room as there is no law on the relation between systematic errors and locations.

According to the conventional methods, in addition to the multipath signals, the amplitude of the received signal that depends on the location could be one of the reasons. Therefore, we conducted simulations that consider the received amplitude of real-environment experiments. Figure 9 shows the results of these simulations of the chirp method. These figures show that the systematic errors change in response to the received amplitude. Thus, in the conventional methods, the received amplitude is a factor in the difference of the systematic error between simulation and real-environment experiments.

B. Random error of demodulation

In this section, we discuss the reason why the standard deviation of the proposed method tends to be larger than the OFDM method, as shown in Section IV. Figure 10 shows the error of each symbol for the 16-symbol sequence (Table I) repeated 15 times at the received location with maximum standard deviation. Although the errors of the chirp method in Figure 10a contains periodic systematic errors and random errors, its random error is smaller than that of the proposed method (Figure 10b) as the signal length used in the OFDM method is twice as long as in our proposed method. Therefore, our proposed method has a disadvantage in terms of SNR, and its performance might be worse than conventional methods when systematic errors are small.

VI. CONCLUSIONS

In this paper, we proposed highly precise localization and communication methods using short-time and narrow-band acoustic signals. The simulation and real-environment experiments showed that our proposed method could reduce systematic errors compared to the conventional methods as interference between the acoustic signals could be avoided.

APPENDIX

The inner product of the sine wave and the complex sine wave can be defined as

$$\begin{aligned}&\int_0^T \sin(2\pi f_a t+\phi)\exp(-j2\pi f_b t)dt\\ =&\frac{T}{2j}\exp(j(\frac{2\pi(f_a-f_b)T}{2}))\mathrm{sinc}(\frac{2\pi(f_a-f_b)T}{2})\\ &-\frac{T}{2j}\exp(-j(\frac{2\pi(f_a+f_b)T}{2}+\phi))\mathrm{sinc}(\frac{2\pi(f_a+f_b)T}{2})\end{aligned} \tag{34}$$

where $\mathrm{sinc}(x)$ is the sinc function $\mathrm{sinc}(x) = \sin(x)/x$. If $2\pi(f_a + f_b)T/2$ is set to a large enough value,

$$\begin{aligned}&\int_0^T \sin(2\pi f_a t+\phi)\exp(-j2\pi f_b t)dt\\ &\approx\frac{T}{2j}\exp(j(\frac{2\pi(f_a-f_b)T}{2}))\mathrm{sinc}(\frac{2\pi(f_a-f_b)T}{2})\end{aligned} \tag{35}$$

If $(f_a - f_b)T$ is an integer and non-zero value, Equation (35) is 0. This means that the sine wave $\sin(2\pi f_a t + \phi)$ and the complex sine wave $\exp(-j2\pi f_b t)$ are orthogonal.

REFERENCES

[1] J. Xiao, Z. Zhou, Y. Yi, and L. M. Ni, "A survey on wireless indoor localization from the device perspective," ACM Comput. Surv., vol. 49, no. 2, 2016, pp. 1–31.

[2] H. Shen, S. Machineni, C. Gupta, and A. Papandreou-Suppappola, "Time-varying multichirp rate modulation for multiple access systems," IEEE Signal Processing Letters, vol. 11, no. 5, 2004, pp. 497–500.

[3] R. Dutta, A. B. J. Kokkeler, R. v. d. Zee, and M. J. Bentum, "Performance of chirped-fsk and chirped-psk in the presence of partial-band interference," in Proc. of SCVT, 2011, pp. 1–6.

[4] F. Höflinger et al., "Acoustic self-calibrating system for indoor smartphone tracking (assist)," in Proc. of IPIN, 2012, pp. 1–9.

[5] P. Lazik and A. Rowe, "Indoor pseudo-ranging of mobile devices using ultrasonic chirps," in Proc. of Sensys, 2012, pp. 99–112.

[6] M. O. Khyam, M. J. Alam, A. J. Lambert, M. A. Garratt, and M. R. Pickering, "High-precision ofdm-based multiple ultrasonic transducer positioning using a robust optimization approach," IEEE Sensors Journal, vol. 16, no. 13, 2016, pp. 5325–5336.

[7] M. O. Khyam, S. S. Ge, X. Li, and M. Pickering, "Orthogonal chirp-based ultrasonic positioning," Sensors, vol. 17, no. 5, 2017, pp. 1–14.

[8] M. O. Khyam, S. S. Ge, X. Li, and M. R. Pickering, "Pseudo-orthogonal chirp-based multiple ultrasonic transducer positioning," IEEE Sensors Journal, vol. 17, no. 12, 2017, pp. 3832–3843.

[9] F. J. Álvarez, T. Aguilera, and R. López-Valcarce, "Cdma-based acoustic local positioning system for portable devices with multipath cancellation," Digital Signal Processing, vol. 62, 2017, pp. 38–51.

[10] M. Hazas and A. Hopper, "Broadband ultrasonic location systems for improved indoor positioning," IEEE Trans. on Mobile Computing, vol. 5, no. 5, 2006, pp. 536–547.

[11] M. Alloulah and M. Hazas, "An efficient cdma core for indoor acoustic position sensing," in Proc. of IPIN, 2010, pp. 1–5.

[12] C. Sertatıl, M. A. Altınkaya, and K. Raoof, "A novel acoustic indoor localization system employing cdma," Digital Signal Processing, vol. 22, no. 3, 2012, pp. 506–517.

[13] J. Chen, J. Benesty, and Y. A. Huang, "Time delay estimation in room acoustic environments: an overview," EURASIP Journal on Advances in Signal Processing, vol. 2006, no. 1, 2006, pp. 1–19.

[14] I. Rishabh, D. Kimber, and J. Adcock, "Indoor localization using controlled ambient sounds," in Proc. of IPIN, 2012, pp. 1–10.

[15] T. Akiyama, M. Nakamura, M. Sugimoto, and H. Hashizume, "Smart phone localization method using dual-carrier acoustic waves," in Proc. of IPIN, 2013, pp. 1–9.

[16] M. Nakamura, T. Akiyama, M. Sugimoto, and H. Hashizume, "3d fdm-pam: Rapid and precise indoor 3d localization using acoustic signal for smartphone," in Proc. of UbiComp, 2014, pp. 123–126.

[17] H. Hashizume, A. Kaneko, Y. Sugano, K. Yatani, and M. Sugimoto, "Fast and Accurate Positioning Technique Using Ultrasonic Phase Accordance Method," in Proc. of IEEE TENCON, 2005, pp. 1–6.

[18] M. Nakamura, T. Akiyama, H. Hashizume, and M. Sugimoto, "A spot-controllable data transfer technique using cots speakers," in Proc. of IPIN, 2016, pp. 1–8.

Polymer Photonic Crystal Membrane for Human Body Thermoregulation

*Mohamed Boutghatin, Salim Assaf, Michèle Carette, Vincent Thomy, Abdellatif Akjouj, Bahram Djafari- Rouhani, Yan Pennec**

Institute of Electronic, Microelectronic and Nanotechnology (IEMN), Université de Lille

Villeneuve d'Ascq, France

*e-mail : mohamed.boutghatin@univ-lille.fr; salim.alhajj-assaf@univ-lille.fr; michele.carette@univ-lille.fr; vincent.thomy@univ-lille.fr; abdellatif.akjouj@univ-lille.fr; bahram.djafari-rouhani@univ-lille.fr; *yan.pennec@univ-lille.fr*

***Abstract*—We study the optical properties of a polymer photonic membrane to keep the human body in thermal comfort. We show theoretically that the periodic structuration of the membrane with air holes modulates the optical response in the Mid-Infrared range. We found that the modulation of the optical spectrum allows to decrease the required ambient temperature by about 0.5 °C to maintain the normal skin temperature of 34 °C. The structured membrane is flexible and can easily be added to usual textiles.**

Keywords-photonic membrane; Mid-Infrared; thermal comfort.

I. INTRODUCTION

A large part of the energy consumed is used to regulate the temperature of residential buildings. Reducing this consumption will have a positive impact on the economy and the environment. In previous studies, the importance of personal thermoregulation was investigated and demonstrated in different ways [1][2]. Photonic crystals have been recently proposed to control the propagation of electromagnetic waves in the Mid-Infrared range for several applications from thermophotovoltaic systems to thermal textile [3]. For radiative cooling, Raphaeli et al. presented a metal-dielectric photonic structure, reflective in the visible and having high emissivity in the Mid-Infrared [4]. More recently, we have demonstrated the efficiency of a structured polymer membrane to maintain an individual thermal comfort in indoor rooms [5]. Our objective here is to demonstrate that a polymer membrane can act both as a sensor by the modification of its structural parameters and as a passive actuator by modifying its thermal properties.

In this work, we propose to study numerically a polyethylene (PE) membrane drilled with air holes following a triangular array, as illustrated in Figure 1. The structured membrane is characterized by three geometrical parameters, the thickness (h), the diameter of the hole (D) and the period of the array (P).

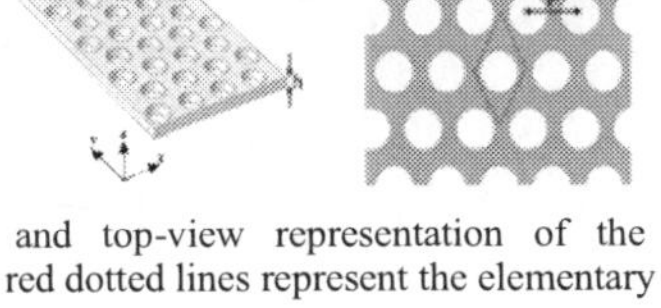

Figure 1. 3D and top-view representation of the polymer photonic membrane. The red dotted lines represent the elementary unit cell.

In section II, we discuss the effect of structuration of the PE membrane in the Mid-IR range. In section III, we investigate the thermal properties of the photonic membrane to maintain the thermal comfort of the human body.

II. OPTICAL PROPERTIES

We performed the numerical calculation with the help of the Finite Element Method (FEM), considering an incident wave coming from the human body and launched in air medium normally to the photonic membrane. To simulate the interaction wave-photonic membrane, we used the commercial COMSOL software to solve the Maxwell equations. The elementary unit cell is defined Figure 1, where we applied the Periodic Boundary Conditions (PBC) along the two directions x and y to build the periodic membrane. We thus calculated the reflection (R) and transmission (T) coefficients and deducing the absorption coefficient (A) by the formula $A = 1 - R - T$. Figure 2(a) shows the evolution of the reflection R (black), transmission T (blue) and absorption A (red) in the wavelength range [5-15 µm] for a non-structured membrane of thickness $h = 4$ µm. The blue light shaded area corresponds to the human body radiation calculated at 34 °C following the Planck law. One can see that, for a thickness $h = 4$ µm, the transmission is comprised between 80% and 100% with an average absorption less than 10%. It means that the PE membrane is almost transparent in the Mid-IR.

Figure 2 (b) reports the same calculation of the coefficients when the membrane is structured with the set of geometrical parameters: $h = 4$ µm, $D = 5.5$ µm and $P = 7$ µm. The comparison between the spectrum of the simple membrane (a) and the structured one (b), shows the occurrence of new peaks and dips between 6 and 7 µm (see Figure 2(c)). It means that the structuration clearly affects the scattering coefficients at low wavelength. The modulus of the calculated electric field shows that the two peaks (A and C) correspond to guided modes inside the membrane. With respect to the middle plane of the membrane, the first one (A) is antisymmetric while the second one (C) is symmetric. The peak B corresponds to a mode confined in the air hole. This latter gives rise to an asymmetric peak and comes from the interaction of the localized mode B with the incident wave, known as a Fano-like resonance.

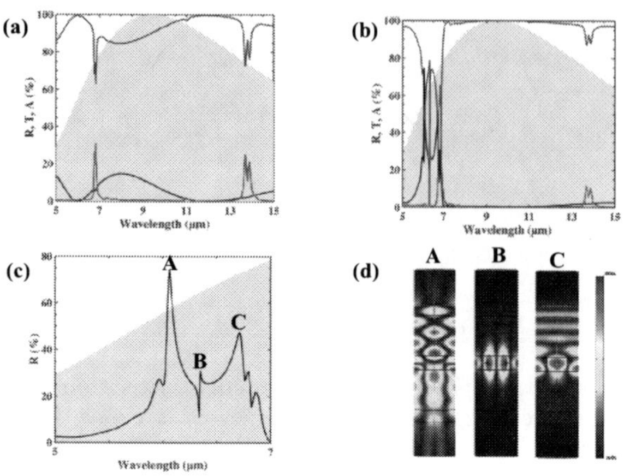

Figure 2. (a, b) Reflection (black), transmission (blue) and absorption (red) spectra for the (a) non structured and (b) structured PE membrane with the geometrical parameters: h = 4 µm, D = 5.5 µm and P = 7 µm. (c) Magnification of the reflection curve in (b) in the wavelength range [5-7] µm. Human body radiation at 34 °C is indicated by the shaded region. (d) Snapshots of the modulus of the electric field for the three peaks of reflection A, B and C.

In order to show the effect of geometrical parameters on the photonic membrane spectrum (that could happen when using active polymer reacting to parameters, such as temperature or humidity), we homothetically increase the three parameters h, D and P. Figure 3 shows the spectrum for the set of geometrical parameters: h = 5.1 µm, D = 7.1 µm and P = 9 µm.

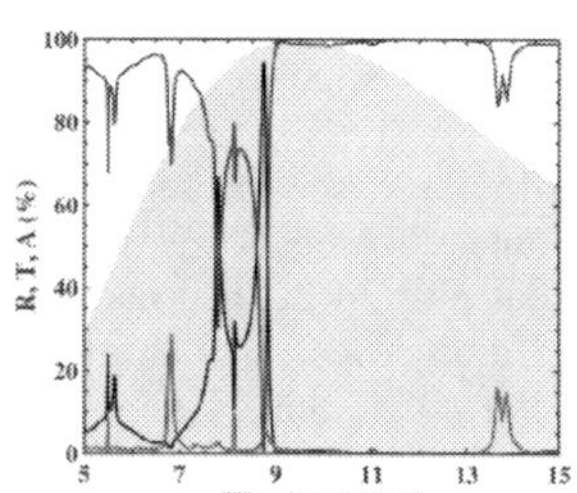

Figure 3. Reflection (black), transmission (blue) and absorption (red) spectra for the structured PE membrane with the geometrical parameters: h = 5.1 µm, D = 7.1 µm and P = 9 µm.

One can see that the photonic effect has been shifted to higher wavelengths. With these chosen parameters, peaks and dips now occur in the vicinity of 9 µm. Therefore, a variation of the geometrical parameters offers the possibility to span the full range of radiation of the human body at the skin temperature 34 °C.

III. THERMAL PROPERTIES

We then investigated the thermal properties of the photonic membrane, considering an unidimensional heat model previously developed [2]. The two volumes of control in our case are: the human body standing and relaxed and the PE membrane. The emissivity of the human body and environment is assumed to be equal to the unity. In the thermal model, we have considered all conduction, convection and radiative heat flows between the human body and the indoor room, through the photonic membrane. The resolution of the thermal equations leads to a balance where the temperatures depend on the scattering coefficients calculated in the previous part.

To estimate the efficiency of the photonic membranes we proceed to the calculation of the required ambient temperature to achieve the skin temperature of 34 °C. This latter is considered as a reference for a comfort feeling of the human body.

Figure 4 represents the evolution of the required ambient temperature as a function of different set of parameters of the photonic membrane. The blue curve corresponds to the ambient temperature for a non-structured membrane, drawn as a reference. For the structured one, we have considered different scaling factors, taking from reference [5]: α_1 (h = 4 µm, D = 5.5 µm, P = 7 µm), α_3 (5.1 µm, 7.1 µm, 9 µm), α_5 (6.3 µm,8.6 µm, 11 µm), α_7 (7.4 µm, 10.2 µm, 13 µm) and α_9 (8.6 µm, 11.8 µm, 15 µm). Figure 4 shows that for the non-structured membrane with a thickness of 8.6 µm (α_9), the comfort skin temperature of 34 °C can be reached with an ambient temperature of 25.5 °C.

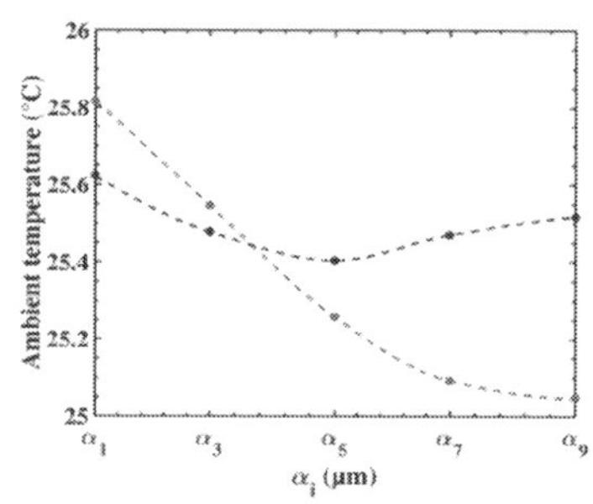

Figure 4. Evolution of the required ambient temperature to achieve 34 °C as a function of geometrical parameters for a skin covered with a non-structured (blue) and structured (red) membrane.

On the other hand, when the same membrane is drilled with air holes of diameters 11.8µm and a period of 15 µm, an ambient temperature of 25 °C is sufficient to achieve the skin comfort. It means that the latter structured membrane minimizes the necessary external temperature to maintain the human body in thermal comfort by almost 0.5 °C.

IV. CONCLUSION AND FUTURE WORK

In conclusion, we have demonstrated theoretically that a change in the structuration parameters of a polymer membrane can modulate the optical coefficient in the Mid-IR range. We show that, with an appropriate design of polymer photonic membrane, we can efficiently modulate the thermal radiation emitted from the human body. Compared to a regular PE textile, the photonic membrane maintains the thermal comfort of the human body with a lower ambient temperature of 0.5 °C. In addition, we seek to study photonic membranes based on active polymer, sensitive to ambient temperature, to study a textile membrane which acts both as a sensor and a passive actuator.

ACKNOWLEDGMENT

This work was supported by the European Interreg project 'Photonitex'.

REFERENCES

[1] P.-C. Hsu et al., "Personal Thermal Management by Metallic Nanowire-Coated Textile", Nano Lett., vol. 15, no 1, p. 365-371, janv. 2015, doi: 10.1021/nl5036572.J. Clerk Maxwell, A Treatise on Electricity and Magnetism, 3rd ed., vol. 2. Oxford: Clarendon, pp. 68–73, 1892,

[2] J. K. Tong, X. Huang, S. V. Boriskina, J. Loomis, Y. Xu, and G. Chen, "Infrared-Transparent Visible-Opaque Fabrics for Wearable Personal Thermal Management", ACS Photonics, vol. 2, no 6, pp. 769-778, juin 2015, doi: 10.1021/acsphotonics.5b00140.

[3] W. Li and S. Fan, "Nanophotonic control of thermal radiation for energy applications [Invited]", Opt. Express, vol. 26, no 12, p. 15995, juin 2018, doi: 10.1364/OE.26.015995.

[4] E. Rephaeli, A. Raman, and S. Fan, "Ultrabroadband Photonic Structures To Achieve High-Performance Daytime Radiative Cooling", Nano Lett., vol. 13, no 4, pp. 1457-1461, avr. 2013, doi: 10.1021/nl4004283.

[5] S. Assaf et al., "Polymer photonic crystal membrane for thermo-regulating textile", Sci Rep, vol. 10, no 1, pp. 9855, déc. 2020, doi: 10.1038/s41598-020-66731-1.

Bi-Directional Communication Between Infra-Structure and Mobile Device Based on Visible Light Communication

Paula Louro, Manuela Vieira, Manuel Augusto Vieira,
ADEETC/ISEL/IPL
R. Conselheiro Emídio Navarro, 1959-007
Lisboa, Portugal

CTS-UNINOVA
Quinta da Torre, Monte da Caparica, 2829-516,
Caparica, Portugal
e-mail: plouro@deetc.isel.pt, mv@isel.ipl.pt, mv@isel.pt

***Abstract*—A visible light bi-directional data transmission system based on visible light communication using white tri-chromatic LEDs is presented. The proposed communication system allows indoor navigation for a mobile autonomous picking robot moving in a warehouse. Downlink communication from the infrastructure to the mobile device allows positioning, navigation services and data transmission. White LEDs are used at the lamps infra-structure to illuminate the space and to transmit data and provide positioning. An a-SiC:H/a-Si:H pin-pin photodiode is used at the receiver unit to decode the transmitted data and infer location. Different coding schemes are proposed, considering the need to prevent flickering effects in downlink communication.**

Keywords- visible light communication; white LED; on-off keying, indoor navigation; bidirectional communication.

I. INTRODUCTION

The connection of people and physical objects with the Internet gave rise to new demands on the performance of communication networks, regarding essentially, transmission data rates. This created new challenges to develop communication networks operating at higher data rates and reduced latency, ensuring simultaneously energy saving and cost reduction solutions. The combination of these features is thus the key for higher system capacity and massive device connectivity. In order to accomplish this goal, it is expected that the next-generation of communication networks will integrate several different complementary access technologies, addressing thus the challenge to explore other ranges of the electromagnetic spectrum, also suitable for communication.

Non-guided optical communications are currently a competitive technology, that in a few application areas can be considered as alternative to radio transmission systems or guided optical communication systems. It operates in the near infrared or visible range, using lasers or Light emitting Diodes (LED) as optical sources. Wireless Optical Communication (WOC) technology can be used indoor or outdoor, using four generic system configurations, i.e., directed Line-Of-Sight (LOS), non-directed LOS, diffused, and quasi diffused. Outdoor wireless optical communication operating in the infrared range are also named as Free-Space Optical (FSO) communication. Optical communication operating in the visible range, either indoor or outdoor, are labelled as Visible Light Communication (VLC) and use white LEDs or single-color LEDs [1], to code and transmit the information data [2].

In VLC, data are basically transmitted by switching on and off the LEDs at a higher rate that the human eye can discern [3]. This technology is nested on the ubiquitous use of LEDs for lighting solutions. LEDs provide high energy efficiency when compared to conventional, almost obsolete, incandescent and fluorescent lamps, and at the same time are much more reliable and environmentally friendly, as they are mercury free. Thus, VLC is a precursor optical communication technology for large scale integration with other conventional widespread communication technologies, either indoor or outdoor [4][5].

Main advantages when compared to radio technology are free licensed spectrum, immunity from electromagnetic interference and, less power and weight/volume requirements [6]. Therefore, VLC finds application in many fields ranging from smart systems (transportation, targeted advertisement, health care monitoring), safe communication at RF hazardous places (petrochemical industries, mining) or RF undesirable locations (hospitals, aircrafts), indoor navigation and localization services [7], specific networks (underwater, near field, high speed data communication, Internet of Things network) to energy efficient systems as home automation and domotics [8].

Indoor navigation based on VLC are attractive solutions for Indoor Positioning Systems (IPS), as Global Positioning Systems (GPS) signals are strongly absorbed by the buildings and other wireless solutions need to be used. IPS based on VLC can be used for multiple purposes. Main applications include accessibility aids for visually impaired, navigation in large indoors areas (such as museum guided tours, shopping malls, airports, bus or train stations, parking lots), targeted advertising, augmented reality, indoor robotics, asset tracking and warehouses, among others.

Nowadays, retail market has several online and offline channels of sales and services like same day delivery or store pickups. Costumers preferences have evolved forcing companies to reduce the order-to-delivery time which demands an increased logistics and new enterprise models based very often on technological innovation [9].

Warehousing is designed to provide value and service quality to clients and customers, which corresponds simply to deliver in the shortest possible time [10]. In this field, flexible automation is the best solution for warehouses to gain a competitive advantage. Order picking is one of the most labor intensive and expensive activity in every warehouse, where high efficiency is a demand to improve the delivery process. Any underperformance of the order-picking process can affect the whole supply chain and lead to unsatisfactory service and high operational cost for the warehouse. Thus, under the dual goal of efficiency and save labor costs, modern warehouses are evolving to new levels of automation using a diverse type of driverless vehicles, such as, mobile picking robots, self-driving forklifts, autonomous inventory robots or unmanned aerial vehicles [11].

Mobile robotic picking solutions that provide the transport of goods to the packaging station operated by a human worker can add a new level of efficiency to the process. These autonomous machines typically carry carts or racks following a previously defined route in the warehouse to move products to the packaging stations. These autonomous vehicles take advantage of sensing technology development and advanced algorithms to infer optimized routes. The vehicle movement inside the warehouse lays on indoor localization and indoor navigation techniques based on WiFi communication technology [12][13].

In this paper, we propose an indoor localization system [14][15] designed with white RGB LEDs and a pinpin photodiode based on a-SiC:H/a-Si:H with a simple On-Off modulation scheme [16][17]. The system is designed to establish bidirectional communication between a static infrastructure and the mobile picking robot. The LED luminaires at the warehouse ceiling are used to lighten the warehouse space, and to transmit information about positioning and available racks. The picking robots communicate with the ceiling luminaires to send information about the rack that is being removed and carried to the packaging station. The system uses bi-directional communication which demands different codification schemes to establish both uplink and downlink communication between LED luminaires and mobile robots. This communication uses three different communication channels ensured by 3 different wavelength emitters of white tri-chromatic LEDs.

During the past decades, channel coding has been used extensively in most digital transmission systems. It is now widely used also in optical communication, which, however, brings in several challenges to the code design and implementation. In the specific case of optical links based on VLC, the use of on-off keying intensity modulation (OOK IM) to carry digital information into LED light signal may affect the light brightness. This is due to the distribution of information bits 1's and 0's in the transmitted data frames, as LEDs are turned on or off whether the data bits are 1 or 0. This procedure is prone to produce unbalanced light intensity as long runs of 1's and 0's may cause light intensity fluctuation over a short period, which may exceed the persistence of the human eye and cause noticeable brightness change, i.e., flicker.

To ensure a stable and dimmable illumination, modulation and coding technologies of VLC systems must be able to provide flicker mitigation and dimming support [18] to avoid perceivable brightness fluctuation, as suggested in IEEE Standard 802.15.7 [19].

Different approaches to overcome this undesirable effect make use of Forward Error Correction (FEC) codes followed by DC-balanced Run-Length Limiting (RLL) line codes (e.g., Manchester codes), which break long runs of the same symbols in the code word (i.e., 1 s or 0 s). However, as RLL line codes have code rates less than 1, the transmission efficiency of VLC systems can be decreased, which in certain applications will affect the system performance. Other solutions use auxiliary coding techniques, such as code puncturing, scrambling, RLL line codes or even advanced coding schemes such as Low-Fensity Parity Check (LDPC) codes and turbo codes [8]. In the proposed application, the transmission speed is not a critical issue, as the whole process is mainly dependent on the mobile robot speed along the warehouse. Thus, the use of run-length limiting line codes is adequate as far as the code word for downlink communication balances the distribution of symbols. In uplink communication these effects are negligible as the optical source from the mobile robot is used only for data communication and not for illumination.

The simultaneous use of three different wavelengths corresponds to wavelength multiplexing which demands demultiplexing of the generated photocurrent signal by the photodiode receiver. This task was accomplished using a photodetector based on a-SiC:H/a-Si:H with operation in the visible spectrum. Its sensitivity to different wavelengths can be tuned using steady state light illumination [20]. This feature is used in the decoding strategy to infer the optical signals received by the photodetector [21].

II. COMMUNICATION CHANNELS

The proposed VLC system includes an indoor scenario of bidirectional infrastructure-to-device communication. The LED luminaires at the warehouse ceiling are used to perform three tasks, namely, room illumination, position/navigation services and data transmission. The picking robots communicate with the ceiling luminaires to send information about the rack that is being removed and carried to the packaging station.

The proposed system is composed of the transmitter and the receiver modules, located at the infra-structure and at the picking robot. Downlink communication is established from the ceiling luminaires to the picking robots and uplink communication is from the picking robot to the correspondent ceiling lamp where the movable rack belongs. The optical source of the transmitter at the ceiling lamps is composed of four white RGB LEDs while at the robot it is a multicolor LED or three different single-color LEDs placed at the top of the robot. Coding and modulation of the transmitters allow the transmission of the encoded data signal using on-off modulation. Different coding schemes are proposed to establish uplink and downlink communication. The receiver modules are placed at the ceiling lamps and at the robot. It includes demodulation and decoding of the electrical signal generated at the photodiode. The transmission channel of the optical link is free space propagation. In Figure 1, it is displayed the communication channels established between the lamps and the mobile robots.

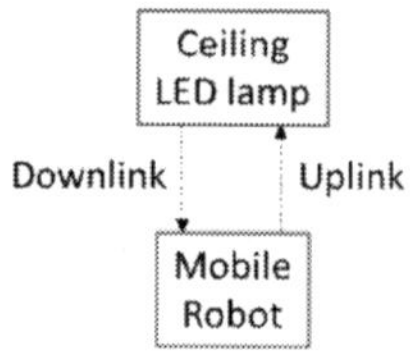

Figure 1. Communication channels established between the lamps at the ceiling and the mobile robots.

A. Transmitters and receivers

The transmitter proposed in this VLC system uses ceiling lamps based on commercial white LEDs with red, green and blue emitters (w-RGB LEDs). Each LED luminaire at the ceiling is composed of four white LEDs placed at the corners of a square. The w-RGB LEDs are designed for general illumination providing therefore, high output power (550 mcd, 850 mcd and 320 mcd, for the red, green and blue emitters, respectively) and wide viewing angle. Analysis of the output light spectrum demonstrates the presence of three distinct gaussian peaks located in the blue (460 nm – 480 nm), green (520 nm – 540 nm) and red (619 nm – 624 nm) regions.

The receiver module includes a photodetector to transform the light signal into an electric signal that is later demodulated and decoded to extract the transmitted information. The photodetector used for the transduction of the optical signal is a monolithic heterojunction composed of two pin structures based on a-Si:H and a-SiC:H and built on a glass substrate between two transparent electrical contacts. The device operates in the visible spectrum and exhibits two different absorption regions due to the presence of the two absorber layers in each pin structure. Selective absorption of long and short wavelengths can be achieved by adding steady state illumination of short wavelength (400 nm) to the photodetector. When this background light soaks the device, from the side of the a-SiC:H pin structure (front illumination), long wavelengths (red and green) provide amplification of the photocurrent, while short wavelengths (blue) attenuate the signal. Under background illumination, from the side of the a-Si:H pin structure (back illumination), the behavior is reversed. Signal amplification is obtained for shorter wavelengths and attenuation for longer wavelengths. The quantification of the signal amplification under front and back optical bias is evaluated by the optical gain, defined at each wavelength as the ratio between the signal magnitude measured with and without optical bias. For the red, green and blue light the front optical gain under 400 nm background light is, respectively, 5, 3.5 and 1.3, while the back optical gains, is, for the same wavelengths, 0.6, 0.6 and 1.7.

In Figure 2, it is displayed the configuration of the luminaire with the four tri-chromatic white LEDs. With this configuration all emitters (red, green and blue) are switched on to provide uniform white lighting in the indoor area. However, only specific emitters are modulated at a frequency imperceptible to the human eye.

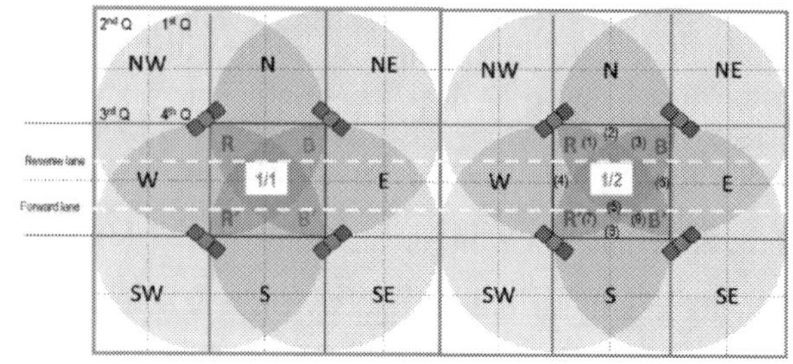

Figure 2. Configuration of the RGB white LEDs of the ceiling lamp showing the optical patterns generated by the red and blue modulated emitters (red emitters at each left side: R and R', and blue emitters at each right side: B and B').

Each of these lamps illuminates an area as shown Figure 2. All green emitters of the lamp are modulated with the same coding scheme to transmit the unique identification of the lamp. Red emitters at the left corners of the square are also modulated, using different frequencies, while the blue emitters remain on in a steady state. The top emitter is pulsed at half frequency of the bottom one. At the right side, a similar modulation scheme is used for the blue emitters, and here the red emitters stay on in steady state. Under this configuration the illumination pattern in the area covered by the light supplied by the lamps allows the definition of the unit navigation cell. Inside this area any receiver will be able to receive the identification of the emission luminaire (supplied by the green emitters) and make the correspondence to the spatial position. Increased position accuracy within each navigation cell is obtained through the optical pattern established by the red and blue modulated emitters of each lamp. Top emitters are assigned to the north cardinal direction inside the navigation cell, while bottom emitters to the south, and left and fight emitters, respectively, to the west and east directions. The illumination of the indoor space is done using different luminaires placed contiguously at the ceiling, which enables successive identification of each luminaire. In Figure 3, it is displayed the spatial organization of adjacent navigation cells with the illustration of the different nine cardinal sub-sections. Each of these regions can contain 4 racks, which spatial position is assigned by the correspondent quadrant (first, second, third and fourth).

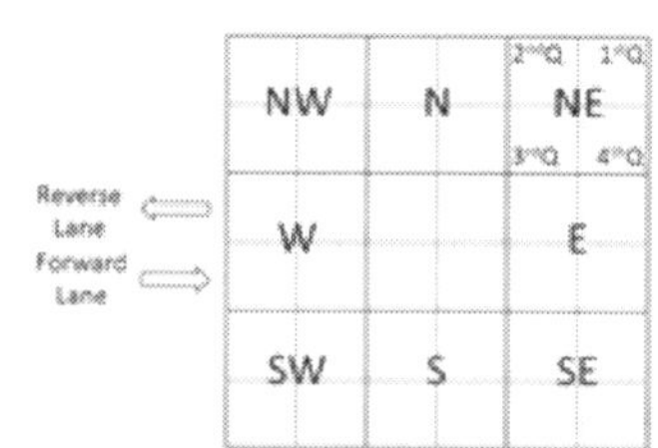

Figure 3. Spatial organization of the navigation cell and respective cardinal sub-sections.

B. Network topology

The network established between the luminaires and the mobile robots demands the definition of specific coding schemes to enable the accurate identification of signal transmitters and receivers. The downlink channel from the ceiling lamps to the mobile robot provides positioning information which enables navigation services and information about the available racks in each area. The uplink channel from the mobile robot to ceiling lamps provides information about the removed rack by each robot. Ceiling lamps provide information about location and about the presence of racks in the area covered by the unit navigation. As these luminaires use slow and fast modulated red/blue emitters and green emitters, the data frame structure is defined differently, depending on the type of emitter. In the downlink coding scheme, each frame in each channel is a word of 32 bits, divided into four blocks. An on-off keying modulation scheme was used with a 32-bit codification (logical state 1: light on and logical state 0: light off). The first and the last blocks ensure synchronism between the emitter and the receptor for correct demodulation of the transmitted signal. The first block (4 bits) is composed of two idle bits (logical value 1) and two start bits (logical value 0) and the fourth block by two stop bits (logical value 0) and two idle bits (logical value 1). The second block is a word of 12 bits. In the fast and slow red and/or blue emitters, this word contains the information on the position within the navigation cell, which is assigned to the frequency. Slow emitters have a frequency half of the fast emitters. The green emitter is used to carry the identification of the unit cell. Its format was designed to ensure safe decode of the signals and prevent errors. It is a 12 bits word where the logic state of each bit never changes simultaneously with the other fast and slow red and blue emitters. The format of the word code is 0XXXX00YYYY0, where XXXX addresses the line and YYYY the column of the unit navigation cell. The third block of every emitter is a 12 bits word, reserved for the transmission of the information related to the available racks inside each navigation area. As the area covered by the navigation unit comprises nine cardinal sub-sections containing four quadrants each, it is necessary 9 x 4 = 36 bits to infer which of these spatial positions, i.e. racks, are available. Each of the channels (12 bits available) transmits information about 3 sub-sections, using 4 bits for each. The first bit is assigned to the first quadrant, the second to the second quadrant and so on. Slow emitters of each navigation cell transmit information about northwest, north and northeast directions, fast emitters at the bottom about southwest, south and southeast, and the green emitters about west, center and east positions.

When the picking robot reaches the desired position defined by the route, it will remove the rack and carry it to the packaging station. It will be necessary for the robot to inform the ceiling lamp which rack will be removed from the correspondent navigation cell. Thus, a dedicated channel establishing communication from the picking robots to the ceiling lamps is needed to register which rack will be temporarily out of the corresponding position inside the navigation unit. This communication will be enabled by VLC using a multicolor LED or three different single-color LEDs placed at the top of the robot. The establishment of communication demands the identification of both partners (lamp and robot). The uplink channel uses three wavelengths and the info is coded in a 3x32 bits word with a simple structure of four blocks: two synchronization blocks (2x4 bits) located at the beginning and at the end of the word and two informative blocks (2x12 bits) in the middle. The first 12 bits block contains the identification of the ceiling luminaire that is illuminating the robot (red emitter) and the identification of the robot responsible for picking the rack (green emitter). Bits of the blue emitter identification block are all assigned to zero. This will demonstrate that the origin of the communication comes from the robot, as in the words from the ceiling luminaires this block is sequentially fulfilled of ones and zeros codes. Flickering effects are negligible, as these LEDs are used only to transmit information and not for lighting.

III. RESULTS AND DISCUSSION

The test case used to validate the proposed communication scheme is displayed in Figure 4, that shows the specific blocks of the 32 bits word of each emitter assigned to the lamps and to the mobile robot.

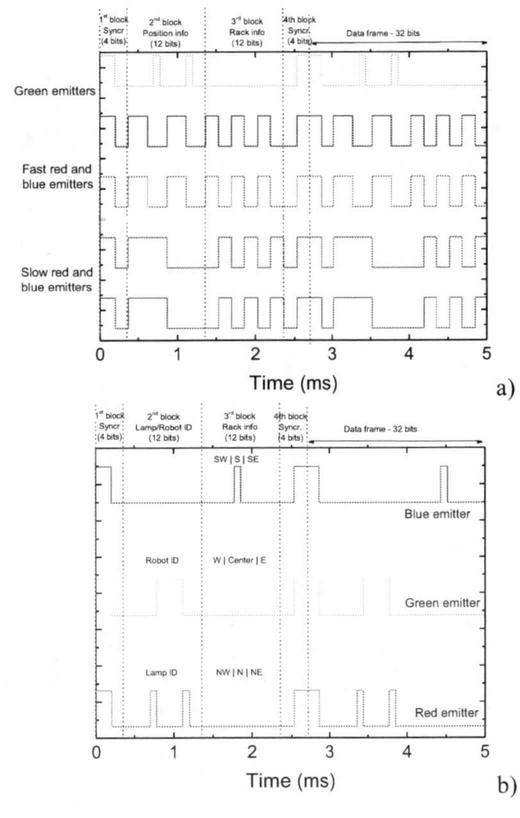

Figure 4 Codification of the optical signals transmitted by the: a) ceiling lamp; b) mobile picking robot.

In the code transmitted by the ceiling lamp (Figure 4a), the green transmitters send the code 1100 | 000010000100 | 0000 0000 0000 | 0011, which corresponds to the navigation cell with identification 1-2 (line 1: 0001, column 2: 0010) and to the information that there is no rack placed in the position west, center and east of the same cell. Slow emitters transmit the 1100 | 111111000000 | 0011 0011 0011 | 0011 code which identifies them as top emitters inside the navigation unit cell and states that in northwest, north and northeast sub-sections the third and fourth quadrants contain available racks that can be picked by the robot. In these quadrants, the 1st and 2nd quadrants are empty of available racks. Fast emitters transmit the code 1100 | 111000111000 | 1100 1100 1100 | 0011 which represents their position as bottom emitters in the navigation unit cell and informs that in the southwest, south and southeast sub-sections the 1st and 2nd quadrants contain available racks to be moved while the 3rd and 4th racks are not accessible as they are empty

In Figure 5, it is displayed the photocurrent signal measured by the mobile robot under variable conditions of optical bias (without and with front/back steady state background light). The signal was acquired in position (9) of the navigation cell 1-2, when the picking robot moves in the forward lane to remove a rack of the first quadrant of sub-section southwest (SE).

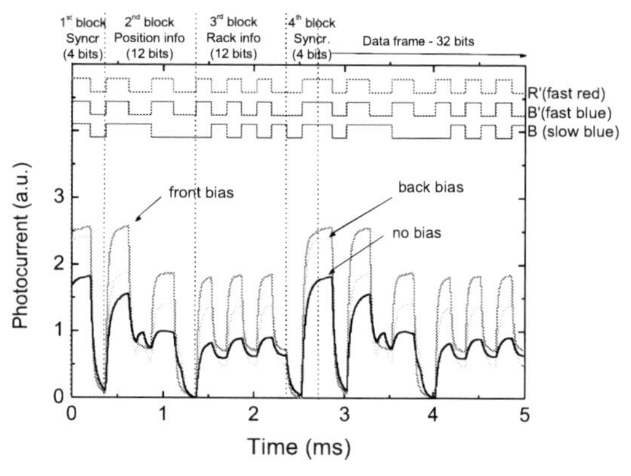

Figure 5 Photocurrent signal (measured without and with front/back steady state light) measured at position (9) of the navigation cell 1-2 after removing the contribution from the green emitters At the top it is displayed the optical signal of each emitter.

The signal was acquired in position (9) of the navigation cell 1-2, when the picking robot moves in the forward lane to remove a rack of the first quadrant of sub-section southwest (SE). At this position the optical excitation comes from the fast red and blue emitters and from the slow blue emitter. The displayed output signal has already been removed of the contribution due to the green optical excitation. In the graph, the trigger event allows easy synchronization and identification of each transmitted frame. This is noticeable by the highest peaks of the front photocurrent signal (represented in the graphs by the magenta line), as well as by the idle bits (all emitters are set to 1). This combination results in photocurrent amplification when the device is soaked by front steady state illumination. By opposition, the same signal under back background light is decreased.

Then, it is necessary to decode the next blocks of the data frame. It is assumed that in the front photocurrent the highest levels correspond to the presence of the red light, while the lowest ones to its absence, which allows the immediate recognition of the ON-OFF states for the red channel. The same reasoning can be used to analyze the back-photocurrent signal. Here the highest levels are assigned to the presence of the blue input signal and the lowest levels to its nonexistence, which allows the decoding of the blue channel. However, at the regions where there are two different signals transmitted by the same wavelength, this approach is not feasible, as it is necessary to infer which of these is channels is on or off. The approach used to decode each optical state was based on the use of a calibration curve. This was obtained by scaling all the possible signal output levels (Figure 6, solid black line) and measuring the photocurrent signal under front optical bias using two red and two blue optical signals. The driving current of each LED emitter was adjusted to provide different levels of photo excitation. On the right side of the picture in Figure 6, it is shown the label of the modulated emitters that correspond to each photocurrent level.

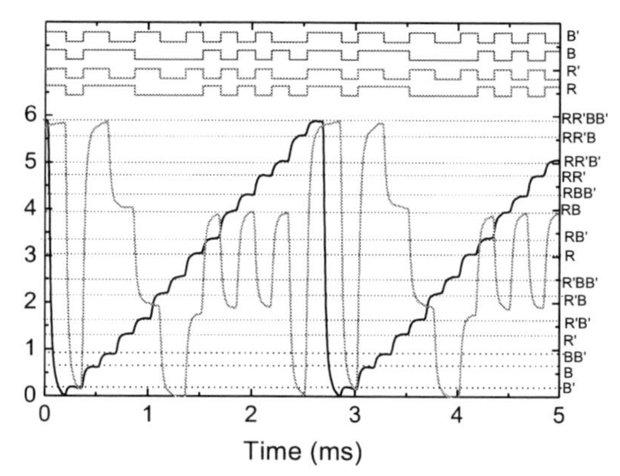

Figure 6 Front photocurrent signal acquired along the forward path at position (9). In superposition it is displayed the calibration grid. Contribution from the green emitters has been removed.

In Figure 7, it is displayed the front photocurrent signal due to the optical signal transmitted by the robot after removing a specific rack at the third quadrant of the south sector inside the navigation cell 1-2.

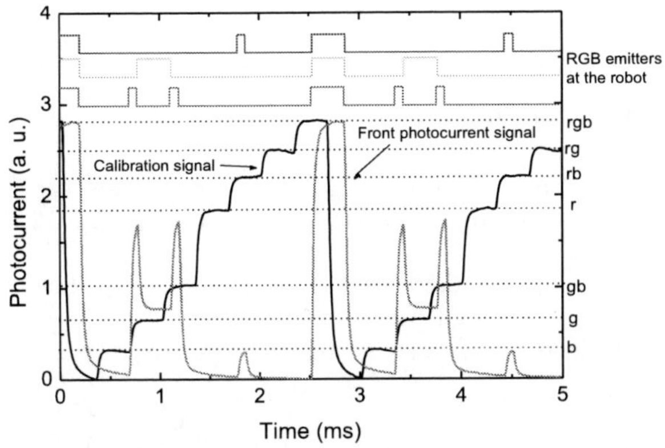

Figure 7 Front photocurrent signal transmitted by the robot when removing a rack. In superposition it is placed the calibration curve with 8 levels.

The calibration curve obtained with the 8 possible combinations is also displayed for decoding purposes.

IV. CONCLUSION

Simultaneous navigation and data transmission based on visible light communication was presented and discussed using bidirectional communication between infrastructure and autonomous vehicle in an indoors scenario. The infrastructure is the ceiling luminaire and the autonomous vehicle a mobile warehouse picking robot. The transmitted data is encoded in a 32 bits word, defined using specific data frames in each direction of the communication to ensure information transmission. Codification of the optical signals ensured synchronization between frames and was also designed to shield the decoding process from errors that might provide wrong identification of the correspondent spatial position and to minimize flickering effects.

ACKNOWLEDGMENT

This work was sponsored by FCT – Fundação para a Ciência e a Tecnologia, within the Research Unit CTS – Center of Technology and systems, reference UID/EEA/00066/2019 and by IPL/2020/Geo-Loc_ISEL.

REFERENCES

[1] N. Kumar and N R. Lourenço, "LED-based visible light communication system: a brief survey and investigation", Journal of Engineering and Applied Sciences, vol. 5, nº4, pp. 296-307, 2010.

[2] A. Jovicic, J. Li, and T. Richardson, "Visible light communication: opportunities, challenges and the path to market".

[3] W. Zhang and M. Kavehrad, "A 2-D indoor localization system based on visible light LED," in Proc. IEEE Photonics Society Summer Topical Conf.—Optical Wireless Systems Applications, pp. 80–81 (2012).

[4] W. Zhang, S. Chowdhury, and M. Kavehrad, "Asynchronous indoor positioning system based on visible light communications", Opt. Eng. 53 (4), pp. 045105-1 - 045105-9, 2014.

[5] Z. Jia, "A visible light communication based hybrid positioning method for wireless sensor networks", Intelligent System Design and Engineering Application (ISDEA) 2012 Second International Conference, pp. 1367-1370, 2012.

[6] E. Ozgur, E. Dinc, and O. B. Akan, "Communicate to illuminate: State-of-the-art and research challenges for visible light communications", Physical Communication 17, pp. 72-8 Z. Zhou, M. Kavehrad, and P. Deng, Opt. Eng. 51(8), (2012)5, 2015.

[7] Z. Zhou, M. Kavehrad, and P. Deng, "High-accuracy indoor positioning system based on visible light communication", Opt. Eng. 51(8), (2012).

[8] T. Komiyama, K. Kobayashi, K. Watanabe, T. Ohkubo, and Y. Kurihara, "Demonstration of Visible light Text data transmission system using LED lamp", Proceedings of SICE Annual Conference, IEEE, 2011, pp. 1926–1928.

[9] W. Ding, "Study of Smart Warehouse Management System Based on the IOT". In: Du Z. (eds) Intelligence Computation and Evolutionary Computation. Advances in Intelligent Systems and Computing, vol 180. Springer, Berlin, Heidelberg (2013).

[10] R. Koster, T. Duc, and K. Roodbergen, "Design and control of warehouse order picking: A literature review", European Journal of Operational Research, 182 (16), 2007, pp. 481-501.

[11] J. Gu, M. Goetschalckx, and L. McGinnis "Research on warehouse operation: A comprehensive review", European Journal of Operational Research, 177 (1), 2007, pp. 1-21.

[12] P. R. Wurman, R. D'Andrea, and M. Mountz, "Coordinating Hundreds of Cooperative, Autonomous Vehicles in Warehouses", Al Magazine, 29 (1), 2008, pp. 9 – 20.

[13] Z. Xiaoguang and L. Wei, "The research of network architecture in warehouse management system based on RFID and WSN integration", 2008 IEEE International Conference on Automation and Logistics, Qingdao, 2008, pp. 2556-2560.

[14] P. Louro, V. Silva, M. A. Vieira, and M. Vieira, "Viability of the use of an a-SiC: H multilayer device in a domestic VLC application", Physica Status Solidi (C) Current Topics In Solid State Physics, 11 (11–12) pp. 1703-1706, 2014.

[15] P. Louro, J. Costa, M. Vieira, and M. A. Vieira, "Indoors positioning through VLC technology using an a-SiC:H photodetector", Proc. SPIE 10453, Third International Conference on Applications of Optics and Photonics, 104530H (22 August 2017).

[16] P. Louro, V. Silva; J. Costa; M. A. Vieira, and M. Vieira, "Added transmission capacity in VLC systems using white RGB based LEDs and WDM devices ", Proc. SPIE 9899, Optical Sensing and Detection IV, 98990F (April 29, 2016).

[17] M. A. Vieira, M. Vieira, V. Silva, and P. Louro, "Optical signal processing for indoor positioning using a-SiC:H technology" Proc. SPIE 9891, Silicon Photonics and Photonic Integrated Circuits V, 98911Z (May 13, 2016).

[18] S. Rajagopal, R. D. Roberts, and S. K. Lim, "IEEE 802.15. 7 visible light communication: Modulation schemes and dimming support," IEEE Commun. Mag., vol. 50, no. 3, pp. 72–82, Mar. 2012.

[19] IEEE Standard for Local and Metropolitan Area Networks–Part 15.7: Short-Range Wireless Optical Communication Using Visible Light, IEEE Std. 802.15.7-2011, Sep. 2011, pp. 1–309.

[20] P. Louro, M. Vieira, and M. A. Vieira, "Coding schemes in a communication system based on visible-light communication", Proc. SPIE 10947, Next-Generation Optical Communication: Components, Sub-Systems, and Systems VIII, 109470G (1 February 2019); doi: 10.1117/12.2510103.

[21] P. Louro, J. Costa, M. Vieira, and M. A. Vieira, Y. Vygranenko, "Use of VLC for indoors navigation with RGB LEDs and a-SiC:H photodetector", Proc. of SPIE, vol 10231, Optical sensors 2017 (102310F-2).

Multi-Sensor Data Fusion and Artificial Neural Network to Estimate the Velocity of Sportive Turfgrass in Putting Green Areas

Lorena Parra[1, 2], Pedro V. Mauri[1], Jaime Lloret[2], Salima Yousfi[1] and José F. Marín[3]
[1]Instituto Madrileño de Investigación y Desarrollo Rural, Agrario y Alimentario (IMIDRA), Finca "El Encin", A-2, Km 38, 2, 28800 Alcalá de Henares, Madrid, Spain
[2] Instituto de Investigación para la Gestión Integrada de Zonas Costeras Universitat Politècnica de València, Valencia, Spain
[3] Area verde MG Projects SL. C/ Oña, 43 28933 Madrid, Spain
Email: pedro.mauri@madrid.org, loparbo@doctor.upv.es, jlloret@dcom.upv.es, salima.yousfi@madrid.org, jmarin@areaverde.es

Abstract—**Although the use of sensors is extended in the environmental monitoring, there are some variables which cannot be directly measured and must be estimated. The velocity of sportive turfgrass is one of them. In this paper, we attempt to estimate the velocity in two putting greens of a golf course, before and after a maintenance action, by the measurement of agronomic variables with digital devices. We measure the soil moisture and temperature, the canopy temperature and the Normalised Difference Vegetation Index. The measurements are performed during five months in two putting greens of *Agrostis stolonifera*. The results indicated that the monitoring of a single agronomic parameter is not useful to evaluate the recovery of the putting green. The agronomic variables showed a total recovery 22 after the maintenance action. Meanwhile, the data of velocity indicates that full recovery was not achieved after 124 days. Finally, we use the agronomic variables to estimate the velocity. A multiple regression model was defined with Normalised Difference Vegetation Index, soil moisture, and soil temperature. Then, those variables are included in an artificial neural network model to generate graphics, which can be used by greenkeepers to estimate the velocity. The model archived 70% of correctly classified cases. Graphics of classification to be used by the greenkeepers, which include the estimated velocity based on soil moisture and Normalised Difference Vegetation Index, for four different temperatures are generated.**

Keywords-velocity of the putting greens; soil moisture; soil temperature; Normalized Difference Vegetation Index; turfgrass

I. INTRODUCTION

In the last decades, the use of sensing devices for environmental monitoring has become more and more popular. One of the areas in which the use of sensors has arisen more useful is the motorisation of crops. The use of Wireless Sensor Networks (WSN) in agriculture, as part of precision agriculture systems, provides higher sustainability and profitability of the activity. The sensors can be used to monitor the soil, the plants or the water as it was said in a survey about the Internet of Things (IoT) for agriculture [1]. The same systems can be applied for turfgrass monitoring in gardens or sportive areas such as golf courses, Football or Rugby camps.

Nonetheless, in many cases, there are variables which cannot be easily measured with the current sensors or digital devices. Some examples are the sportive parameters of turfgrass such as velocity, firmness or traction. Nowadays, for the measurement of the aforementioned variables, analogic devices must be used, which require from the human action and cannot be connected with a WSN of an IoT system. Even though autonomous digital devices cannot measure those parameters, there exist the possibility to estimate them upon other parameters. It is usual to combine different easy-to-measure parameters to estimate another parameter, which is not possible to measure it directly. This technique is known as multi-sensor data fusion, and we can find several examples of its applications for agriculture such as phenotyping [2], or estimating the evapotranspiration [3].

In some cases, a simple linear regression model can be used to estimate the seek parameters. Nonetheless, occasionally the use of artificial intelligence (AI) systems must attain better results. In [4], authors proposed the use of soil temperature, moisture and pH values to estimate farmland soil carbon sink factors using multi-sensor data fusion and artificial neural network (ANN). Therefore, we can affirm that these techniques have been already used to estimate parameters in agriculture.

Though, none of these techniques or methods has been used in sportive grass management. Unlike other examples found in agriculture, the use of estimating parameters in sportive turfgrass has a low direct impact on the sustainability of the activity. Nonetheless, the estimation of parameters such as velocity, firmness or traction of grass has an impact on the quality of the game of the users. Apart from the assumption that not all the greenkeepers have the devices or the time to monitor the status of the turfgrass, the measurement of velocity is one of the most tedious actions. It is generally measured only before a tournament. Besides this, the velocity is an excellent indicator of putting green status. The velocity might be controlled by changing some of the management variables. Some of the maintenance actions, such as aeration, have a dramatic effect on the velocity causing an abrupt reduction.

The aim of the paper is to evaluate if the data gathered from digital sensing devices can be used to estimate the green velocity to monitor its recovery after aeration. The objective is to reduce the time required in the regular field monitoring in the golf courses. To have enough data to test the effectiveness of the results of ANN, we gathered measures before and after the maintenance action during several months. Data is analysed to determine which parameter or parameters can be used to estimate green velocity. We want to confirm two hypotheses, the first one if a single variable can be used to estimate the putting green recovery as it can be done with the velocity. The second one is to determine if Multi-sensor data fusion and ANN can be used to estimate the velocity.

The remainder of this paper is structured as follows. Section 2 outlines the related work in the field of turfgrass monitoring. The test bench is described in Section 3. Section 4 presented our results and their applicability. Finally, the conclusions are summarised in Section 5.

II. RELATED WORK

In this section, we described the existing efforts in turfgrass monitoring and multi-sensor data fusion with AI in agriculture.

Although the interest in turfgrass monitoring is lower than in other farming systems, we can found several examples. Marin et al. [5] proposed the use of remote sensing to evaluate the turfgrass coverage by analysing the histograms of gathered images. They work oriented to ornamental lawns rather than sportive grasses. Parra et al. presented a new methodology for the identification of the weed plant in sportive turfgrass [6]. The authors use remote sensing images and image processing techniques based on edge detection to detect weed plants.

Straw et al. measured multiple parameters in natural turfgrass sports fields to identify short-term spatiotemporal relationship [7]. The authors gather data about soil and plant variables finding some interesting correlations, for example, between Normalized Difference Vegetation Index (NDVI) and surface hardness. Nonetheless, in this paper, no sportive variables are measured, estimated or correlated. More examples of the multi-sensor approach are found for grasslands. In [8], Ouyang et al. analysed vegetation dynamics by utilising the standardised NDVI data gathered with different remote sensing sources. By combining NDVI values, they were able to estimate the biomass. A parallel proposal was presented by Reddersen et al. [9]. In this case, the authors select and extensively managed grassland and several measures are gathered in the experimental area. The measured parameters included Leaf area index, ultrasonic sward height, and 12 vegetation indices to estimate the biomass for different species. The combination of different measured variables offers reasonable estimations of plant biomass. The objective in [8] and [9] was somehow similar to our aim, determine the value of a parameter which is hard to measure (the biomass) with other easy-to-measure variables (NDVI).

Focusing on our objective, the estimation of velocity in the putting green, no one paper has been found that details the existence of a relation of agronomic variables and velocity. The only paper where the velocity of the putting green was measured we found is [10]. In [10], Rana and Askew evaluate the if *Poa pratensis* (one of the species that composes the green) has an effect on ball rolling behaviour. To do so, they measure the rolling behaviour in the putting gree, using a high-speed camera. Their results indicate that no effect was found on ball velocity regardless of tested surface (different grass species). Nonetheless, we are going to analyse more parameters to find a correlation between surface and velocity.

We can affirm that currently there is no one technique which can be used to measure in-situ the green velocity, which can be integrated into IoT systems. Furthermore, no one authors have presented the possibility to estimate the velocity basing on multi-sensor data fusion with or without AI system.

III. TEST BENCH

In this section, the description of the studied area, the measured parameters and used equipment are detailed.

A. Description of the studied area

The studied area is two greens, green two and green 17, of the "Encin Golf Course" located at the region of Madrid (Spain). The greens are the part of the golf course in which the velocity becomes critical; therefore, it is essential to measure this parameter. Although many greens might have a low or null slope in the studied greens, we can identify areas with certain slopes as can be seen in Figure 1.

The green is composed of *Agrostis stolonifera* T1 and presents a small incidence of *Poa annua* as an undesired plant. The greens are mowed, as average, three times per week. The height of the grass in the green area is between 3 and 4mm. The greens are irrigated every day after sunrise according to the recommendations of the Food and Agriculture Organization. In each one of the greens, we have identified three areas to be measured.

After starting the measurements, a maintenance action, green aeration, was carried out. Among the existing techniques for improving the green aeration, we have applied the half-inch-diameter hollow tines. It was done from 23rd to 29th of March. The first measurement was carried out the 24th of February of 2020 with the green in normal status. In the 2nd of April, the greens were monitored after the maintenance actions. After this date, the greens are monitored once or twice per month according to the time disposal and the restrictions due to the COVID. A total of 8 records have been performed, finishing the experiment on 31st of July of 2020. Table 1 details the days in which the greens are monitored and the label that we are going to use for each day. The label indicates the time pass after the maintenance action.

B. Measured parameters

We measure a total of four agronomic parameters (two forms the soil and two from the vegetation) using digital devices, and the green velocity as a sportive parameter. The monitored parameters are the soil moisture (SM), soil temperature (ST), canopy temperature (CT), and NDVI.

Figure 1. Image of Green 2 took on 1/07/2020

TABLE I. SUMMARY OF MEASUREMENTS

Nº of measurement	Day	Label	Description
1	24/02/2020	-1	Before the maintenance action
2	02/04/2020	0	Just after the maintenance action
3	20/04/2020	1	After the maintenance action
4	19/05/2020	2	
5	02/06/2020	3	
6	16/06/2020	4	
7	17/07/2020	5	
8	31/07/2020	6	

The soil moisture is measured with the TDR 350 FieldScout [11] at 5cm. In each point, we gather three measurements and only the mean value is used in this paper. The TDR was configured according to the instructions, and the selected soil type was set on the sand. The soil temperature is also measured with the TDR at 5cm. Again, three records are done in each one of the measured points.

The CT is measured using an infrared thermometer. We have used the Fluke 561 [12]. Three records are performed in each one of the monitored areas, and again, the mean value is used. For the NDVI measurement, we have used the Handheld Crop Sensor GreenSeeker [13]. Since this device allows to perform a scan of the measured area, and the mean value is automatically calculated, we used this option. Both devices are considered as remote sensing devices and have been used at 1m above the soil.

Finally, to measure the green velocity, we have used a stimpmeter. The stimpmeter is a tool designed by the United States Golf Association in 1930 used to measure the velocity of a golf ball in the green area. This measurement is performed manually using the stimpmeter and three golf balls. Although this is the official process to obtain the velocity of the green and it is used in before the most important championships, the process is tedious and might be affected by the person who is performing the measures.

IV. RESULTS

In this section, we present our results. First, the evolution of monitored parameters after the aeration is displayed. Then, the existing correlations and the use of ANN are analysed.

A. Evolution of sensed variables

In order to verify one of our main hypothesis, we are going to present the recorded values of all monitored parameters (including the measured with digital devices and with stimpmeter).

First, we present the measured values of soil measurements. Figure 2 a) and b) represent the mean and the Fisher Least significant difference (LSD) intervals of measured soil moisture and soil temperature for the studied period. Regarding the soil moisture, Figure 2 a), the detected change is a constant increase of soil moisture, unless in data gathered in the second measurement after the maintenance. This increase is explained by a modification in irrigation due to the increase in the temperature, which must be compensated by a higher amount of applied irrigation. Apparently, no relation between the green recovery and the soil moisture can be detected. Concerning the soil temperature, Figure 2 b), again the general trend is due to the changes in environmental conditions. Nonetheless, we can identify that just after the aeration of the green (measure 0) the temperature of soil increases. This fact is caused by the change of surface during the aeration action, when part of the surface, previously covered by grass, changes to sand. Since the sand has different thermic properties than the green plants, the value of soil temperature increases. After 22 days (measure 1), the soil temperature lowers again and present similar values than before the maintenance action. Therefore, we can affirm that in terms of soil temperature, the disturbance caused by the aeration of the greens is recovered after 22 days.

Following, we are going to detail the results of monitored vegetation variables, see Figure 3 a) and b). The results of CT, Figure 3 a) are similar to the results of soil temperature. Although the values are a bit lower due to the capability of reducing the temperature of healthy plants, the observed trend is the same. There is an increase of CT just after the maintenance action due to the introduced modification in the surface. The increase of CT is corrected in the next measure (Measure 1).

Concerning the NDVI, Figure 3 b), the measured NDVI just after the maintenance was much lower than the NDVI before the maintenance. Again, this alteration is corrected after 22 days. Thus we can affirm that considering the agronomic variables, the disturbance of the aeration of greens is recovered in less than 22 days. Finally, we analyse the evolution of green velocity in Figure 4.

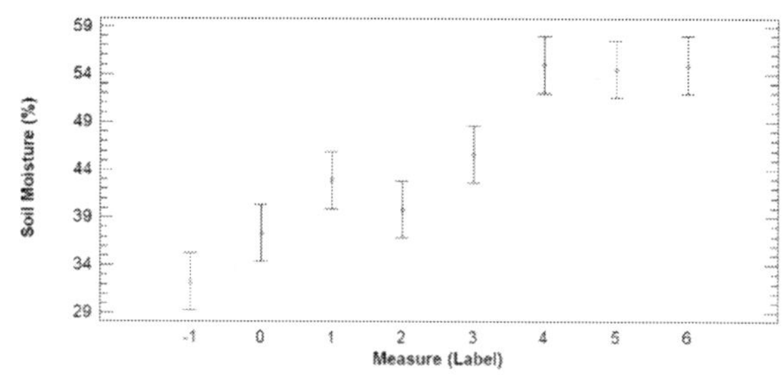

a)

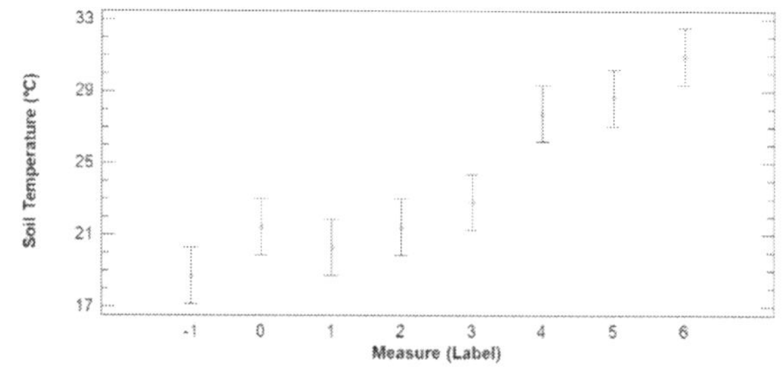

b)

Figure 2. Evolution on measured soil variables as mean value and Fisher LSD intervals

This is the variable that truly indicates us the recovery of the green after the aeration. We can identify that although there is a recovery in measures 1 and 2, the green is not entirely recovered after measure 6 (31/07/2020). We must clarify that the velocities of 7 feet are appropriate for playing. Even so, we cannot consider that green is recovered until the measured velocity is equal to the velocity measured in measure -1 (before the action).

Thus, we can affirm that the simple measure of agronomic variables cannot inform us about the recovery of the green after maintenance action, at least in the case of aeration. According to the measured agronomic variables, we will establish the recovery of the green in Measure 1, 22 days after the aeration. On the other hand, attending to the green velocity, the recovery of green will be reached in Measure 6, 124 days after the aeration. Therefore we need to discard our first hypothesis.

B. *Using agronomic variables to predict the green velocity*

Our second hypothesis is that the combination of two or more agronomic values can be used to predict the green velocity, allowing the evaluation of the recovery. In order to evaluate this option, different tools are proposed. First, a multiple regression, including agronomic variables as independent variables and the velocity as dependent variables, is presented.

Following, and with the purpose of developing a graphics useful for greenkeepers, the application of the ANN is proposed. Despite there are other AI more powerful than ANN, such as Support Vector Machine (SVM), we focus on ANN as the first step of applying AI to gathered data. Other authors compared the performance of SVM with ANN of biological data and SVM showed slightly better accuracy, 80% for ANN and 85% for SVM[14].

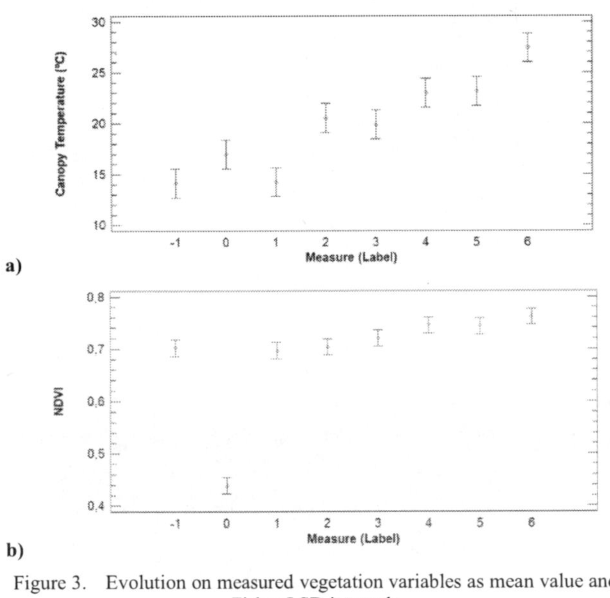

Figure 3. Evolution on measured vegetation variables as mean value and Fisher LSD intervals

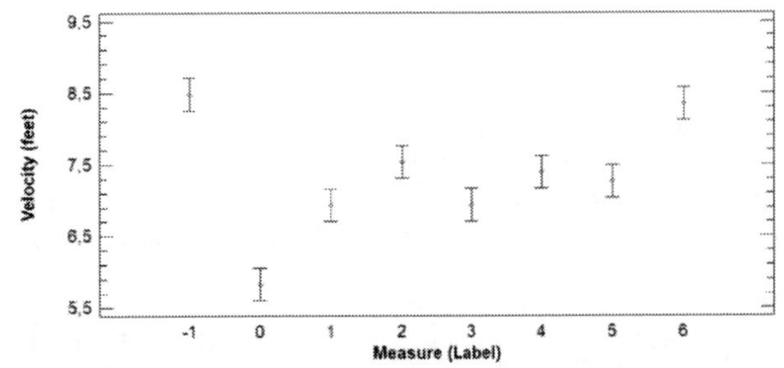

Figure 4. Evolution on measured velocity as mean value and Fisher LSD intervals

Concerning the multiple regression, a first attempt is performed including all the variables and selecting the ordinary minimum squares as adjusting procedure. The generated model has an R^2 of 0.63. Nonetheless, the results of statistical software pointed out that some of the CTs might be extracted to simplify the model. After extract this value from the model, the R^2 has not changed; its value is 0.63. In Figure 5, we can compare the observed value of velocity and the predicted value according to the generated model. We can identify that the lower errors are linked to values of velocity between 6.7 and 7.8 feet. The proposed mathematical model is presented in (1).

$$V\,(feet) = 3.296 \times SM\,(\%) + 7.059 \times NDVI + 0.115 \times ST\,(^{\circ}C) \quad (1)$$

where:

V is the velocity of the green
SM is the soil moisture
ST is the soil temperature

Although the proposed model confirms our hypothesis, the combination of three agronomic variables can be used to estimate the green recovery or velocity, and one more step must be carried out. Besides the application of proposed above model can be useful and its accuracy indicated by the R2, it is almost useless for the daily monitoring activities. Considering the different tasks of greenkeepers if we expect that the proposed model is adopted we need to avoid the use of equations and present the results in a more easy-to-apply and straightforward way. Therefore, and with the aim of generating a series of graphics, an ANN model is created. It will be easier for the greenkeepers to use the classification graphics of the ANN than the application of (1).

The proposed ANN has three input neurons (soil moisture, soil temperature and NDVI), two hidden layers, and six output neurons. In order to simplify our variables, the velocity was included without decimals in the model. The velocity values go from 5 to 10 feet. The rest of the variables are maintained as they are. The probability was set as proportional to the observed and the cost of error equal to all groups. Finally, the sphere of influence was determined by jackknifing.

From the total of 48 observations, most of the cases have a measured velocity of 7 and 8 feet, with 25 and 15 observations. The optimised value of jackknifing during the training was set on 0.073. The results of the proposed ANN pointed out that 70.83% of cases were classified correctly. The percentage of correct classification is shown in Table 2.

According to our results, we can affirm that as found in the regression, the highest error are linked to the most extreme velocities (5, 9 and 10 feet with 0% of correct classified cases). The best accuracy, 88% of correct classified cased, is related to the central velocity, 7 feet. Now, we compare the results of ANN with the regression model. Even that we use the discrete values of velocity values in the regression, the R2 of the newly generated model is 0.60. Thus, we can affirm that ANN not only offers a more straightforward way to use their results for greenkeepers, the classification graphics but also offers the best accuracy compared with regression models.

Finally, we present in Figure 6, the summary of classification graphics obtained. Since in our model, we have three variables we include as x and y-axis the SM and NDVI, and four different graphics are presented for four different ST.

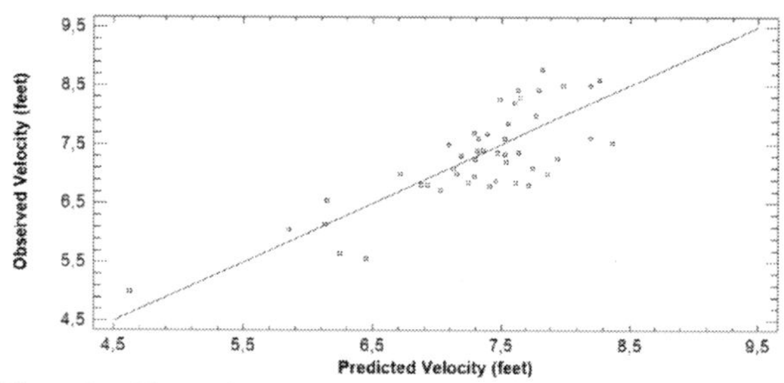

Figure 5. Observed vs predicted values of velocity with the proposed mathematical model

The objective is that those graphics can be easily used by the greenkeepers to estimate the velocity of their greens in the daily monitoring. Figure 6 a) shows the estimated velocity for a soil temperature of 10ºC. We can identify that the higher the NDVI, the faster the velocity. Meanwhile, the soil moisture has the opposite effect, the higher the soil moisture, the slower the green velocity. The same trend is found in Figure 6 b) for 20 ºC, Figure 6 c) for 30ºC and Figure 6 d) for 40ºC. For scenarios with 10ºC, the maximum expected velocity will be 8 feet. The predicted velocities increase with the temperature, and for scenarios with 30 ºC or more, velocities of 10 feet can be expected.

TABLE II. SUMMARY OF CLASSIFIED CASES

Velocity (feet)	Number of observations	Correct classified percentage
5	1	0,0
6	4	50,0
7	25	88,0
8	15	66,6667
9	2	0,0
10	1	0,0
Total	48	70,8333

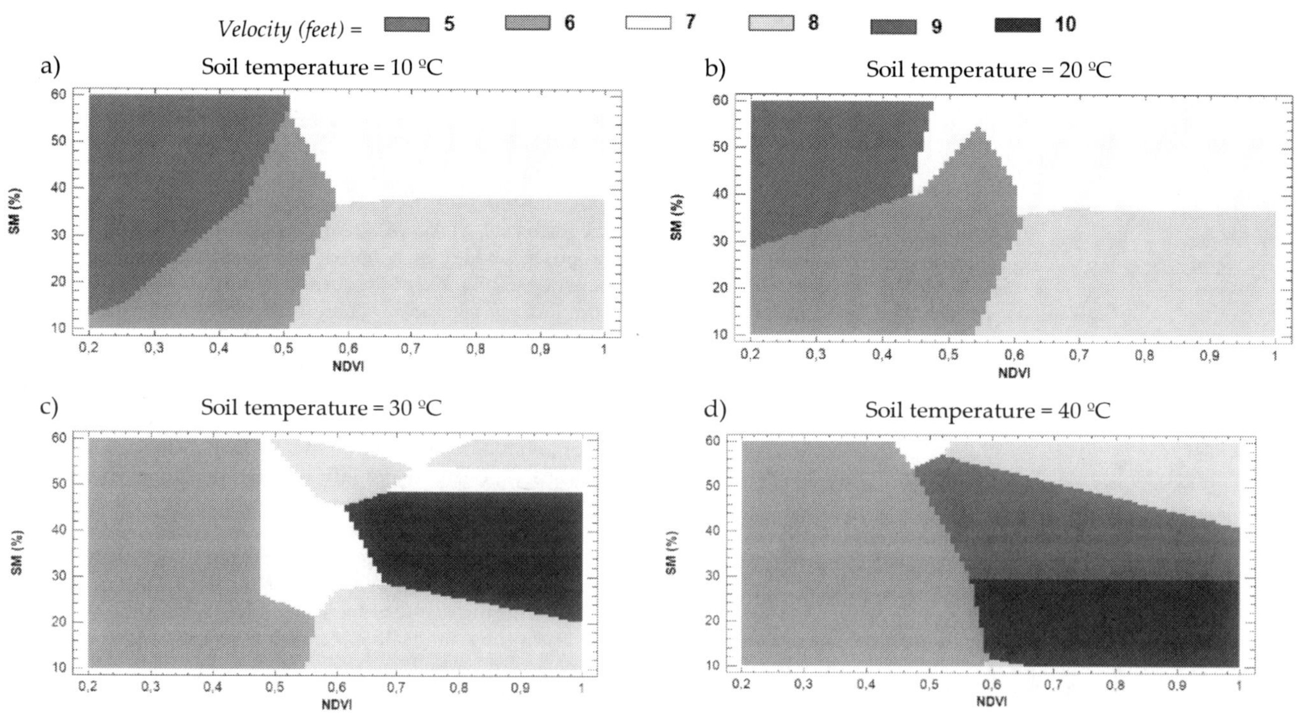

Figure 6. Classification results of ANN applied to gathered data to estimate the velocity from SM, NDVI and ST.

It must be noted that, although the data included in this ANN model is limited, include just one type of grass coverage, and it is affected by the maintenance action, the results are promising. The main limitation of this study is the fact that most of our measured have a similar velocity, between 7 and 8, see Table 2. It is necessary to increase the measuring time to obtained more data under different circumstances.

In addition, results are aligned with the empirical experience of greenkeepers. The knowledge of greenkeepers indicates that the greens are faster when they are dry. Those dry conditions correspond to low soil moisture. Therefore, we have demonstrated that although in previous papers authors have pointed out that no relation was found between ball velocity and surface [10] there is a correlation between soil conditions (NDVI, SM, and ST) and ball velocity. These papers follow the ideas developed in [8] and [9], to estimate parameters, which are hard to measure from NDVI.

V. Conclusion

In this paper, we have dealt with the use of sensing devices to monitor the changes in the velocity in two greens of *Agrostis stolonifera*. The objective is to obtain a way of using the data of the employed digital devices to estimate the velocity, which measurements are a tedious and time-consuming practice.

Our study is performed before, during and after a maintenance action that produces a decrease in the velocity. The results indicated that the measurement and analysis of a single variable are not enough to characterise the velocity of the green. Nonetheless, the combination of soil moisture, soil temperature and NDVI can be used to estimate the velocity. This was demonstrated with a multiple regression model and with the ANN model. The proposed ANN model offers a series of graphics, which can be used by the greenkeepers to estimate the velocity in the daily routine.

The future work will be focused on extending the amount of data from the greens performing more measurements and including more variables. Furthermore, the comparison of our results with other AI techniques will be considered, as well as validate and test the obtained machine learning model with new data. In addition, we will start to monitor greens composed of other grass species and greens with a higher percentage of *Poa annua*. This must be considered since other species have different colourations and might affect to the NDVI measures.

Acknowledgment

This work has been partially funded by AREA VERDE-MG projects, Projects GO-PDR18-XEROCESPED funded, by the European Agricultural Fund for Rural Development (EAFRD) and IMIDRA, and by Conselleria de Educación, Cultura y Deporte with the Subvenciones para la contratación de personal investigador en fase postdoctoral, grant number APOSTD/2019/04.

References

[1] L. García, L. Parra, J. M. Jimenez, J. Lloret, and P. Lorenz, P. "IoT-Based Smart Irrigation Systems: An Overview on the Recent Trends on Sensors and IoT Systems for Irrigation in Precision Agriculture," *Sensors*, 20(4), 2020, pp. 1042.

[2] M. Maimaitijiang et al., "Unmanned Aerial System (UAS)-based phenotyping of soybean using multi-sensor data fusion and extreme learning machine," *ISPRS Journal of Photogrammetry and Remote Sensing*, 134, 2017, pp.43-58.

[3] K. A. Semmens et al., "Monitoring daily evapotranspiration over two California vineyards using Landsat 8 in a multi-sensor data fusion approach," *Remote Sensing of Environment*, 185, 2016, pp.155-170.

[4] W. Qiulan, G. Xia, L. Yong, and X. Hongli, "Research on multi-sensor data fusion algorithm of soil carbon sink factors based on neural network," In Proceedings of the IEEE 2013 International Conference on Mechatronic Sciences, Electric Engineering and Computer (MEC 2013), December 20-22, 2013 Shenyang, China, pp. 637-641

[5] J. Marín et al. "Urban lawn monitoring in smart city environments," *Journal of Sensors*, 2018, pp. 2018.

[6] L. Parra et al. "Edge detection for weed recognition in lawns," *Computers and Electronics in Agriculture*, 176, 2020, pp. 105684.

[7] C. M. Straw, R. A. Grubbs, and G. M. Henry, "Short-term spatiotemporal relationship between plant and soil properties on natural turfgrass sports fields," *Agrosystems, Geosciences & Environment*, 3(1), 2020, pp. e20043.

[8] W. Ouyang, et al., "Integration of multi-sensor data to assess grassland dynamics in a Yellow River sub-watershed," *Ecological indicators*, 18, 2012, pp.163-170.

[9] B. Reddersen, T. Fricke, and M. Wachendorf, "A multi-sensor approach for predicting biomass of extensively managed grassland," *Computers and electronics in agriculture*, 109, 2014, pp. 247-260.

[10] S. S. Rana and S. D. Askew, "Measuring Canopy Anomaly Influence on Golf Putt Kinematics: Does Annual Bluegrass Influence Ball Roll Behavior?" *Crop Science*, 58(2), 2018, pp. 911-916.

[11] TDR 350 Manual. Available at: https://www.specmeters.com/assets/1/22/6435_TDR_350_manual_(web).pdf. Last access on 19/10/2020

[12] Fluke 561 Infrared & Contact Thermometer manual. Available at: https://dam-assets.fluke.com/s3fs-public/56x_____umeng0000.pdf. Last access on 19/10/2020

[13] GreenSeeker Information. Available at: http://trl.trimble.com/docushare/dsweb/Get/Document-475150/022503-1123A_GreenSeeker_DS_MarketSmart_USL_0415_LR_web.pdf. Last access on 19/10/2020

[14] H. Bisgin et al., "Comparing SVM and ANN based machine learning methods for species identification of food contaminating beetles," *Scientific reports*, 8(1), 2018, pp.1-12.

A CPW-SIW Planar Dual-Band Antenna for ISM Applications

Radhoine Aloui[1], Zied houaneb[2], Hassen Zairi[3]
Research Laboratory Smart Electricity ICT, SEICT,
LR18ES44, National Engineering School of Carthage
University of Carthage.
Tunis, Tunisia.
[1]Radhoine.aloui1990@gmail.com [2] zied_houaneb@yahoo.fr
[3] hassen.zairi@gmail.com

Fermin Mira[1], Ignacio Llamas-Garro[2]
Centre Tecnologic de Telecomunicacions de Catalunya
(CTTC/CERCA)) Castelldefels, Barcelona,
Spain.Castelldefels, Barcelona, Spain.
[1]fermin.mira@cttc.cat, [2]ignacio.llamas@cttc.es

Abstract—**A dual-band low cost antenna for Industrial, scientific and medical (ISM) applications with circular polarization at 5.8 GHz is presented. The proposed antenna is excited through a single feed line connected to the patch. Two omni-directional radiation patterns are obtained for the two ISM bands. The proposed antenna is patterned on an RF30 rectangular dielectric (28 mm x 40 mm) with 1.52 mm thickness. The antenna exhibits a super-wide frequency bandwidth from 5.4 GHz to 6.4 GHz centered at 5.8 GHz, and 0.5 GHz bandwidth for the first resonance frequency, centered at 2.4 GHz. An improvement in return loss has been obtained by introducing a Coplanar Waveguide (CPW) feed implemented in Substrate Integrated Waveguide (SIW) technology. A prototype antenna is fabricated using standard PCB fabrication. Measured results show a good agreement between simulation and measured results.**

Keywords- Dual-band; ISM antenna; Single layer; micro-strip; SIW technolgy.

I. INTRODUCTION

ISM-band antennas are a crucial component in sensor nodes, used for high quality data transmission in wireless sensor networks. A dual-band antenna made on a simple planar layer has the flexibility and simplicity required to be integrated into chemical sensors, operating at infrared wavelengths [1]. In previous years, researchers have been interested in developing the called Substrate-Integrated Waveguide (SIW) [2], a simple technology compatible with planar circuits with ease of integration with other components, thus with characteristics that can improve the performance or packaging of RF circuits. The SIW technology is compatible with rectangular waveguides and microstrip or CPW technology. SIW planar technology involves simple PCB fabrication techniques and has been used for ISM band applications [3]-[5]. Many passive circuits have been developed using SIW technology [6]-[10]. Highlighting antenna development, several multiband antennas have been presented in previous years for specific applications. In [11], an antenna for MIMO application works at a single frequency with two different modes of operation. A multiband multimode antenna can be found in [12]; the antenna design has a circular patch on the top of the structure, where a SIW cavity is used for the outer antenna, and includes a perpendicularly placed connector. The antenna has a degraded gain for the TM02 first mode and a high gain for other modes. A dual-band antenna working in the ISM band with low profile for body centric communications is presented in [13]; the antenna has low gain for the first band with an omnidirectional radiation pattern and an unidirectional radiation pattern for the second resonance frequency. The antenna uses two connectors perpendicular to the top patch.

In this paper, a planar dual-band antenna fabricated on a single layer of dielectric material is described in section II. The antenna includes a microstrip line and ground plane as shown in Figure 1. The proposed ISM antenna is used for wireless sensor data transmission. The two antenna frequency bands of operation can be independently tuned as discussed in section III, by adjusting the microstrip line dimension parameters, and the width of the ground plane. The measurement and simulation results are presented in section IV. Finally, section V provides a conclusion for this work.

II. PROPOSED ISM ANTENNA STRUCTURE

The proposed antenna with and without CPW-SIW technology is composed of micro-strip lines patches, as shown in Figure 1. The designs can be connected using a simple SMA connector attached to the substrate side. The microstrip line is designed to resonate at the frequencies of 2.4 GHz and 5.8 GHz, as shown in Figure 2. RF30 material is used as the substrate, with a dielectric constant value of 3.35, loss tangent of 0.001, and substrate thickness of h=1.52 mm. The design of the microstrip patches is based on conventional theory. The width and length of the patch were calculated using the following standard expression [14].

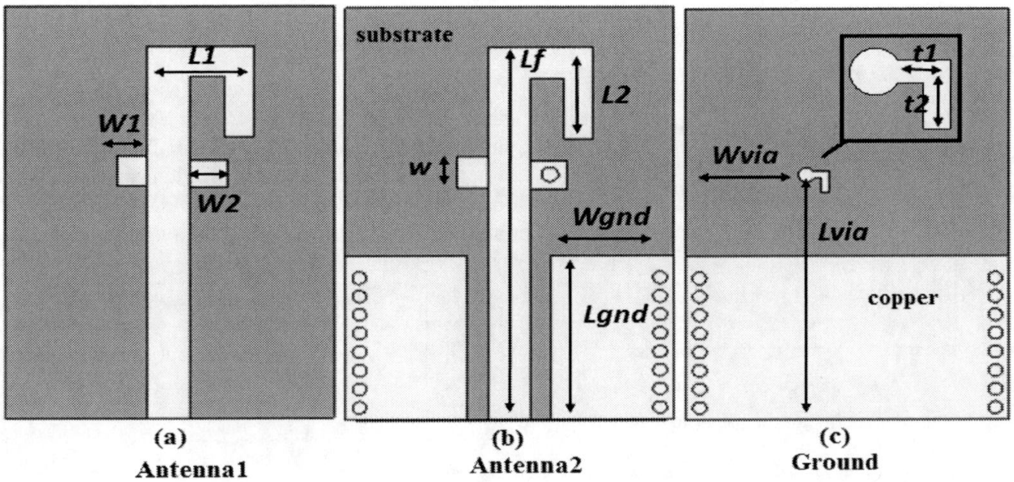

Figure 1. Proposed antenna, (a) Top view antenna without SIW, (b) Top view with SIW, (c) Bottom view.

$$Width = \frac{c}{2f_0\sqrt{\frac{\varepsilon_r+1}{2}}} \qquad (1)$$

$$Length = \frac{c}{2f_0\sqrt{\varepsilon_{eff}}} - 0.824h\left[\frac{(\varepsilon_{eff}+0.3)\left(\frac{W}{h}+0.264\right)}{(\varepsilon_{eff}-0.258)\left(\frac{W}{h}+0.8\right)}\right] \qquad (2)$$

The proposed antenna is made on a sheet of low permittivity substrate with dimensions 28mm x 40mm x 1.52mm. Table I summarizes the design parameter value used to produce the antenna. In this paper, a single layer structure, with simple side interface with the connector is used. The proposed antenna involves microstrip lines, coplanar waveguide (CPW) and SIW technology. The bottom ground plane dimension must also be carefully taken into account to provide the desired band of operation.

TABLE I. DIMENSION OF STRUCTURE

Parameters	L_{gnd}	W_{gnd}	L1	L2	Lf	W
Value [mm]	24.2	10.4	9	8.8	34	2
Parameters	t1	t2	L_{via}	W_{via}	W1	W2
Value [mm]	1.4	2.05	22.15	10.2	3	3.7

The bandwidth enhancement technique and the VSWR results are demonstrated in the following section. The impedance matching at 2.4 and 5.8 GHz bands can be adjusted with the proposed structure, which was found to be effective in obtaining a high impedance bandwidth in the antenna's upper operating band.

III. RESUSLTS AND DISCUISSON

In this part, an initial proposed antenna has been simulated and compared with the CPW-SIW technology antenna.

A. *Initial design*

The proposed antenna is simulated using CST commercial software; CST software is based on the integral method (FDTD). Figure 2 shows a comparison between simulated results using the proposed antenna with and without using CPW-SIW. The dimensions of the microstrip radiating conductors and the ground plane in the bottom part of the antenna are shown in Figure 1.

Through numerical analysis, the reflection coefficient in the ISM bands in minimized, while the reflection coefficient is maximized elsewhere. According to the result in Figure 2, an improvement is obtained when the CPW-SIW structure is introduced. The VSWR is below 3 dB for the two ISM bands, centered at 2.4 GHz and 5.8 GHz. Figure 2 and Figure 3 show an improvement in results between the two antennas, according to the S-parameters and VSWR, obtained. From the simulation results of Figures 2 and 3, an impedance bandwidth with $|S11| < -10$ dB is obtained, with ranges from 2.2 to 2.9 GHz (30%) and 5.2 to 6.8 GHz (80%), where 19% VSWR is achieved. Fig.4 shows the improvement obtained when inducing the CPW-SIW structure in terms of radiation pattern at 2.4 GHz and 5.8 GHz. The maximum gain of the proposed antenna is approximately 3.4dB. The simulated spinning linear radiation patterns in two orthogonal planes (xoy and yoz) for the two resonance frequencies of 2.4 GHz and 5.8 GHz are plotted in Figure 4, respectively.

The radiation pattern shows an improvement when the CPW-SIW technology is used, with an omnidirectional radiation pattern at 2.4 GHz and an unidirectional one at 5.8 GHz.

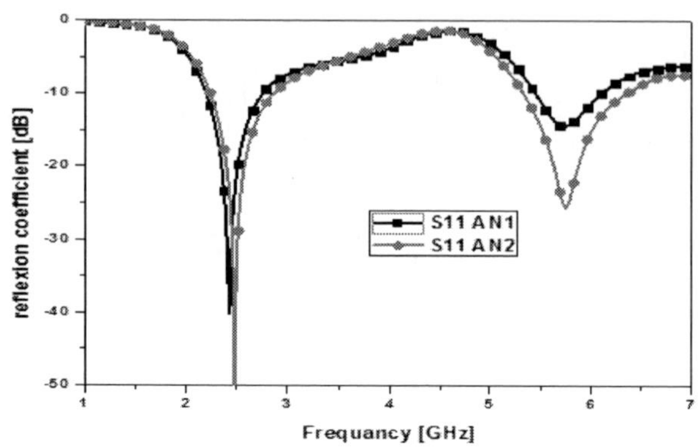

Figure 2. Reflexion coefficient comparaison.

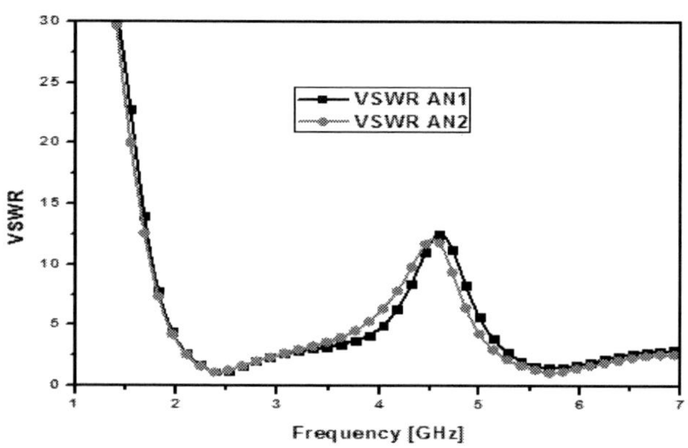

Figure 3. VSWR of the antennas versus frequency.

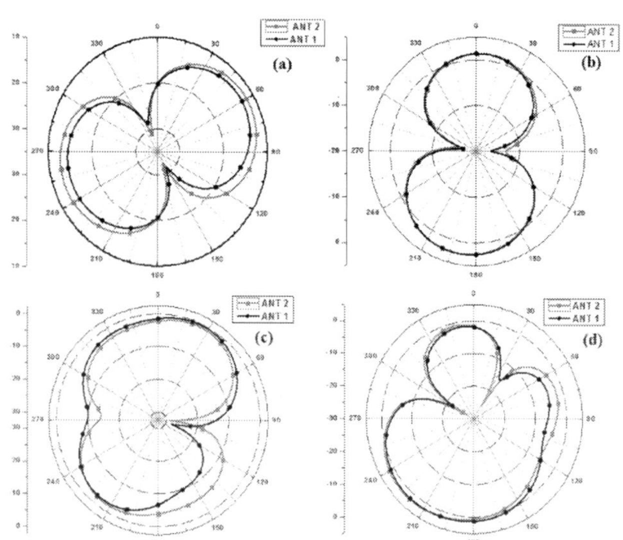

Figure 4. Radiation pattern (a) E field 2.4 GHz (b) H-field 2.4 GHz (c) E-field 5.8 GHz and (d) H-field 5.8 GHz

B. *Band tuning technique analysis.*

Although the precedent design resonates at 2.4 GHz and 5.8 GHz exactly, the resonant frequencies are not independently tunable. A dual-band and dual-mode antenna is attractive and very useful when a single band frequency can be tuned to the desired frequency of specific applications, while keeping the other band fixed.

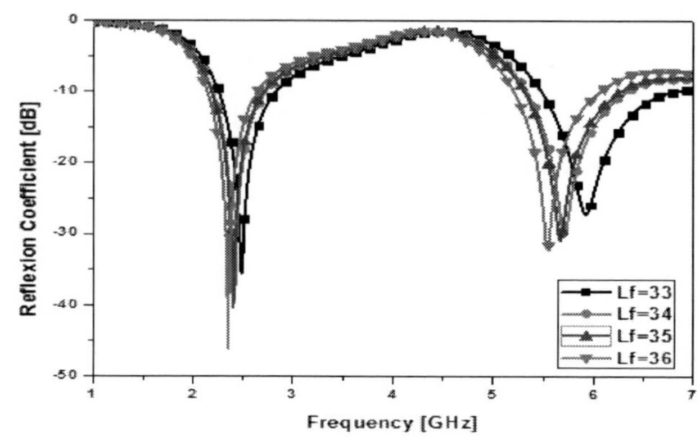

Figure 5. Reflexion coefficient versus L_f.

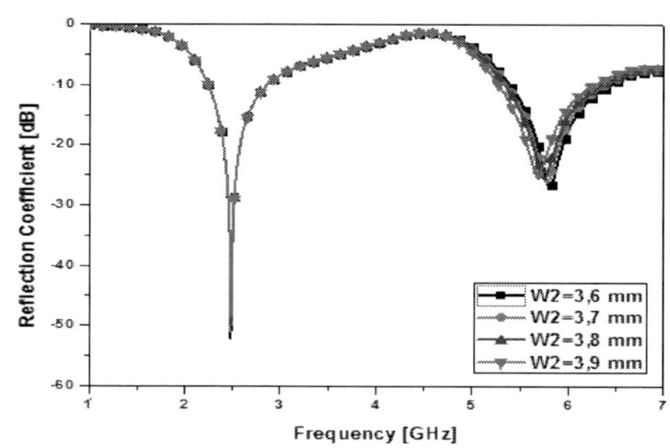

Figure 6. Reflexion coefficient versus W_2.

In this paper, to independently tune the resonant milti-band frequencies of the antenna, design parameters are varied as follows. Lf and W2 are the most important parameters for frequency tuning. Figure 5 shows the different reflection coefficients vs Lf parameters. This result illustrates that the two bands can be tuned at the same time, so it is not reasonable to adjust the two bands at once. On the other hand, we can tune the high resonance frequency (5.8GHz), where W2 can be adjusted to modify the second resonance frequency. Figure 6 showns the reflection coefficient versus frequency for different W2 parameters. Figure 5 and Figure 6 contain the reflection coefficients versus Lf and W2 parameters, respectively. Increasing the parameters produces decreased resonance frequencies. While, increasing W2 provides modifying the sencond resonance frequency independently, while the first resonance stays fixed.

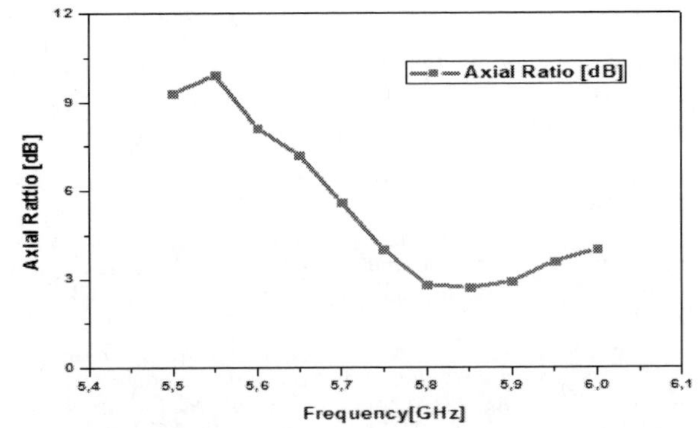

Figure 7. Simulated axial ratio versus frequency of the proosed antenna.

IV. EXPERIMENT RESULTS

The proposed ISM antenna is simulated using CST studio software, based on FDTD method (integral method). The antenna was mesured in the frequency range from 2 to 6 GHz. SIW technology is used with vias having a diameter of 1.2 mm. The diameter of the vias hole at the microstrip line defining the antenna is 1.4 mm. The antenna prototype is fabricated and measured in an anechoic chamber after optimization performed through simulations. A photograph of the antenna top side is shown in Figure 8.

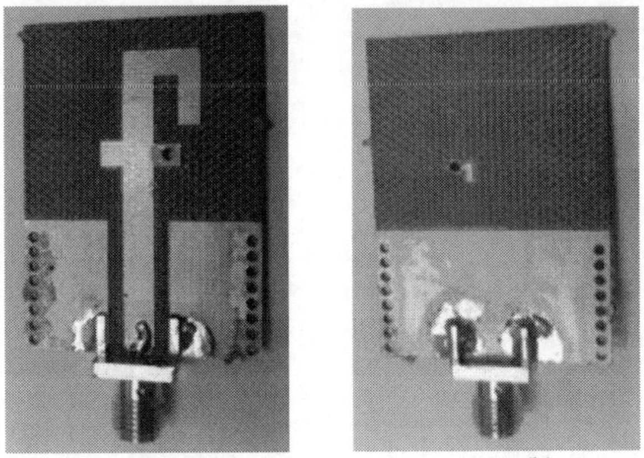

(a) (b)

Figure 8. Photograph of the antenna prototype (a) top side (b) bottom view

The simulated and measured reflection coefficient results are shown in Figure 9. The measured and simulated results show a good agreement, except for slight frequency shift at 5.8 GHz, which may be caused to the probe-feed position after fabrication, fabrication tolerances and soldering. The measured relative bandwidth for the first mode is 500 MHz. At 5.8 GHz, the bandwidth is 1000 MHz bandwidth. The bandwidths of operation are 8% and 20% at 2.4 GHz and 5.8 GHz, respectively. The simulated antenna gains are about 2.71 dB and 3.43 dB at 2.4 GHz and 5.8 GHz, respectively. Antenna radiation patterns are shown in Figure 10, corresponding to the frequencies of 2.4 GHz and 5.8 GHz. The antenna radiation patterns results show agreement between measurement and simulation, obtained for the two antenna bands of operation. For antenna measurements, an extended ground plane was used using copper tape.

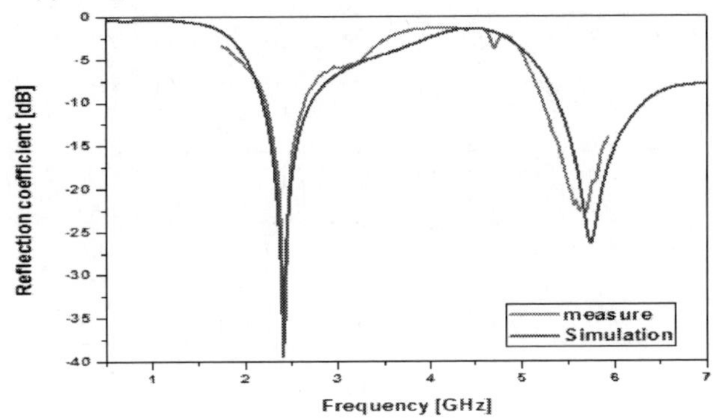

Figure 9. Simulation and measured reflection coefficient of the antenna.

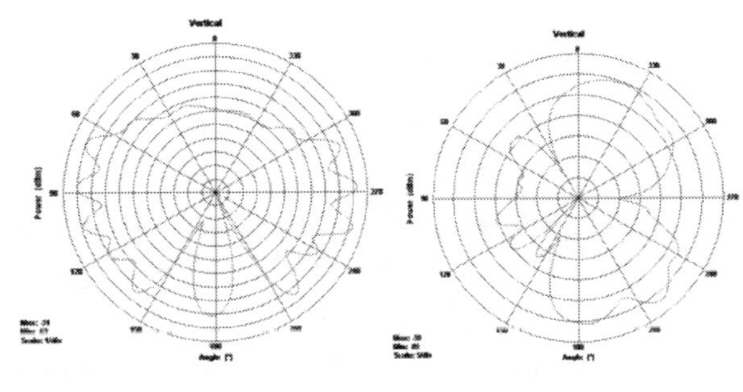

(a)

(b)

Figure 10. Measured radiation pattern of the antenna (a) E-field and H-field at 2.4 GHz; (b) E-field and H-field at 5.8 GHz.

Table II shows a comparison among ISM antennas. The proposed antenna has good gain with bandwidths of 250 MHz and 1 GHz at 2.4 GHz and 5.8GHz, respectively. The proposed antenna exhibits circular polarization for the second resonant mode. Figure 7 showns the axial ratio for the frequency range from 5.4 to 6.1 GHz.

TABLE II. ISM ANTENNA COMPARAISON

Parameter	Frequency	[15]	[16]	[17]	[18]	Proposed antenna
Gain	F1=2.4	1.73	2.07	2.02	2.01	2.72
[dB]	F2=5.8	5.4	1.17	4.06	3.45	3.22
Bandwidth	F1=2.4	48.7	250	200	350	350
[MHz]	F2=5.8	200	250	650	1000	1000
Polarization	F1=2.4	L.	L.	L.	L.	L.
Linear/Circular	F2=5.8	L.	L.	L.	L.	Cir.

V. CONCLUSION

In this paper, a circular polarization, dual-band antenna for ISM band is reported. An improvement is achieved when using a coplanar waveguide at the input feed including an SIW structure. The CPW-SIW structure improves the antenna response S-parameters and gain. To be able to use this design for sensor networks, the proposed dual-band design can be independently tuned in frequency and bandwidth of operation. The planar antenna structure and its performance makes it a suitable candidate for integration with ISM applications and sensor nodes.

ACKNOWLEDGEMENT

This work is supported by NATO SPS project G5640 and the Spanish ministry of defence project SensorQ. Spanish ministry of science and innovation, project RTI2018-099841-B-I00, Generalitat de Catalunya, grant 2017 SGR 891.

REFERENCES

[1] E. Fontana, J.-M. Kim, I. Llamas-Garro and G. O. Cavalcanti,"Microfabricated Otto chip device for surface plasmon resonance based optical sensing," Applied Optics, vol. 54, pp.9200– 9204, November 2015.

[2] S. S. Sabri, B. H. Ahmad, and A. R. Othman "Design and Fabrication of X-Band Substrate Integrated Waveguide Directional Coupler", IEEE Symposium on Wireless Technology andApplications, (ISWTA).

[3] D. H. Yang and al.,"E-band SIW H-plane horn antenna development," COMPEL - The international journal for computation and mathematics in electrical and electronic engineering , vol. 32, no. 2, pp. 431-441, Sep. 2015.

[4] H. Y. Tsao and al. , "W-Band SIW H-plane Horn Antenna Development ," COMPEL -The international journal for computation and mathematics in electrical and electronic engineering, 2013.

[5] R. Aloui, Z. Houaneb, I. Llamas-Garro, H. Zairi, "Substrate integrated waveguide dual-band ISM antenna for wireless sensors", Microwave Journal, Microwave Journal, Vol. 63, No. 9, September 2020.

[6] A. Nasri, et al., "A compact SIW mixer for millimeter-wave applications," International Journal of Electrical and Computer Engineering (IJECE), Vol. 4, No. 6, 902–908, 2014.

[7] S. Doucha, et al., "A leaky wave antenna design based on half-mode substrate integrated waveguide technology for X band applications," International Journal of Electrical and Computer Engineering (IJECE), Vol. 7, No. 6, 3467–3474, 2017.

[8] Z. He, J. Cai, Z. Shao, X. Li, and Y. Huang, "A novel power divider integrated with SIW and DGS technology," Progress In Electromagnetics Research, Vol. 139, 289–301, 2013.

[9] Z. Sotoodeh, B. Biglarbegian, F. Hojjat-Kashani, and H. Ameri, "A novel bandpass waveguide filter structure on SIW technology," Progress In Electromagnetics Research Letters, Vol. 2, 141–148, 2008.

[10] I. Llamas-Garro, F. Mira, P. Zheng, Z. Liu, L. Wu, Y. Wang, All resonator based LTCC diplexer using substrate integrated waveguides , Electronics Letters, Vol. 53, No. 21, pp. 1410-1412, November 2017.

[11] N. Herscovici, C. Christodoulou, E. Rajo-Iglesias, O. Quevedo-Teruel, and M. Sainchez-Ferflifldez, "Compact multimode patch antennas for MIMO applications," IEEE Antennas Propag. Mag., Vol. 50, No. 2, 197–205, Apr. 2008.

[12] D., Z. Guan, Qian, W. Cao, L. Ji, and Y. Zhang, "Compact SIW annular ring slot antenna with multiband multimode characteristics," IEEE Antennas Propag. Mag., Vol. 63, No. 12, 5918–5922, Dec. 2015.

[13] Z. G. Liu, and Y. X. Guo, "Dual-band low profile antenna for body centric communications," IEEE Trans. Antennas Propag., Vol. 61, No. 4, 2282–2285, Apr. 2013.

[14] R. Waterhouse, R. Microstrip Patch Antennas: A Designer's Guide; Springer Science & Business Media: Berlin/Heidelberg, Germany, 2013.

[15] Z. G. Liu and Y. X. Guo, "Dual band low profile antenna for body centric communications," IEEE Trans. Antennas Propag., vol. 61, no. 4, pp. 22822285, Apr. 2013.

[16] J-I Moon and S-O Park, "Small Chip Antenna for 2.4/5.8-GHz Dual ISM-Band Applications," IEEE Anten. and Wireless prog. Letters., vol. 2, 2003.

[17] I-F Chen, C-M Peng, and S-C Liang, "Single Layer Printed Monopole Antenna for Dual ISM-Band Operation," IEEE Trans. Antennas Propag., vol. 53, NO. 4, APRIL 2005.

[18] N. O. Parchin, H. J. Basherlou , R. A. A.-Alhameed and J. M. Noras, "Dual-Band Monopole Antenna for RFID Applications," Future Internet, vol. 11, NO.31, 2019.

Simulation Model of the Integrated Hall Element Implemented in Verilog-A

Damjan Berčan, Janez Trontelj
Laboratory for Microelectronics
Faculty of Electrical Engineering, University of Ljubljana
Tržaška cesta 25, 1000 Ljubljana, Slovenia
e-mail: damjan.bercan@fe.uni-lj.si, janez.trontelj@fe.uni-lj.si

***Abstract*—The paper describes the development of the improved simulation model based on a six terminal Hall element implemented in the hardware description language Verilog-A. The new simulation model considers temperature effects, offset voltage, influence of mechanical stress, external magnetic field and internal magnetic field generated by the internal microcoil. To obtain the best accuracy of the Verilog-A based model, all key parameters of the simulation model were determined and characterized by measuring the manufactured Hall plate bonded into a ceramic package. The verification of the improved simulation model was performed in the Cadence Spectre simulator. The Hall element simulation model was designed in the 0.18µm technology but can be easily adapted to any technology to a certain extent by adjusting its parameters according to the measurement results.**

Keywords-Hall element; simulation model; Verilog-A.

I. INTRODUCTION

Hall sensors are still widely used in the magnetic sensors market, although the emerging magnetoresistive sensors, such as Anisotropic Magneto-Resistance (AMR), Giant Magneto-Resistance (GMR) and Tunnel Magneto-Resistance (TMR) are showing impressive performance results. Recently, a comprehensive sensor market study has been taken. It concludes, that Hall-effect sensors will still lead the future of the sensor market exceeding $1.2 billion in 2030, although the Hall effect in semiconductor has been extensively studied in the past few decades [1]. The Complementary Metal Oxide Semiconductor (CMOS) Hall sensors are used to measure relative or absolute position, electric current, energy, speed, angle, Earth's magnetic field, etc. The main reasons why CMOS Hall effect sensors lead the field of magnetic sensors are their linearity over a wide dynamic range, their low process costs compared to their competitors due to their compatibility with standard CMOS technology and their robustness. There are also many disadvantages of the Hall element compared to its magnetoresistive competitors, which need to be solved by researches. The low sensitivity, high power consumption and low signal to noise ratio are just a few of them. The next is the relatively large offset voltage, which is a function of geometry and production errors. However, the high offset voltage and 1/f noise can be greatly reduced by applying the well-known current spinning technique [2], which is commonly used in the art of designing a magnetic microsystem with the Hall elements. The second is the temperature variation of the sensitivity of the Hall element. The variation of sensitivity is non-linear and depends on the mechanical stress. One way to overcome the problem is to use an integrated microcoil that generates an internal reference magnetic field to calibrate the sensitivity of the magnetic microsystem [3].

The magnetic system with an array of N Hall sensors is used to measure the spatial distribution of the magnetic field or to increase the low sensitivity of the Hall element by the factor N, to increase the signal to noise ratio and to minimize the offset by a factor $\sqrt{N}$ [4]. The second is the use of ferromagnetic structures, also known as magnetic concentrators, where they are used as planer magnetic amplifiers [5]. Basically, the magnetic concentrator converts the parallel magnetic field into a magnetic field that is orthogonal to the surface of the Hall element. The mentioned disadvantage of the solution is an additional step in the production of the System on Chip (SoC).

To reduce the power consumption of the magnetic microsystem, the bias current of the Hall element can be pulsed during signal processing. In order to simulate and design the high performance magnetic microsystem, an accurate simulation model of the Hall element must be used. Such a simulation model should take into account the offset voltage, the external magnetic field, the internal magnetic field, the mechanical stress and the temperature variations of the sensitivity [6]. Sometimes integrated circuit manufacturers do not provide all the necessary technological parameters required for a successful implementation of the Hall element model in e.g. multiphysics software such as COMSOL. In a case, where the technological parameters are treated as confidential, the Hall element model can be created using the measured results and know-how.

The rest of the paper is structured as follows. In Section 2, the theory and the measured results of the Hall element designed and manufactured in the 0.18µm Bipolar CMOS Double Diffused Metal Oxide Semiconductor (DMOS) (BCD) technology are collected. In Section 3, the development and verification of the Verilog-A model are presented. Finally we summarize the paper in Section 4.

II. THEORY AND MEASURED RESULTS

The Hall effect in semiconductor can be briefly described as a deflection of charge carriers caused by the Lorentz force when the magnetic field is present. If the magnetic field is perpendicular to the semiconductor surface and the Hall element is connected to the power supply, i.e., the current flows through the semiconductor then, the small Hall voltage appears at the edges of the Hall plate [7]. The Hall element can be biased with current or voltage. This means that the Hall voltage can be described as a function of the selected bias [8]. If the Hall element is voltage biased, the Hall voltage is given by (1),

$$V_H = G\frac{W}{L}\mu_H V B_z, \qquad (1)$$

where the correction factor G depends on the shape of the Hall element, W and L are the width and length of the sensor, respectively, μ_H is the Hall mobility, V is the supply voltage and B_z is the applied magnetic field orthogonal to the surface of the Hall element. Secondly, the Hall element can be biased using the current source. In this case, the Hall voltage is expressed as (2):

$$V_H = G\frac{r_H}{qnt} I B_z, \qquad (2)$$

where r_H is the Hall factor, q the electron charge, n the doping concentration in n-doped silicon, t the thickness of the active N-well region and I the bias current flowing through the Hall element [8].

The Verilog-A model is based on the six terminal Hall element model presented in [9] and serves as the starting point for a new Hall element model. The simplified electrical Hall element model and its cross-shaped layout model with four contacts *U – Up*, *D – Down*, *L – Left* and *R – Right* are shown in Figure 1. The electrical model consists of four N-well resistors representing the N-well Hall element resistance. The cross-shaped Hall element is widely used due to its 90° symmetry, which reduces potential mask misalignment errors. It is also useful when current spinning technique, i.e., electrical rotation of its terminals, is used to minimize the offset voltage. The complete cross-shaped Hall element with integrated microcoil is shown in Figure 2. The active area width of the Hall element is 13 µm. It is worth mentioning that the minimization of the Hall element is crucial, e.g. to increase the spatial magnetic field resolution and the bandwidth of the magnetic microsystem. One of the disadvantages of miniaturization is a larger offset and errors e.g. due to etching. In addition, the efficiency of the microcoil is increased because it is closer to the active area of the Hall element. The number of microcoil turns is another parameter that is important when designing the internal reference magnetic field. The N-well area, microcoil and metal contacts are shown in Figure 2 as well. The complex electrical circuit schematic of the six terminal Hall element model is shown in Figure 3 [9]. The Hall element has four basic contacts *U, D, L, R* and an auxiliary contact *B* for the simulation of the external magnetic field. In addition, there are two more contacts *CI, CO* each representing the input and output of the internal microcoil. The resistance of the Hall element is represented by four N-well resistors connected in the resistor bridge. Four resistors are added between *U* and *ua*, *D* and *da*, *L* and *la* and *R* and *ra* as current sensing element. The value of each resistor is 1 Ω. This means that the voltage drop across the resistors directly represents the bias current of the Hall element. At each branch, 8 Voltage Controlled Resistors (VCR) and 8 Current Controlled Current Sources (CCCS) form a current loop. Four pairs (red current loops) are active when the external magnetic field is present and the other four pairs (green current loops) are active when the internal magnetic field is generated. VCRs only work for positive values (positive resistance), so two current loops are added to each branch. The value of the four VCRs when the external field is applied is determined by the voltage drop across the sensing resistors caused by the bias current of the Hall element. The others value is 0. The current in each loop depends on the CCCS controlled by the current flow (*vm*) through the resistor connected between contacts *B* and *gnd*. The mentioned current depends on the voltage signal at terminal *B*, which represents the external magnetic field. Similarly, when the internal magnetic field is applied, the current in the other four loops depends on the current flowing (*vs*) through the 50 Ω resistor, which represents the resistance of the microcoil. The electrical model contains 8 Voltage Controlled Voltage Sources (VCVS) representing the offset voltage of the Hall element. The controlled voltage depends on the voltage drop across the current sensing resistors caused by bias current of the Hall element. The four current sensing resistors are used to maintain the symmetry of the resistor

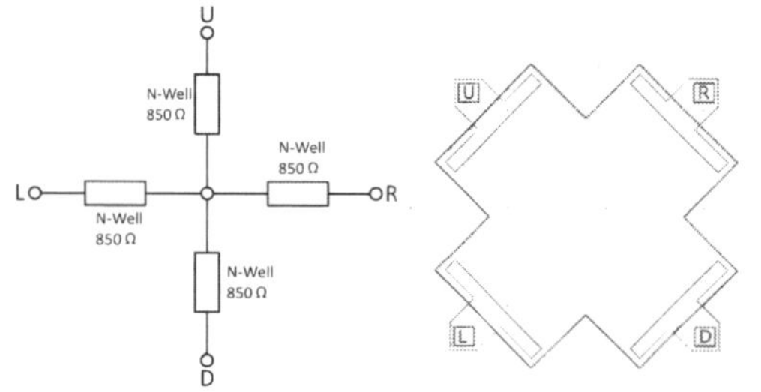

Figure 1. The simplified electrical model of the Hall element (left) and its cross-shaped layout model (right).

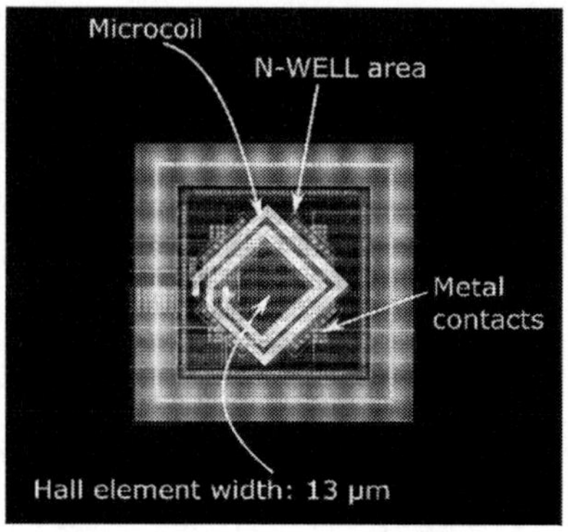

Figure 2. The complete cross-shaped Hall element with microcoil.

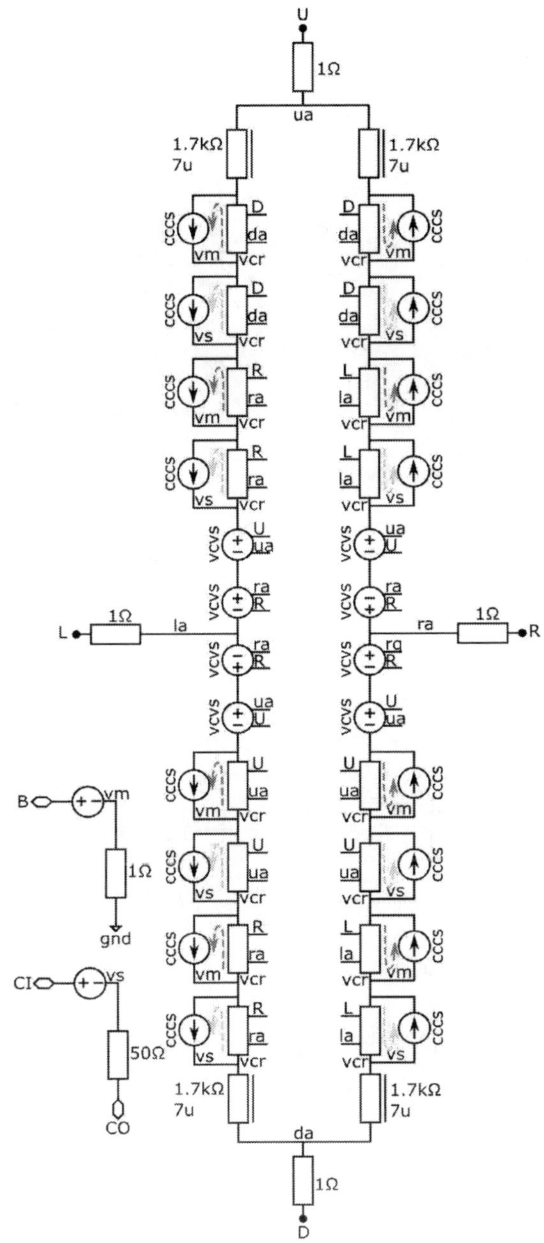

Figure 3. The complex electrical schematic of the six terminal Hall element model in 0.18 μm BCD technology.

bridge. From a functional point of view, only two of them could be used. The microphotography of the Hall element manufactured in the 0.18 μm BCD technology is shown in Figure 4. The Hall element was bonded with 30 μm bond wires into a ceramic package. The Hall element was exposed

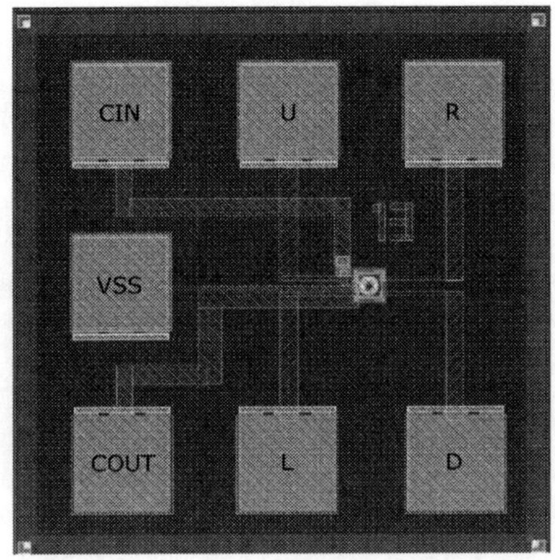

Figure 4. The microphotography of the Hall element with corresponding contacts.

to an external magnetic field of 34 mT or 340 G between two circular magnetic coils - Helmholtz pair, which generated an almost uniform magnetic field. Thermal tests were carried out in the temperature chamber from -40 °C to 120 °C. First, the offset voltage was measured at different temperatures and in different bias modes without applied magnetic field. The average measurement results of the offset voltage based on N=20 samples are gathered in Table 1. When the Hall element is voltage biased, the bias current *Ib* decreases with temperature due to the positive temperature coefficient of the N-well. This means that the N-well resistance increases with increasing temperature and consequently influences the offset voltage *Voff*. When the Hall element is current biased, the changes in offset voltage are greater due to the applied constant current. The results show that the Hall element suffers from a large offset voltage (mV) therefore current spinning technique should be used to reduce it to (μV). The

TABLE I. OFFSET VOLTAGE MEASUREMENT RESULTS

	Voltage Biased		Current Biased	
T (°C)	*Voff (mV)*	*Ib (mA)*	*Voff (mV)*	*Ib (mA)*
-40	-0.324	2.000	-0.324	2
-20	-0.445	1.918	-0.465	2
0	-0.529	1.828	-0.588	2
20	-0.656	1.733	-0.768	2
40	-0.793	1.636	-1.005	2
60	-0.926	1.542	-1.247	2
80	-1.050	1.445	-1.531	2
100	-1.168	1.360	-1.838	2
120	-1.272	1.280	-2.167	2

offset voltage changes locally from die to die or globally from wafer to wafer, so it is a random function. In this case, the offset voltage could be expressed as a third order polynomial:

$$V_o(x) = 2 \cdot 10^{-8}x^3 - 2 \cdot 10^{-5}x^2 - 0.0042x - 0.297, \quad (3)$$

where x represents a temperature. The polynomial is found as a line that best fits the measured data. Equation (3) is used later in Verilog-A description of the Hall element.

Then, the sensitivity of the Hall element to the external and internal magnetic field was measured. The results are shown in Table 2. The measurement was performed for both bias modes. Figure 5 and Figure 6 show the average measurement results of the current related sensitivity *SI* and voltage related sensitivity *SV* respectively for N=20 samples. The temperature coefficient of the Hall element sensitivity depends on the carrier mobility, the Hall element factor and the mechanical stress. To describe the absolute value of the current-related sensitivity variation with temperature, the relative error δ_{SI} can be added as:

$$\delta_{SI}(x) = 8.83 \cdot 10^{-6}x^2 - 1.50 \cdot 10^{-3}x - 0.0035, \quad (4)$$

where x stands for the temperature. In this case, the relative error 0 at 0 °C is selected. Again, equation (4) is found as a line that best fits the measured data, so the relative error deviates slightly from 0 at 0 °C.

The sensitivity of the Hall element to the internal magnetic field generated by the integrated microcoil is 26 V/AA or 26 μV at 1 mA of the bias current of the Hall element and 1 mA of the current flowing through the microcoil. The integrated coil generates a magnetic field of 0.52 mT or 5.2 G at 1mA DC current. The resistance of the microcoil also changes with temperature, so the temperature coefficient of the microcoil should not be neglected. Its measured value is $3 \cdot 10^{-3}$ /°C.

With the measurement results obtained, the Verilog-A based Hall element model can be developed.

TABLE II. THE MEASURED RESULTS OF THE HALL ELEMENT SENSITIVITY

T(°C)	SV (V/VT)	SI (V/AT)
-40	0.034	54.2
-20	0.032	51.9
0	0.029	50.1
20	0.027	48.8
40	0.025	48.0
60	0.023	47.5
80	0.022	47.4
100	0.020	47.2
120	0.019	47.4

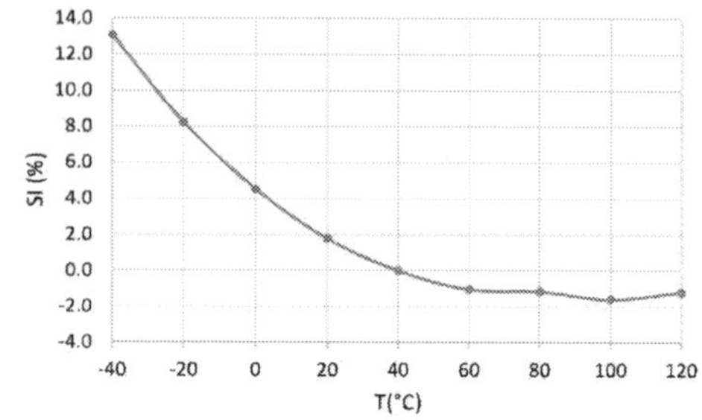

Figure 5. Current related sensitivity of the Hall element.

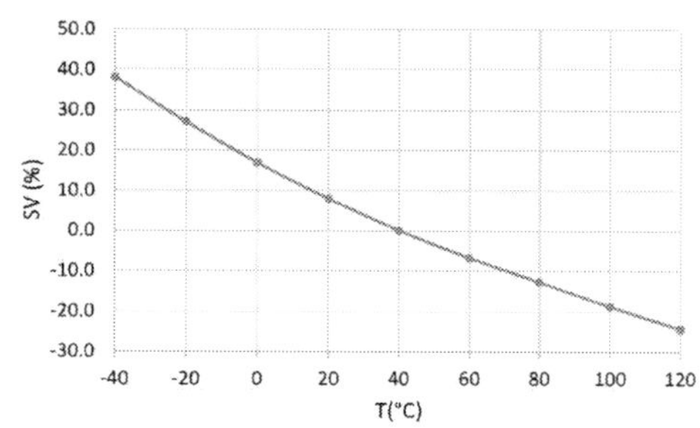

Figure 6. Voltage related sensitivity of the Hall element.

III. DEVELOPMENT OF THE VERILOG–A BASED HALL ELEMENT MODEL

In this Section only a crucial part of the Verilog-A code will be analysed as, the rest is a top level description of the Hall element shown in Figure 3. The first part of the code is shown in Figure 7 and describes the VCR. The value of the resistor is represented by the voltage drop between *p2* and *n2*.

```
// VerilogA, VCR
`include "constants.vams"
`include "disciplines.vams"
        module vcr (p2, n2, p1, n1);
        inout p2, n2, p1, n1;
        electrical p2, n2, p1, n1;
        real vctrl;
analog begin
        vctrl=V(p2,n2);
        if (vctrl<1e-05) begin
                vctrl=1e-05;
                I(p1,n1)<+V(p1,n1)/vctrl; end
        else
                I(p1,n1)<+V(p1,n1)/vctrl; end
endmodule
```

Figure 7. VCR description in Verilog-A.

The current through *p1* and *n1* is proportional to the voltage difference between terminals *p1* and *n1* divided by *vctrl*. To avoid division by zero error or negative resistance, the *vctrl* is limited to $1 \cdot 10^{-5}$. This is achieved by using a conditional statement.

The second part of the code is shown in Figure 8 and represents CCCS. The *I(out)* depends on the voltage drop

```
// VerilogA, CCCS
'include "constants.vams"
'include "disciplines.vams"
        module cccs (pi, ni, p, n);
        inout p, n, pi, ni;
        electrical pi, ni, p, n;
        parameter real gain=1;
        parameter real rm=1;
        branch (p, n) out;
        branch (pi, ni) in;
        parameter real pt=($temperature-273.15);
        parameter real ksen3=0;
        parameter real ksen2=0;
        parameter real ksen1=0;
        parameter real nsen=0;
        parameter real sen=0;
        real ksen=0;
analog begin
        if (sen==1) begin
ksen=(ksen3*(pt)*(pt)*(pt)+ksen2*(pt)*(pt)+ksen1*(pt) + nsen);end
        else if (sen!=1) begin ksen=0; end
        I(out)<+((1+ksen)*(gain*V(in)))/rm; end
endmodule
```

Figure 8. CCCS description in Verilog-A.

V(in) across the current sensing resistor, which represents the current that controls CCCS. The value of the current depends on the ports used (*branch (pi, ni) in*). First, when the input port *B* is selected, the current depends on the input voltage applied to port *B*, which represents external magnetic field. Second, when input terminal *CI* is selected the current depends on the input voltage applied to terminal *CI*, which represents internal magnetic field. The variable *pt* represents temperature. The absolute value of sensitivity to the external or internal magnetic field can be adjusted by the *gain* parameter. The polynomial *ksen* with the corresponding coefficients *ksen3*, *ksen2*, *ksen1* and *nsen* representing the relative error δ_{SI} is used when the parameter *sen* is equal to 1. If *sen* is 0 then, the relative error or *ksen* is zero.

The third part of the code is shown in Figure 9 and describes the VCVS, which adds the offset in the model of the Hall element. The controlled voltage *vctrl=V(p2,n2)/2*

```
// VerilogA, VCVS
module vcvs (p2, n2, p1, n1);
inout p2, n2, p1, n1;
electrical p2, n2, p1, n1;
parameter real pt=($temperature-273.15);
parameter real koff3=0;
parameter real koff2=0;
parameter real koff1=0;
parameter real noff=0;
parameter real off=0;
real vctrl;
real koff;
analog begin
vctrl=V(p2,n2)/2;
if (off==1) begin
koff=(noff+koff3*(pt)*(pt)*(pt)+koff2*(pt)*(pt)+koff1*(pt)); end
else if (off!=1) begin koff=0; end
V(p1,n1)<+vctrl*abs(koff);
end
endmodule
```

Figure 9. VCVS description in Verilog-A.

depends on the voltage drop across the current sensing resistor, which represents the bias current of the Hall element. The polynomial *koff* with the corresponding coefficients *koff3*, *koff2*, *koff1* and *noff* is added to simulate the offset voltage. The offset voltage can be switched on or off by setting the *off* parameter to one or zero.

Figure 10 shows the Hall element and its parameters which can be set according to the measurement results. The absolute value of the sensitivity can be adjusted by changing the parameters *emf* (external magnetic field) and *imf* (internal magnetic field). The resistance of the N-well resistor can be changed by the parameters *nw* (width) and *nl* (length). The temperature coefficient of the microcoil can be adjusted by changing the parameter *tc_coil*.

The next step in the development is the verification of the Hall element written in Verilog-A. Figure 11 and Figure 12

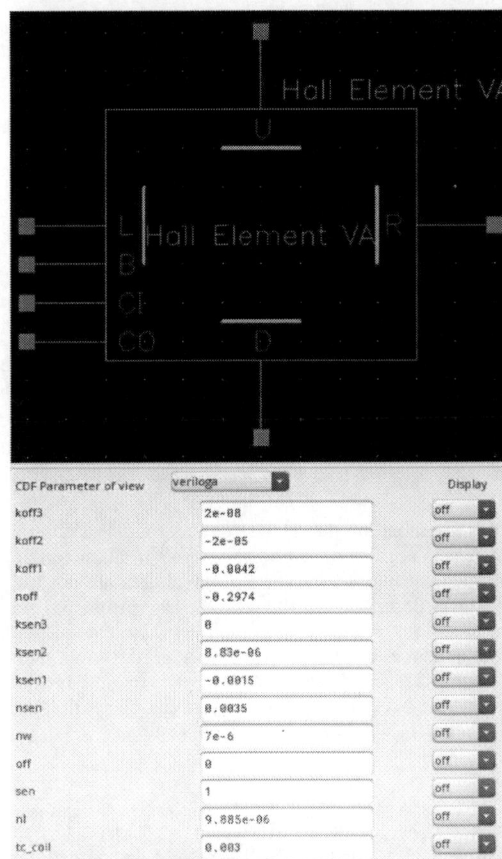

Figure 10. The symbol of the Hall element and its parameters in Cadence Virtuoso®.

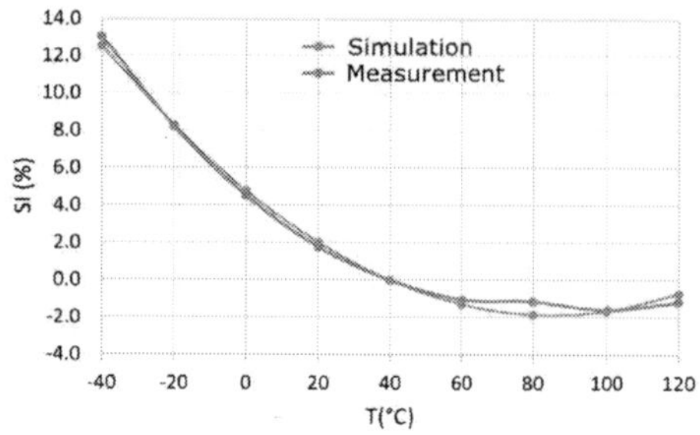

Figure 11. Current related sensitivity of the Hall element.

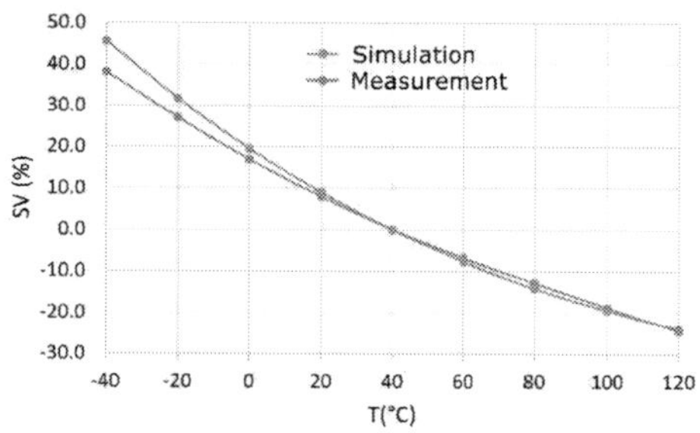

Figure 12. Voltage related sensitivity of the Hall element.

show the comparison between measurement and simulation results. The proposed model shows a good agreement with the measurement results of N=20 Hall element samples bonded into the ceramic packages.

IV. CONCLUSIONS

A development of the Hall element model written in Verilog-A was presented. Some solutions for characterizing the Hall element in case, the technological data are not fully available are described in the paper. The proposed Hall element model takes into account the internal magnetic field, the external magnetic field, and offset voltage, the temperature dependence of the sensitivity of the Hall element and its offset voltage, and the packaging stress. The simulation results show a good agreement with the measurement results.

REFERENCES

[1] R. Dixon, "A Technology Roadmap for XMR Sensors in Automotive Applications", IHS Markit, pp. 6, Mar. 22, 2019.

[2] V. Mosser, N. Matringe, and Y. Haddab, "A Spinning Current Circuit for Hall Measurements Down to the Nanotesla Range", IEEE Trans. Instrum. Meas., vol. 66, no. 4, pp. 637–650, Apr. 2017.

[3] J. Trontelj, D. Berčan, and M. Gradišek, "Novel Integrated Magnetic Sensor Based on Hall Element Array", Sens. Transducers, vol. 237, no. 9/10, pp. 17–22, 2019.

[4] J. Trontelj, "Smart integrated magnetic sensor cell", J. Microelectron. Electron. Compon. Mater., vol. 29, no. 3, pp. 126–128, 1999.

[5] H. Fan, S. Li, V. Nabaei, Q. Feng, and H. Heidari, "Modeling of Three-Axis Hall Effect Sensors Based on Integrated Magnetic Concentrator", IEEE Sens. J., vol. 20, no. 17, pp. 9919–9927, Sep. 2020.

[6] Y. Xu and H.-B. Pan, "An Improved Equivalent Simulation Model for CMOS Integrated Hall Plates", Sensors, vol. 11, no. 6, pp. 6284–6296, Jun. 2011.

[7] A. Karsenty, "A Comprehensive Review of Integrated Hall Effects in Macro-, Micro-, Nanoscales, and Quantum Devices", Sensors, vol. 20, no. 15, pp. 4163–4196, Jan. 2020.

[8] Y. Xu, H.-B. Pan, S.-Z. He, and L. Li, "A Highly Sensitive CMOS Digital Hall Sensor for Low Magnetic Field Applications", Sensors, vol. 12, no. 2, pp. 2162–2174, Feb. 2012.

[9] A. Sešek and J. Trontelj, "A New Model for Six Terminal Hall Element", MIDEM - Journal of Microelectronics, Electronic Components and Materials, pp. 61–66, Mar. 2007.

Optimization Analysis of the Integrated Micro-coil Geometry Parameters Influence on the Uniformity of the Magnetic Field Distribution

Miha Gradišek and Janez Trontelj
Laboratory for Microelectronics, Faculty of Electrical Engineering, University of Ljubljana,
Tržaška cesta 25, 1000 Ljubljana, Slovenia
e-mails: Miha.Gradisek@fe.uni-lj.si, Janez.Trontelj1@guest.arnes.si

***Abstract*— The paper deals with the optimization of the integrated planar micro-coil characteristics with respect to maximizing the generated magnetic field amplitude and its uniformity along the region of interest. The integration calls for as efficient realization as possible otherwise the electrical heating would contribute to reduced performance of the integrated system in which the micro-coil is used. A multi-objective optimization is performed with respect to efficiency and uniformity of the magnetic field distribution. It is optimized in a range of the technological rules to be used in application where precise magnetic field measurement is required.**

Keywords-Integrated planar micro-coil; Magnetic field uniformity; Optimization; Parametrized 3D model.

I. INTRODUCTION

Whenever a new technological product is developed, the engineers strive for the best possible performance to price ratio. To accelerate product development and meet desired performance, various optimization methods are used. Based on the problem to be solved, two approaches are known, the stochastic and the deterministic approach. The former is used when the imitation and evolution of nature phenomenon is used during convergence to the optimal solution, while the latter minimizes or maximizes the criterion function, called the Objective Function (OF), with respect to the deterministic change of the independent Control Variables (CV) deterministically. This work uses a deterministic approach because the geometry of the integrated planar micro-coil (μCoil), realized in a standard Complementary Metal Oxide Semiconductor (CMOS) technology, is limited to the technological parameters dictated by the manufacturing process rules, so the inputs to the simulator are specific numbers and also the output of the simulator is determined by the Partial Differential Equation (PDE) formulation, therefore it is a deterministic object.

There has been a lot of research work on the uniformity of the magnetic field of coils in different constellations [1][2][3]. The most commonly used method to tackle magnetic field uniformity is accomplished with Helmholtz coils, which alleviate the difficulties in achieving the desired magnetic field homogeneity in the center of the system. On the other hand, coil integration in the CMOS process prevents a comparable relative precision of magnetic field variation, as it is inevitable to overcome the mismatch of the planar μCoil geometry as a result of the manufacturing process. Furthermore, the area of interest for magnetic field evaluation in Integrated Circuit (IC) is generally located outside the coil center plane, since the Hall sensor is located at the bottom of the IC, in the diffusion area, while the planar μCoil is realized at higher metal planes. Furthermore, the integration of the planar μCoil inside the die requires an energy efficient realization. Consequently, this work focuses not only on the optimization with respect to the uniformity of the magnetic field in the region of interest, but on electrical losses as a consequence of the μCoil resistance as well. These losses are reflected through the heat dissipation, which is particularly undesirable in the integrated system, where the μCoil is used as a generator of the reference magnetic field for the temperature calibration of the Application Specific Integrated Circuit (ASIC) for which the μCoil is to be used [4].

The paper is structured as follows: The Section II analyzes the optimization problem in relation to the specific ASIC and the possible formulation of the multi-objective function, the Section III describes the workflow from the design of 3D model of the μCoil to its integration into the optimization interface, while Section IV presents the simulation results with observations. Finally, the article concludes with summary of the overall work, and an acknowledgement.

II. OPTIMIZATION PROBLEM

As already mentioned, the integrated μCoil should exhibit high efficiency, i.e., it should generate as large magnetic flux density per μCoil bias current as possible. Therefore, we are staring to increase the magnetic flux density by increasing the number of coil turns N or to minimize the μCoil radius r. According to the Biot-Svart law, the axial component of the magnetic flux density B_Z in the centerline of the circumference is acquired after integration over all elements dL of the closed curve, e.g., μCoil (1) shown in Figure 1.

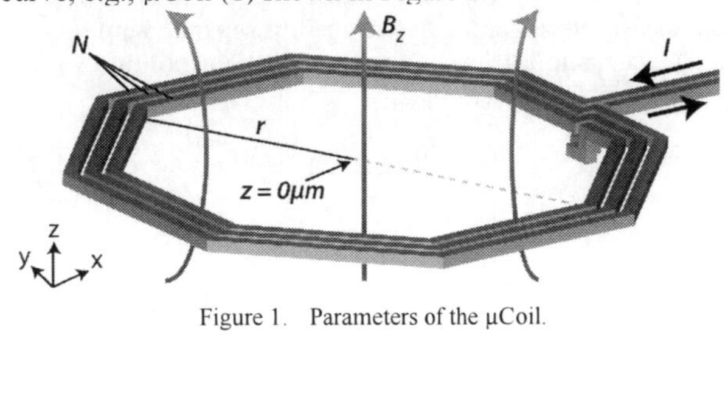

Figure 1. Parameters of the μCoil.

$$B_Z = \frac{\mu_0 INr}{4\pi\sqrt{(r^2+z^2)^3}} \oint dL. \qquad (1)$$

Where, μ_0 is the permeability of free space, I current through N turns with radius r while z denotes the distance pointing from the center of the μCoil to an on-axis observation point. However, a higher number of μCoil turns N increases the total resistance R_{coil}, which means higher ohmic heat losses, or on the other hand larger variation of the magnetic flux density, B_Z when too small μCoil radius is chosen.

These variations are especially problematic when high uniformity of the magnetic field at the sensor location is desired, i.e., in the ASIC with temperature compensation of the Hall sensor and the overall system sensitivity. The Hall sensor is implemented in the strongly temperature dependent n-well diffusion region of the CMOS process. The sensitivity of the sensor to magnetic field is therefore temperature dependent, which is why a compensation technique should be introduced. The compensation approach is based on the simultaneous measurement of the external magnetic field and the reference magnetic field generated by the μCoil. Both signals are modulated at high frequency and later, after signal processing, demodulated back to a signal proportional to the external magnetic field and an additional signal containing information about Hall sensor sensitivity, based on the response of the overall ASIC sensitivity to a known reference magnetic field generated by the μCoil. The reference magnetic field should be constant over the entire modulation time. It should also be uniformly distributed over the entire Hall sensor volume, otherwise a parasitic signal component is sneaked into the signal of the measured magnetic field during the demodulation process. The aforementioned non-uniformity causes signal distortion, as shown in Figure 2, so the μCoil should generate as uniformly distributed reference magnetic field as possible. Taking into account the above criteria, an optimal realization of the μCoil should be designed, which calls for an optimization procedure.

The optimization should reduce μCoil resistance and at the same time decrease magnetic field gradient in the area of Hall sensor. Calculation of the rectangular cross-section planar μCoil resistance R_{COIL}, where current is not evenly distributed, as in wires with circular cross-section, is complicated therefore an electromagnetic simulator is mandatory. Objective function Q_R for the resistivity R_{coil} (2) has the minimum value of 0 for single turn coil N=1 with minimum radius r_{min}=10μm, which is half of the Hall sensor maximum dimension. Before the objective function Q_R is evaluated, the maximum, minimum R_{coil_min} and the average R_{coil_avg} resistance of the μCoil are determined in separate simulation run. The constant k_R is used to normalize the maximum value of Q_R compared to other objective function maximum.

$$Q_R = \frac{R_{COIL} - R_{MIN}}{R_{AVG}} * k_R \qquad (2)$$

Objective function Q_{stdB}, which evaluates the uniformity of the magnetic field (3), is composed of the standard deviation of the magnetic flux density σ_B over the cross-section line where Hall sensor is positioned, marked in red in Figure 3. For comparable σ_B at different magnitudes of magnetic flux densities B_Z for different μCoil radius, the normalization of σ_B is accomplished by the magnetic flux density in the center of the μCoil B_{Z0}. The minimum $(\sigma_B/B_{Z0})_{MIN}$ and maximum $(\sigma_B/B_{Z0})_{MAX}$ ratios of standard deviation to magnetic flux density are again acquired in separate simulation runs to calculate $(\sigma_B/B_{Z0})_{AVG}$ as well. Normalization constant is represented by k_{stdB}.

$$Q_{stdB} = \frac{(\frac{\sigma_B}{B_{Z0}}) - (\frac{\sigma_B}{B_{Z0}})_{MIN}}{(\frac{\sigma_B}{B_{Z0}})_{AVG}} * k_{stdB} \qquad (3)$$

The purpose of the third objective function (4), which is composed of Q_R and Q_{stdB}, is to compare and find an optimal solution when both Q_R and Q_{stdB} have equal weight. Nevertheless, the objective function $Q_{combined}$ could be reformulated based on the design preferences for Q_R or Q_{stdB} to achieve a different significance of the specific objective function.

$$Q_{combined} = abs(1 - \frac{Q_R}{Q_{stdB}}) \qquad (4)$$

All objective functions are formulated in such a way that they converge to 0 when the resistance (2) decreases, the relative uniformity of the magnetic flux density (3) decreases and when the two above mentioned function values converge to each other (4). Three objective functions form the multi-objective function $Q(r,N)$, for which the optimizer should find a minimum value (5). The optimizer search for the solution in the space of the possible parameters, i.e., the objective variables. Additionally, constraint of the minimum magnetic flux density B_{Z_min}=1mT in the region of Hall sensor from $-r_{min}$ to $+r_{min}$ is specified to attain sufficient magnetic field. The control variables ranges are listed in Table 1. All simulations are carried out for a μCoil bias current of 10mA.

$$min\, Q(r, N) \qquad (5)$$

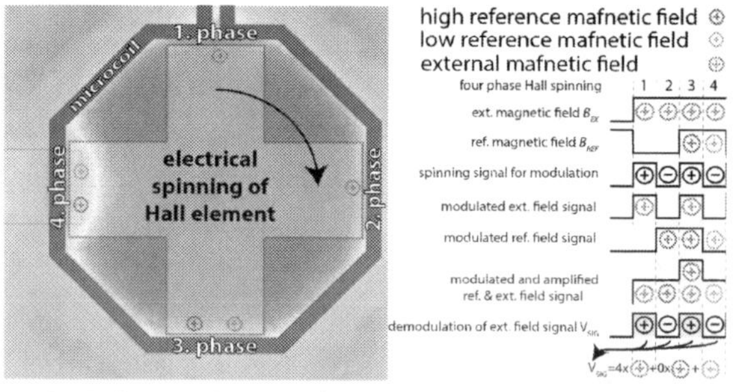

Figure 2. Influence of non-uniformly distributed reference magnetic field on the signal error.

TABLE I. OPTIMIZATION PARAMETERS

Control variable / Constraints	*Symbol*	*Lower bound*	*Upper bound*
μCoil radius	r	10 (μm)	50 (μm)
Number of μCoil turns	N	1	3

III. SIMULATION ENVIRONMENT

For the simulation purpose, Comsol Multiphysics in combination with Solidworks is used. The chart flow of the optimization procedure is presented in Figure 4.

Firstly, a parametrized 3D model of the μCoil is constructed in Solidworks according to the recommendation of the 0.35μm CMOS technology semiconductor foundry. The two most important parameters linked to the Comsol Multiphysics simulator are the μCoil diameter r and the number of μCoil turns N. The designed 3D model is imported into Comsol Multiphysics geometry, where the two parameters mentioned above are linked to the control variables that are permutated in the predefined range from the lower to the upper bound during optimization. The planar aluminum μCoil is inserted inside sphere where the electromagnetic evaluation takes place. The μCoil that is inserted into the sphere within the simulation environment with generated mesh is shown in Figure 3. The free tetrahedral mesh should be finer at the boundaries of the different domains and short edges, while it should be coarser, at other locations to avoid memory errors. Since the optimization problem is time independent, the evaluation of the electrical characteristics of the 3D μCoil model is performed by the Comsol Multiphysics "AC/DC Electromagnetic Fields" module with static analysis on the basis of Finite Element Method (FEM). This module is suitable for the calculation of the μCoil resistance and the generated magnetic field distribution, which are the main concerns and have to be considered during the optimization process. Simulator provides many optimization algorithms, but many of them tend to get stuck in local minima, as they iteratively converge to the local optimum [5], based on the value of the multi-objective function from the previous step, as shown in Figure 5. To overcome this problem, the optimization is performed using a Monte Carlo method that randomly sweeps the entire parameter search space with uniform distribution of solver points independently of the previous step to find global optimum. In the optimization interface, multi-objective functions (2-5) and an additional constraint of $Bz_{\_min}$ are specified.

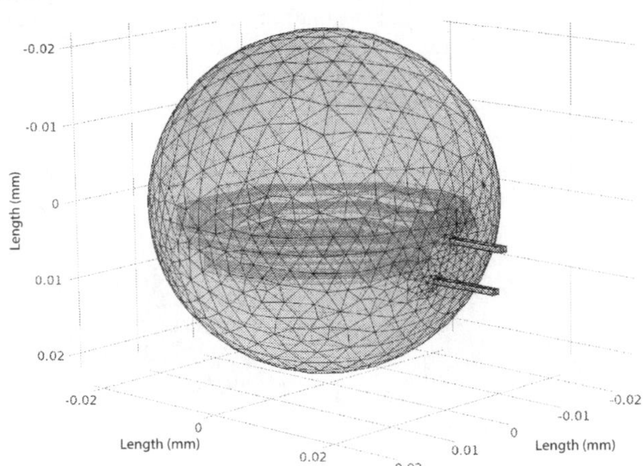

Figure 3. Quality of the mesh dictates accuracy of acquired model evaluation.

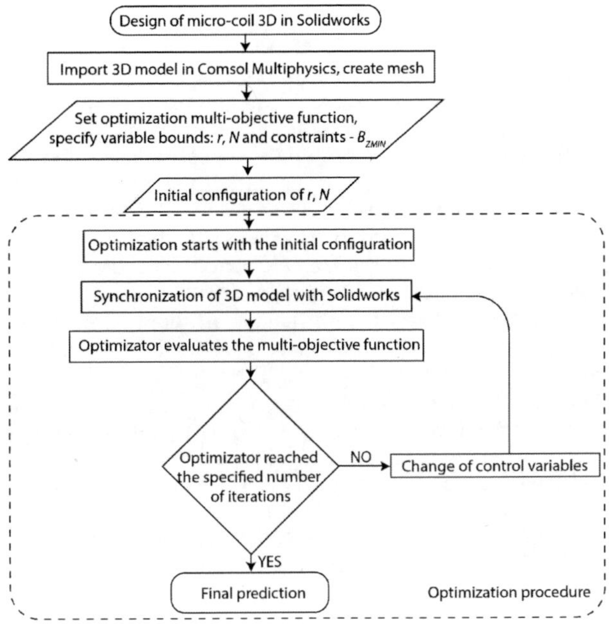

Figure 4. Flow chart of the μCoil parameters optimization.

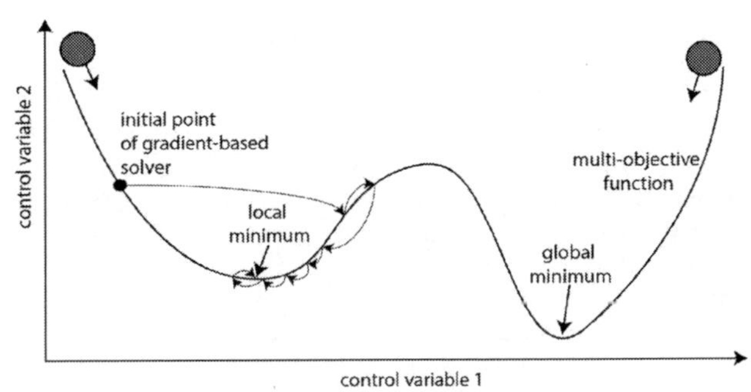

Figure 5. Local and global optimum.

During the optimization process the geometry of the μCoil is changed based on values of the control variable r and N. These two variables are permutated, while the statistical distribution of the values of the multi-objective function is acquired. The optimizer repeats the simulations as long as it does not reach the specified number of iterations.

IV. RESULTS

The optimization of the relatively simple geometry of the μCoil in combination with the Monte Carlo algorithm is quit time-consuming. In addition, the computing power increases exponentially with additional control variables. The optimizer therefore only works with the control variables that are essential for the optimization, while some parameters are evaluated and determined prior to the optimization run, e.g., shape of the μCoil structure, some CMOS technology data such as thickness of the specific metal layer, metal material, etc. The design rules specified in Process Design Kit (PDK), within which the μCoil is developed, restrict the design of curves in the layout, consequently the planar μCoil consists of straight sides only. It can be seen from Figure 6 that variation in the number of sides of the μCoil has a negligible effect on B_z in the center of the μCoil, while the resistance listed in Table 2 decreases as the shape approaches the circumference shape. Table 2 summarizes resistivity for μCoil with N=1 and r=10μm. With regard to resistance and adoption to the maximum dimension of the Hall element, the octagon shape is chosen for the optimization process.

To further reduce the difficulty of the optimization process, four optimization runs were performed separately for each of the four IC metal layers. From the Table 3 where optimization results are given, it is evident when μCoil turn is closest to the Hall sensor, i.e., metal *m1*, the radius *r1* is larger than *r2* for the higher metal layer *m2*. This result is expected because the variations in magnetic flux density at the edge of the coil conductor are at least in the order of 10 greater than the variations in the center of the coil. As a result, the standard deviation of magnetic flux density in a configuration with a small radius and small distance between the source and the sensor of the magnetic field is larger compared to the configuration using the same distance with a larger radius or the same radius but larger distance, which is also shown in Figure 7. Figure 7 confirms that at greater distances between the source of the magnetic field and sensor course of the B_Z has flatter behavior compared to the same radius at smaller distances. Table 3 lists the number of turns on each metal layer, the values of all 3 objective functions and the average magnetic flux density B_Z on the line from $-r_{min}$ to $+r_{min}$ regarding the center of the Hall sensor. Resistance R_{coil} related to Q_R increases with larger radius or coil turns. Optimization without B_{Z_min} constraint results in an optimal solution for the radius in the middle radius search space range in combination with N=2 which is explained by the fact that the weight of both Q_R and Q_{stdB} is normalized. In contrary, optimization with the specified B_{Z_min} constraint, which is necessary to fulfill requirement of the real-world application, leads to a different design realization. Constraint B_{Z_min} cannot be achieved with higher metal levels m3 and m4 while m1 and m2 reach the desired magnitudes as shown in Table 3.

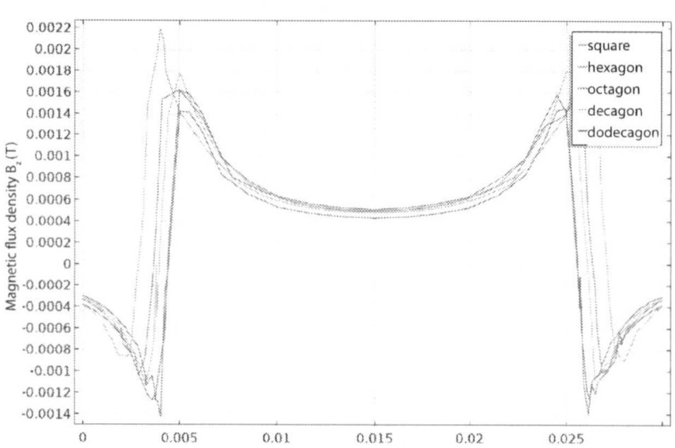

Figure 6. Magnetic flux density for different μCoil shape realizations (r=10μm, N=1).

TABLE II. COIL RESISTANCE FOR DIFFERENT NUMBER OF SIDES

Number of μCoil sides	*μCoil resistance (Ω)*
4	4.40
6	3.98
8	3.84
10	3.82
12	3.76

TABLE III. OPTIMIZATION SOLUTION

i	*Metal layer*	r_i *(μm)*	*N*	Q_R	Q_{stdB}	$Q_{combined}$	B_Z *(mT)*
1	m_i	14.3	3	0.253	0.413	1.053	1.017
2	m_i	12.2	3	0.209	0.363	0.998	1.055
3	m_i	10.6	2	0.084	0.049	0.860	0.643
4	m_i	10.0	3	0.159	0.330	1.007	0.646

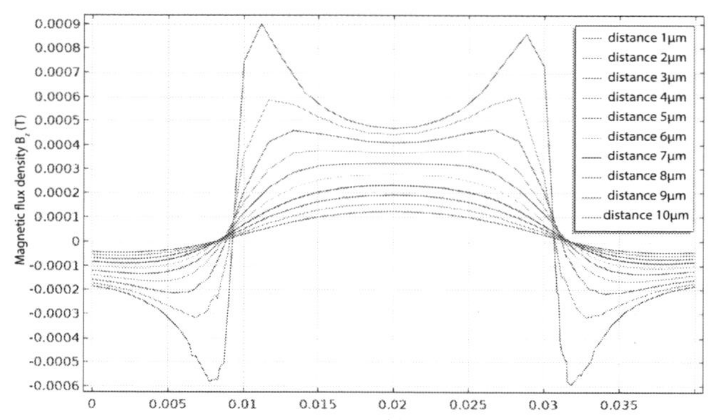

Figure 7. Magnetic flux density B_Z for different distances between magnetic field source and sensor (r=10μm, N=1).

Contribution to the magnetic flux densities of all four separately optimized μCoil layers is super positioned and verified with an additional simulation using the optimized 3D model shown in Figure 8. The total magnetic flux density of 3.76mT is close to the sum of all B_Z values listed in Table 3 which confirms our assumption.

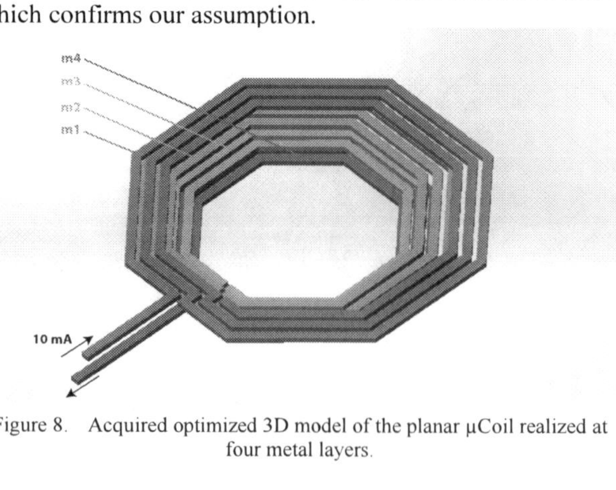

Figure 8. Acquired optimized 3D model of the planar μCoil realized at four metal layers.

The comparison between optimized and non-optimized μCoil is shown in Figure 9. The red line represents the non-optimized μCoil, while the blue line represents the optimized design. Both coils are designed to produce approximately the same average magnetic flux density B_Z=3.76mT. Streamline of magnetic flux density in the sphere volume of the simulation is shown in Figure 10, while magnetic flux density in the region of Hall sensor is shown in Figure 11.

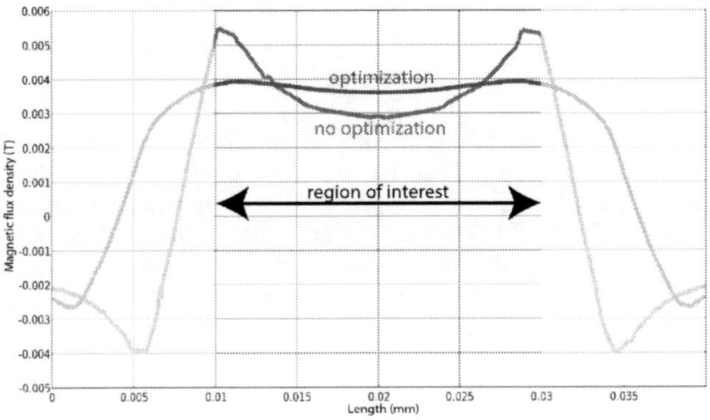

Figure 9. Comparison between optimized and non-optimized μCoil.

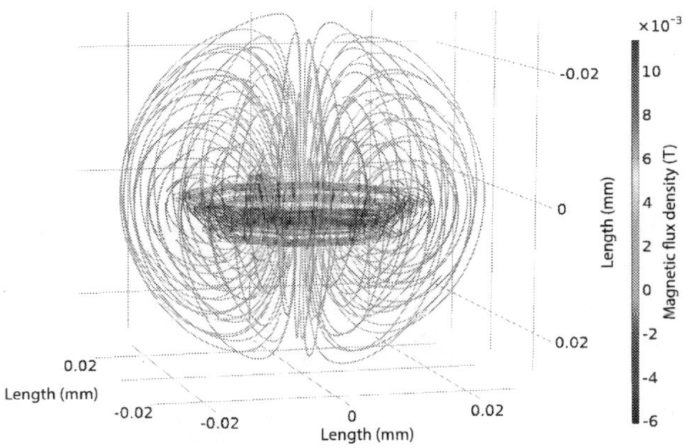

Figure 10. Streamline of magnetic flux density in the volume of simulation.

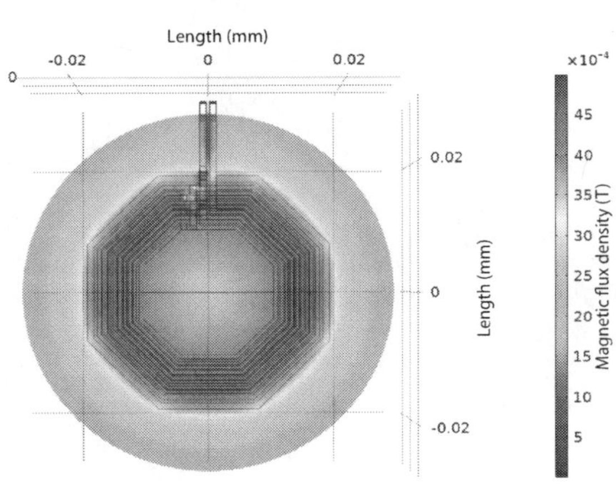

Figure 11. Distribution of magnetic flux density in plane of Hall sensor.

V. CONCLUSION AND FUTURE WORK

The behavior of the planar μCoil used in the ASIC, which incorporate temperature compensation of the sensor sensitivity, was analyzed. Presented work investigated the main disadvantage of on-chip generation of the magnetic field and proposed possible solutions obtained by an optimization process. The optimization was performed in Comsol Multiphysics using the 3D model designed in Solidworks. 3D model was optimized in terms of efficiency and performance to minimize thermal losses and maximize the magnetic field uniformity in the region of interest. The geometry of the 3D model was optimized in a range of possible parameters specified in the IC process. The multi-objective function and the constraints criterion could be modified based on the performance preferences of the μCoil in the specific application, which would lead to a different geometry of the optimized μCoil. Presented results indicated some deviations in magnetic flux density between separately optimized planar μCoils compared to the μCoil composed of all four planar μCoils. The deviations were due to the optimizer precision, as a coarser mesh was used in the composed version of μCoil otherwise too much memory was allocated for simulation run. The future work will focus on reformulating the 3D model meshing for a more efficient use of computer memory and a reasonable optimization time of more complex 3D structures.

ACKNOWLEDGMENT

The present work is part of the program "Systems on chip with integrated micromechanical, THz, magnetic and electrochemical sensors" No. P2-0257 (D) supported by Slovenian Research Agency (ARRS). Author would like to express gratitude to the LMFE department from the Faculty of Electrical Engineering in Ljubljana for expertise to greatly contribute to the success of the research.

REFERENCES

[1] B. J. Darrer, J. C. Watson, P. Bartlett, and F. Renzoni, "Toward an Automated Setup for Magnetic Induction Tomography," IEEE Trans. Magn., vol. 51, no. 1, pp. 1–4, Jan. 2015, doi: 10.1109/TMAG.2014.2355420

[2] S. H. Kim and K. Ishiyama, "Magnetic robot and manipulation for active-locomotion with targeted drug release," IEEE/ ASME Transactions on Mechatronics," vol. 19, no. 5, Oct. 2014, pp. 1651-1659, doi: 10.1109/TMECH.2013.2292595

[3] X. Han, Q. Cao, and L. Li, "Design and Evaluation of Three-Dimensional Electromagnetic Guide System for Magnetic Drug Delivery," IEEE Trans. Appl. Supercond., vol. 22, no. 3, pp. 4401404, Jun. 2012, doi: 10.1109/TASC.2011.2176456

[4] M. Gradišek and J. Trontelj, "Integrated System Based on the Hall Sensors Incorporating Compensation of the Distortions," Adv. Mater. Lett., vol. 11, no. 1, pp. 20011463 (1-4), Jan. 2020, doi: 10.5185/amlett.2020.011463

[5] A. Glotić, "Optimization of electrical power network elements by using evolutionary algorithms," Ph.D dissertation, pp. 2-3, University of Maribor," Maribor, 2011, [retrieved: Sep. 2020, https://dk.um.si/IzpisGradiva.php?lang=slv&id=18250]

On Wafer Characterisation of the Analog Anisotropic Magnetoresistance Sensor

Janez Trontelj ml.
University of Ljubljana,
Faculty of Electrical Engineering
Trzaska 25, 1000 Ljubljana, Slovenia
e-mail: janez.trontelj2@guest.arnes.si

Abstract - **This article presents the solution for a fast evaluation tool of an analog integrated Anisotropic Magnetoresistance Sensor (AMR) on a silicon wafer. It was necessary to evaluate a selected prototype development phase of a custom analog AMR sensor. This approach significantly shortened the development time as no dicing and packaging was required. We will also use this solution later for a final volume production wafer sorting. The biggest challenge was to quickly generate and release an accurate, sufficiently strong magnetic field that is as parallel as possible to the wafer surface. Such a field is needed to measure the peak values of the sine and cosine output signals of the analog AMR sensor.**

Keywords - analog AMR sensor; wafer sort; AMR sensitivity.

I. INTRODUCTION

Magnetoresistance (MR) is the tendency of selected material to change its electrical resistance value when an external magnetic field is present. Several effects are known [1], such as Anisotropic Magnetoresistance (AMR), Giant Magnetoresistance (GMR), Tunnel Magnetoresistance (TMR), Colossal Magnetoresistance (CMR) and Extraordinary Magnetoresistance (EMR). In contrast to isotropic MR materials, anisotropic MR materials [2] have a different resistance depending on the material's orientation in a magnetic field.

We can purchase several inexpensive MR and AMR sensors available on the market today. They are produced by manufacturers like Sensitec GmbH, STMicroelectronics, Honeywell, iC-Haus and many others. They are intended for measuring electric current, for the electronic compass, for the acquisition of linear position, speed or angle in technical equipment and similar [3]. The MR sensors are known for their reliability, accuracy, low cost and extreme resistance to environmental influences [4][5].

In our case, a local company has developed its version of the analog AMR sensor based on their specific needs. Our task was to produce this application-specific sensor. It was also necessary to quickly verify such analog AMR sensor components on silicon wafers to facilitate this task. Although there is a lot of literature about different AMR sensors, we could not find any good literature about the test implementation (including a sensitivity measurement) of an analog AMR sensor on a wafer. Therefore, we describe our solution to this problem in this article.

The ideal analog, variable resistance AMR sensor output, which corresponds to the changing magnetic field of the magnetic tape, shows Figure 1, and Figure 2 shows the equivalent circuit of the AMR sensor. It consists of two Wheatstone bridges. The first has four equal resistors R1, R2, R3 and R4 and the second also has four equal resistors R5, R6, R7 and R8. They are made of a thin tantalum layer. The upper Wheatstone bridge covers one half of the magnetic field period, and the lower Wheatstone bridge covers a second half of the magnetic field period.

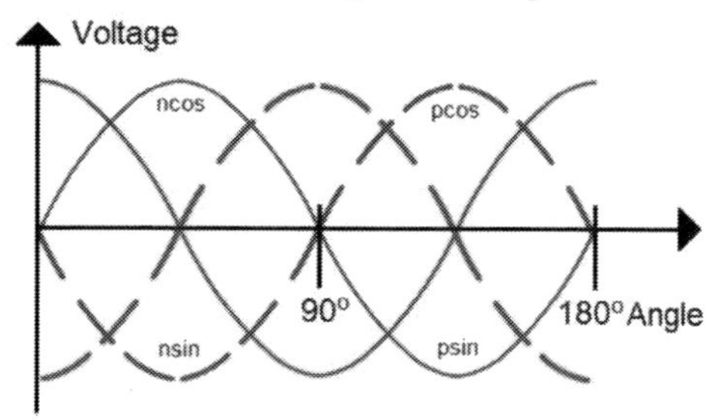

Figure 1. Ideal analog AMR sensor output of ncos, pcos, nsin and psin signals.

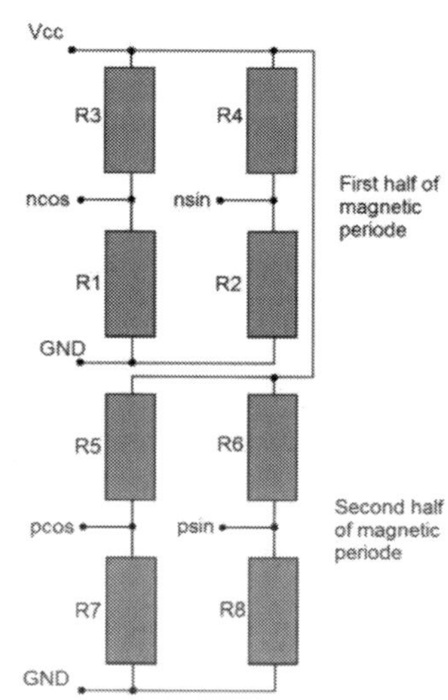

Figure 2. AMR equivalent circuit.

The problem here was to generate an appropriate magnetic field while probing a Device Under Test (DUT) on the wafer prober. The requirement was to immediately obtain a peak value of the sensor sensitivity of the sine and cosine curve. The direction of the magnetic field must be as parallel as possible to the silicon wafer's surface. An additional limiting factor is a small opening in the test probe card (Figure 3) and the fragile contact probes' proximity. The magnet's free space in the middle of the probe-card with six test probes is magnified for better presentation.

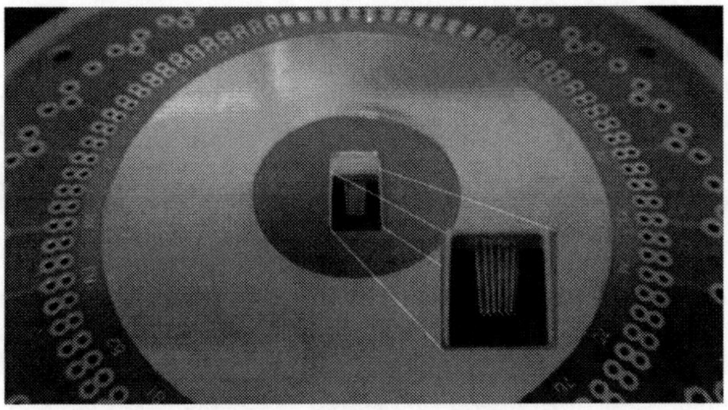

Figure 3. AMR test probe card with twelve test probes in the middle. We need two probes per pad for four-wire measurement.

The test sample's sensitivity level should be as close as possible to the sensitivity level measured near the magnetic tape (Figure 4). The device's most relevant parameters are the signal amplitudes at terminals "ncos-nsin" and "pcos-psin". In addition to the sensitivity, we must also measure each resistance in a double Wheatstone bridge.

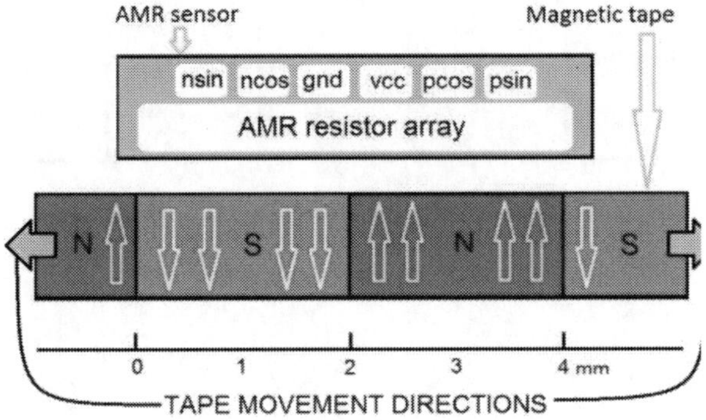

Figure 4. AMR sensor with six pads and resistor array near the magnetic tape.

Other important parameters are the offset voltages at "ncos-nsin" and "pcos-psin" when no magnetic field is present. The current consumption is also a part of the characterization, which is monitored during development and production. A small hysteresis of the outputs we consider, at this stage, is guaranteed "by design" itself. At the moment, the hysteresis can only be measured by using a magnetic tape when we change the direction of tape travel according to the AMR sensor.

Section 2 describes a precise mechanism that allows a magnetic field generation near a silicon wafer's surface and in proximity to the test needles without damaging them. Section 3 describes some AMR sensitivity results, and section 4 describes some ideas for further improvement of the AMR sensor on the silicon wafer characterization procedure.

II. Materials and Methods

To develop the analog AMR sensor's optimal resistor geometry and layer structure, it was necessary to cut a silicon wafer, place the sensor device into a test package, and then measure all the sensor's critical parameters, including the sensitivity. These measurements were performed with specially designed hardware and an alternating magnetized magnetic tape (Figure 4) perpendicular to the AMR sensor. We are talking about a magnetic field with a typical strength of 30mT. Figure 4 shows the top view of the AMR sensor with pads and resistor array. The distance from the 1mm thick tape to the sensor is adjustable from 0.5 to 1.5mm, and the dimension of the sensor is about 1 x 4mm.

To avoid this time-consuming step, we decided to use a small neodymium magnet to create a permanent magnetic field and a special structure to transfer this field close to the silicon wafer's surface. The magnetic field direction should be as parallel as possible to the surface of the silicon wafer. This structure was custom made from a soft ferromagnetic material [6]. After performing some simulations and experimenting with different shapes and materials, we selected a final form shown in Figure 5.

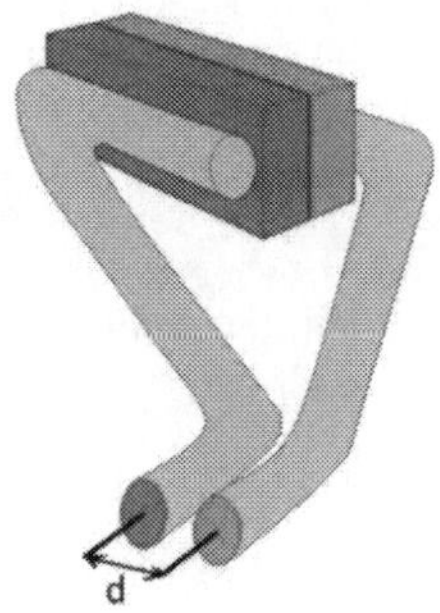

Figure 5. Structure from neodymium magnet and ferromagnetic material. Distance "d" is 2mm

During wafer sorting, it is essential to perform some measurements with and without a magnetic field. It was necessary to develop a precision mechanism (Figure 6) with an actuator.

This mechanism allows us to position the magnetic field with a small joystick within a few micrometer range. The hinge is made of a thin steel sheet. The entire mechanism is screwed onto the test probe card and later adjusted under a microscope.

III. Results

The repeatability of measurements in the magnetic field is in the range of 1.6% of the measured value. By accurately adjusting the magnetic field near the DUT, we can measure the maximum amplitude of the sine and cosine signals. The measured values are almost identical to the values measured later on packaged parts near the magnetic tape. We have the best matching score at the one mm sensor-tape gap. Figure 7 shows a graph of the differences between two sequentially repeated sensitivity measurements for 100 devices. The typical peak amplitude of the sensitivity amplitude is 50 to 60 millivolts and the standard deviation of the difference in repeated measurements is 0.9 mV. Blue colored values in Figure 7 present differences between cosine amplitude and red values present differences between sine amplitude.

Figure 6. Probe card with fine adjustable magnetic field actuator.

During wafer sort, the magnetic field generation and settling time is approximately twenty-five milliseconds, and the total test time per DUT is about 40 milliseconds. The magnetic field is reset to zero as the wafer prober moves the probes to the next device. At this point, the magnetic field actuator increases the distance between the wafer surface and the magnet structure in Figure 4. The gap rises from a few micrometers to about ten millimeters. No magnetic influence on the AMR sensor can then be detected.

Some additional parameters for the optimal exploitation of one device are presented in Table 1. There are some characteristics concerning three different distances of the test AMR sensor sample from the magnetic tape. The typical space in the final application is 0.5 mm.

The sensor's resistance does not change significantly with the magnetic field distance, as shown in the table's second line. The sensitivity at the magnetic field change is also within the required range, and we can also expect some offset values.

IV. Conclusion

With this method we have tested several thousand analog AMR sensors so far. This approach significantly shortened the development time for a customer-specific, analog AMR sensor. Further development in this area is in replacing the mechanical actuator and permanent magnet with a microfine coil with permalloy or soft magnetic composite materials [6] core for even faster magnetic field generation. We have already carried out some experiments in this direction but had problems with the field strength and the limited space near the test probes.

TABLE 1. AMR Sensor Test Sample Results.

	measurement1	measurement2	measurement3	
Tape Distance	0.10	0.50	1.00	mm
Resistance	0.9316	0.9362	0.9418	kOhm
Amplitude sin	66.74	65.91	60.96	mV
Amplitude cos	66.69	65.83	60.85	mV
Offset sin	3.80	4.15	3.97	±mv
Offset cos	4.92	4.94	4.86	±mV
Hysteresis	0.00	0.9	4.24	µm

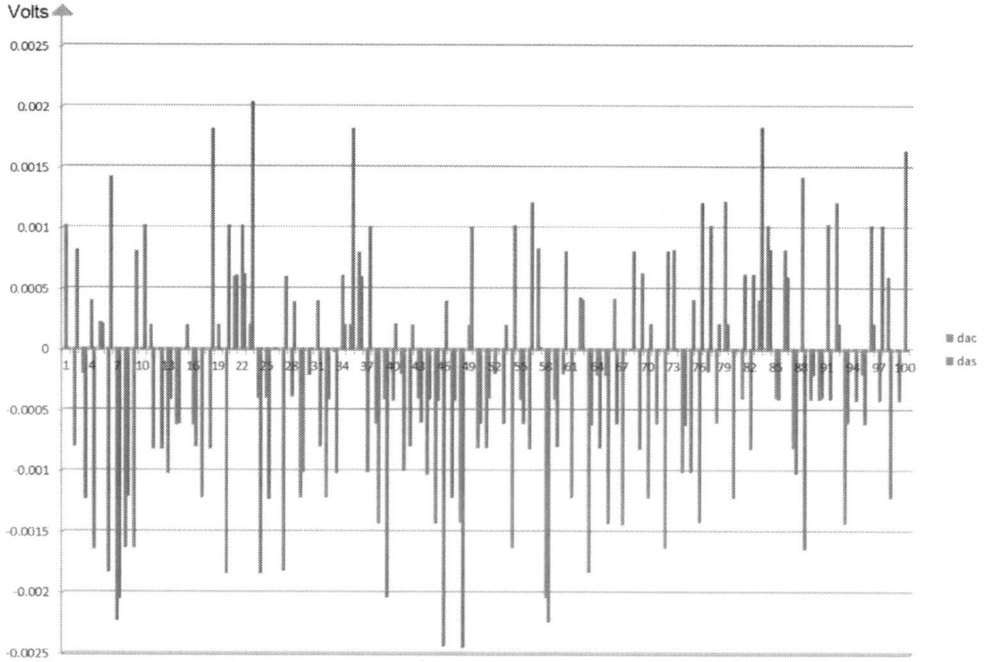

Figure 7. AMR sensitivity repeating measurement difference graph in volts for 100 devices with standard deviation of 0.9mV.

The data in Table 1 were obtained from the described test procedure on the wafer. Measurements were averaged with a 16-bit analog to digital conversion and with hi gain. Accuracy and repeatability were also verified with a calibrated, professional voltmeter.

The hysteresis cannot be measured with the described method. It can only be determined by moving a sensor or magnetic field in both directions (Figure 4). However, our solution to this problem is currently patent pending and will be published shortly.

Additionally, we also see the upgrade of the overall process in the improvement of the AMR sensor geometry and its performance [7][8].

REFERENCES

[1] Wikipedia contributors. "Magnetoresistance," *Wikipedia, The Free Encyclopedia.* Wikipedia, The Free Encyclopedia, 10 Sep. 2020. Web. 20 Sep. 2020.

[2] Wikipedia contributors. "Magnetic anisotropy," *Wikipedia, The Free Encyclopedia.* Wikipedia, The Free Encyclopedia, 27 May. 2020. Web. 20 Sep. 2020.

[3] R. Slatter, "Magnetoresistive (MR) Sensors for Angle-, Path- and Current Measurement in Harsh Environments," *Proc. AMA Conference Sensor 2015 and IRS*^{2}, Nuremberg, pp. 228-233, 2015.

[4] J. Fraden, "Handbook of Modern Sensors: Physics, Designs, and Applications, 5th ed.," *Springer International Publishing Switzerland,* 2016.

[5] S. A. C. Harmon, M. J. Hall, S. Turner, and N. Hillier, "Characterization of magnetic sensors at the operational temperatures of industrial applications," in *IEEE Transactions on Magnetics.,* vol. 51, no. 1, pp. 1-4, Jan. 2015.

[6] F. Fiorillo, G. Bertotti, C. Appino, and M. Pasquale, "Soft Magnetic Materials," *Wiley Encyclopedia of Electrical and Electronics Engineering 1999,* John Wiley&Sons, Inc., Hoboken, NJ, USA, 1999.

[7] C. Wang, W. Su, J. Pu, Z. Hu, and M. Liu, "A Self-biased Anisotropic Magnetoresistive (AMR) Magnetic Field Sensor on Flexible Kapton.," *2018 IEEE International Magnetics Conference (INTERMAG),* Singapore, pp. 1-1, 2018

[8] N. G. Hadjigeorgiou and P. P. Sotiriadis, "Parasitic Capacitances, Inductive Coupling, and High-Frequency Behavior of AMR Sensors," in *IEEE Sensors Journal,* vol. 20, no. 5, pp. 2339-2347, March, 2020.

Inverse Convolution Method for Periodic Media under Deterministic and Stochastic Condition

Xuefeng Li, Mohamed Ichchou, Abdelmalek Zine, Noureddine Bouhaddi
Ecole Centrale de Lyon, France
Email: xuefeng.li@ec-lyon.fr

Christophe Droz
KU Leuven, Division LMSD, Belgium
Email: christophe.droz@ec-lyon.fr

***Abstract*—Wavenumber extraction has attracted widespread attention in periodic structures, sonar, radar and sensor fields. The Inverse Convolution Method (INCOME) is presented and optimized to extract wavenumber of 1D and 2D wave propagating in periodic structures under deterministic and stochastic condition in this paper. This method is one of inverse methods and combines the principle of the Prony series and the Bloch-Floquet theorem based on convolution framework.**

Keywords- Periodic structure; Wavenumber Extraction; Inverse method; Deterministic and Stochastic condition; Wave propagation.

I. INTRODUCTION

Wavenumber extraction has been used in periodic structures field to reveal many unique properties, such as complex band structure which has been applied to many applications, such as damage identification, vibration isolation, unable filters, wave guides and more [1]. The whole frequencies from which wavenumber is extracted can be divided into three regions: low frequency region, medium frequency region and high frequency region. For the low frequency region, traditional model-based analysis methods, such as Transfer Matrix Method (TMM) and Wave Finite Element method (WFEM), have an effective performance to extract wavenumber. But in the medium and high frequency region, these model-based analysis methods generally cause the computational issues and even are invalid. In order to overcome these issues, an amount of inverse methods involving Fourier-based wavenumber estimation methods and improved signal processing methods have been proposed. Fourier-based wavenumber estimation methods contain two-dimensional spatial Discrete Fourier Transform (2D-DFT), McDaniel's method, Inhomogeneous Wave Correlation (IWC) method [2], Inverse Wave Decomposition (IWD) and so on. In particular, IWC method has obvious advantages on identification of guided waves propagating in plates. For example, IWC is smaller sensitive to the boundary condition and the source of force and only requires the sparse signal as input parameters. But as an extension of the Fourier transform, it has itself disadvantages, such as the limitation of wavenumber resolution, which cause the inaccurate results when the number of wavelengths within the signal is few. Additionally, IWC leads to a non-linear optimization problem, maximizing the correlation coefficient between an inhomogeneous wave and the complete wave field. In the past few decades, several improved signal processing methods have been proposed such as Matrix Pencial, ESPRIT, Prony method, MUSIC and HRWA. Prony method and ESPRIT method are limited to 1D application and regard fine periodic measurements as input parameters. Recently, the High Resolution Wavenumber Analysis (HRWA) method proposed by P. Margerit provides an effective way to increase the wavenumber resolution and only requires to solve the linear problem by the combination of ESPRIT algorithm and the ESTER criterion [3]. The signal order is estimated due to the use of ESTER criterion and the complex wavevectors are extracted from the measured frequency response using ESPRIT method. Additionally, from the extracted wavenumber, this method allows the identification of some mechanical properties. But HRWA is implemented without considering the effect of uncertainties factor, such noise and non-periodicity sampling, on the wavenumber extraction. More recently, Boukadia proposed a novel improved signal processing method referred to INCOME as an extension of Prony method [4]. This method can be applied to extract wavenumbers in 1D and process K-space analysis in 2D based on linear algebra. But the periodic measurement is still a strong constraint in this method and the problem of automatic signal order identification needs to be solved. The rest of this paper is organized as follows. Section II introduces the principle of INCOME and uses a beam case to validate the effectiveness of INCOMDE. Section III describes the perspective and conclusion.

II. INCOME PRINCIPLE AND SIMULATION EXAMPLE

A. Principle

The core of the INCOME method is to use the Prony method (commonly used in spectrum estimation) to solve the estimation of the wavenumber in the periodic structure. When only considering the incident wave, the displacement field can be expressed as the sum of complex exponentials including different positive propagation constants.

$$U_n = \sum_{m=1}^{n_w} b_m \lambda_m^{-n} \tag{1}$$

Where b_m is the complex amplitude of propagating wave for m^{th} wave, n_w is the number of waves, λ_m is equal to the propagation constant of mth wave and k_m is equal to wavenumber of mth wave. The corresponding characteristic polynomial with coefficient a_m of the formula (1) is

$$\psi(\lambda) = \sum_{m=0}^{n_w} a_m \lambda^{n_w - m} \tag{2}$$

For INCOME, the input parameter is a series of experimental displacement data. These data can be expressed as an autoregressive matrix with Toeplitz structure and then, convolved with a vector of characteristic polynomial coefficients (product kernel). Finally, the least-squares method is used to estimate the best polynomial coefficients and propagation constant can be obtained by solving the roots of the characteristic polynomial. The out parameter is wavenumber obtained by Bloch-Floquet theorem. The whole process can be regarded as a filtering process and the estimation of the best filter is the key to the method.

B. Simulation example

The effectiveness of INCOME in deterministic condition is validated by the wavenumber extraction of two pairs of bending waves in a Timoshenko beam with resonators. Figure 1 shows a model of Timoshenko beam with resonators and the corresponding results in the positive direction are as follows:

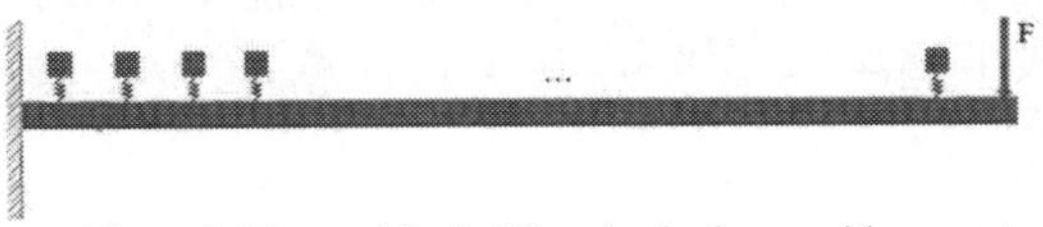

Figure 1. The model of a Timoshenko beam with resonator

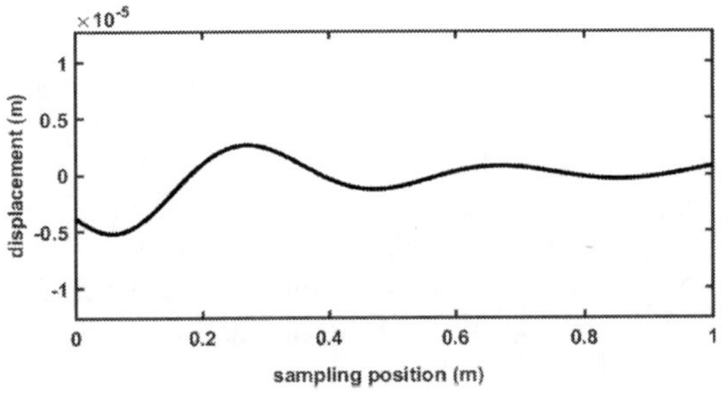

Figure 2. The frequency response curve at 500 Hz

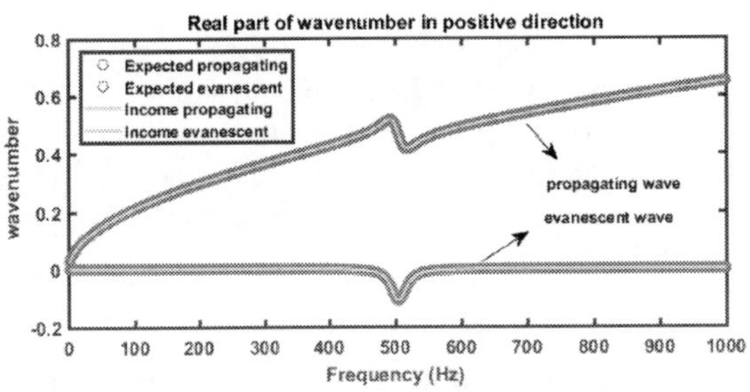

Figure 3. Real part of the complex dispersion curve

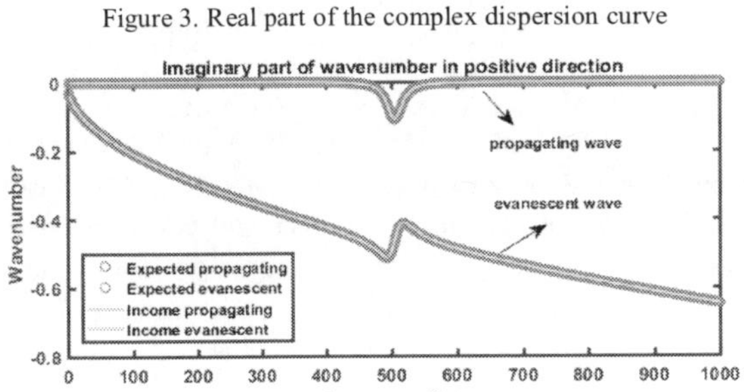

Figure 4. Imaginary part of the complex dispersion curve

The length L of beam is set to 1m and it is divided to 100 elements evenly. The weight and height are set to 2cm and 1cm respectively. The damping, Young's modulus, density and Poisson are set to 0.005, 210 × (1 + 0.005i) GPa, 7800 kg/m^3 and 0.3 respectively. 30 resonators are distributed evenly through the Timoshenko beam. The mass of resonators is equal to 5% of the overall beam. The Natural frequency of resonator is 500Hz and the damping factor of resonator is 0.05. Figure 2 shows the frequency response curve in 500Hz, which shows the amplitude of displacement is decaying exponentially with wave propagating. Figure 3 and 4 present the complex dispersion curve of waves propagating in positive direction, which can illustrate that the INCOME is effective to extract wavenumbers. On the other hand, the dynamic properties of periodic structure can be explained. When the frequency reaches the natural frequency of the spring oscillator, resonance occurs. The energy is dissipated during the process of resonance, leading to the band gap existing near the natural frequency. In the band gap, the wave can't propagate. This principle is mainly reflected by the imaginary part of the wavenumber. For example, in the imaginary part of the dispersion curve, the wavenumber of the propagating wave changes to negative number near the natural frequency of spring oscillator, which leads to the exponential attenuation of displacement and the appearance of band gap.

III. Perspectives and Conclusion

INCOME overcomes the limitations of Fourier-based methods and other traditional model-based analysis methods. The proposed method only relies on linear prediction theory instead of nonlinear optimization and allows a coherent estimate of the full K-Space in deterministic condition and stochastic condition. The theory of INCOME in deterministic condition is established and its effectiveness is validated by different cases in 1D. For stochastic case, it requires to be explored further, such as considering the effect of different kinds of disturbances on wavenumber extraction and the experimental cases need to be implemented to validate the effectiveness of INCOME further.

References

[1] M. I. Hussein, M. J. Leamy and M. Ruzzene, "Dynamics of Phononic Materials and Structures: Historical Origins, Recent Progress, and Future Outlook," J. Applied Mechanics Reviews, pp: 1380-1419, 2014, doi: 10.1115/1.4026911.

[2] M. N. Ichchou, J. Berthaut and M . Collet, "Multi-mode wave propagation in ribbed plates: Part I, wavenumber-space characteristics," J. International Journal of Solids & Structures, Vol.45, pp: 1179-1195, March 2008. Available from: https://doi.org/10.1016/j.ijsolstr.2007.09.032.

[3] P. Margerit, A. Lebée, J. F Caron, K. Ege and X. Boutillon, "The High-Resolution Wavevector Analysis for the characterization of the dynamic response of composite plates," J. Journal of Sound and Vibration, vol. 458, pp:177-196, 2019, dio: 10.1016/j.jsv.2019.06.026.

[4] R. F. Boukadia, E. Deckers, C. Claeys, M. Ichchou and W. Desmet, "An Inverse Convolution Method for Wavenumber Extraction," J. MSSP, in press.

Device for Hemodynamic Parameters Measurement in Veterinary Medicine of Small Animals

Jan Havlík
Faculty of Electrical Engineering
Czech Technical University in Prague
Prague, Czech Republic
email: xhavlikj@fel.cvut.cz, ORCID 0000-0001-9301-6359

Jakub Vitáček
Faculty of Electrical Engineering
Czech Technical University in Prague
Prague, Czech Republic
email: vitacjak@fel.cvut.cz

***Abstract*—The paper describes the design and realization of a device for non-invasive sensing of hemodynamic parameters in veterinary medicine of small animals (dogs and cats). Two main hemodynamic parameters were selected for the measurement blood pressure and heart rate. An oscillometric method was chosen to measure blood pressure. The heart rate is determined from the electrocardiography (ECG) signal, i.e., by sensing the electrical activity of the heart from the body surface. The realized device saves the measured data on the SD card after measuring the signals. To evaluate them, a MATLAB script, which determines the values was implemented. The control of the measuring device and communication with the user is provided by the ESP32 microcontroller. The advantage of the realized device is the possibility of displaying oscillometric pulsations, which is not usually available in commercial devices. Thanks to the simultaneous measurement of the mentioned biological signals, the possibilities of the signal evaluation can be further extended, e.g., by measuring the pulse wave velocity measurement.**

***Index Terms*—hemodynamic parameters, veterinary medicine, blood pressure, heart rate, oscillometric method**

I. Introduction

Hemodynamic parameters are one of the basic clinical parameters, which should inform about an overall health state and indicate potential risks both in human and veterinary medicine. The hemodynamic parameters reflect blood flow in the vascular bed. The primary hemodynamic parameters are heart rate and blood pressure [1].

The first measurements of blood pressure were (invasively) realized at the beginning of 18. century by Stephen Hales [2]. The non-invasive blood pressure was firstly determined in 1896 by Italian physician Scipione Riva Rocci [3]. The blood pressure is a pulsatile pressure in arteries, which is characterized by systolic (maximal), diastolic (minimal), and mean values. In 2007, the recommendation for blood pressure measurement was created by the American College of Veterinary Interna Medicine (AVCIM) [4]. The updated recommendation was published in 2018 [5]. The method, which is frequently used for non-invasive blood pressure measurement currently, is oscillometry measurement [6], [7]. The typical values of blood pressure in veterinary medicine of small animals are roughly 140 mmHg systolic pressure, 77 mmHg diastolic pressure, and 99 mmHg mean arterial pressure for healthy cats [8], and 119 mmHg systolic pressure, 67 mmHg diastolic pressure and 94 mmHg mean arterial pressure for dogs [9].

The heart rate is defined as the number of ventricular contractions per unit time and is usually given in beats per minute (bpm) [10]. There are several methods for heart rate determination, such as photoplethysmography (PPG) [11] or electrocardiography (ECG) [12]. The ECG method offers a straightforward approach to heart rate, which is not influenced by the health state of peripheral vessels; thus, it is the reason this approach was selected for the study. The typical signal, which is frequently used for heart rate determination from ECG, is lead II (electrodes placed on the right arm and the left leg). The amplitude of the QRS complex in lead II is typically about 2 mV for dogs (about 2.5 mV for bigger races) and about 0.9 mV for cats [13].

The study aims to design and realize a device for non-invasive sensing of basic hemodynamic parameters (heart rate and blood pressure) in veterinary medicine of small animals (typically cats and dogs) and to design and implement signal processing methods for the determination of derived hemodynamic parameters, such as pulse transition time and pulse wave velocity.

In Section II, the design of the device is described. The features of blood pressure measurement and ECG measurement parts are specified, and the related signal processing is described. In Section III, proof of the proposed concept is presented. The device was evaluated on a human volunteer. In Section IV, the results and future steps are briefly discussed.

II. Methods

The device is designed as a stand-alone measurement device, which consists of several principal blocks (see Figure 1). The whole device is controlled by a microcontroller ESP32 (240 MHz dual-core microcontroller) with an integrated 802.11 b/g/n (WiFi) transceiver/receiver and dual-mode Bluetooth. The data are stored on an SD card for off-line processing and could also be transferred via WiFi network for processing immediately during data acquisition. The main parts of the device are blood pressure measurement and heart rate measurement blocks. The user interface is realized using buttons and LCD. The device could also communicate by the web interface. The power supply unit is designed both for supply from DC voltage sources, such as DC adaptors or from build-in LiON accumulator.

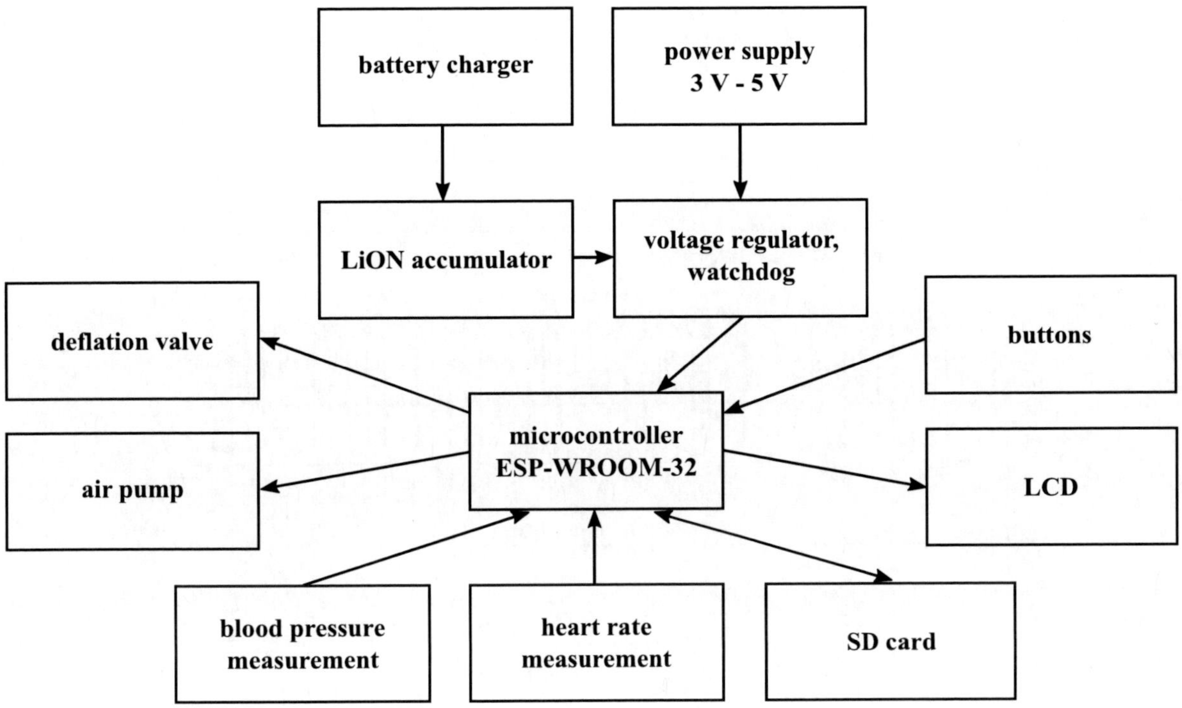

Fig. 1. Block diagram of the device

A. Blood Pressure Measurement

The blood pressure measurement is based on the oscillometry method. The hardware realization of the blood pressure measurement part could be divided into a pneumatic circuit and an electronic part. The pneumatic circuit consists of an air pump for inflating the cuff and a deflation valve. The electronic part includes the pressure sensor MP3V5050 (NXP Semiconductor) [14] and the analog filter (1st order low-pass filter with cut-off frequency 650 Hz) [15]. The signal from the pressure sensor is digitalized by the ADC integrated into the microcontroller. A two-tube newborn size cuff is used for blood pressure measurement.

B. Heart Rate Measurement

The ECG part is based on the single-lead heart rate monitor front-end AD8232 (Analog Devices) [16]. The gain is set to 100 [-], common-mode rejection ratio is at least 80 dB (DC to 60 Hz). Two analog filters are used for a better detection of heart rate by emphasizing the QRS complex in ECG signal. The first one is a 2nd order high-pass filter with cut-off frequency 7 Hz, and the second one is a 2nd order Sallen-Key low-pass filter with cut-off frequency 24 Hz. The additional gain of the filter is 11 [-].

C. Signal Processing

The acquired signals are processed off-line in PC. Firstly, the oscillometry pulsations are extracted from the cuff pressure by band-pass filter with cut-off frequencies 0.5 Hz and 3.5 Hz. Consequently, the envelope of the signal is computed. Afterwards, the mean arterial pressure is determined as a pressure in the cuff at the moment of maximal oscillation (maximum amplitude algorithm) [17]. The systolic and diastolic pressures are determined using the ratio method [18].

Simultaneously, the recorded ECG signal is processed to determine the heart rate. The PanTompkins algorithm is used for ECG signal processing [19].

III. Results

As a proof of concept, the device was evaluated on a human volunteer. The proband was a young healthy woman (25 years, 174 cm, 67 kg). The ECG electrodes were placed on the right arm (RA electrode) and the left leg (LL), the acquired signal corresponding to lead II. The cuff was placed on the left hand. The working range of blood pressure (from 60 mm Hg up to 160 mm Hg) and ECG signal (the amplitude of QRS complex about ones of mV) in human medicine is the same of working range of blood pressure and ECG signal in veterinary medicine of cats and dogs [8], [9], [13].

The acquired ECG signal is shown in Figure 2a in detail, the one-minute record is shown in Figure 2b. All R peaks were detected correctly (highlighted using red triangles). The instantaneous value of the heart rate determined from the ECG signal is shown in Figure 2c.

The signals relating to the blood pressure measurement are shown in Fig 3. The cuff pressure acquired during the deflation of the cuff is shown in Figure 3a. The record of oscillometry pulsations extracted from the cuff pressure is

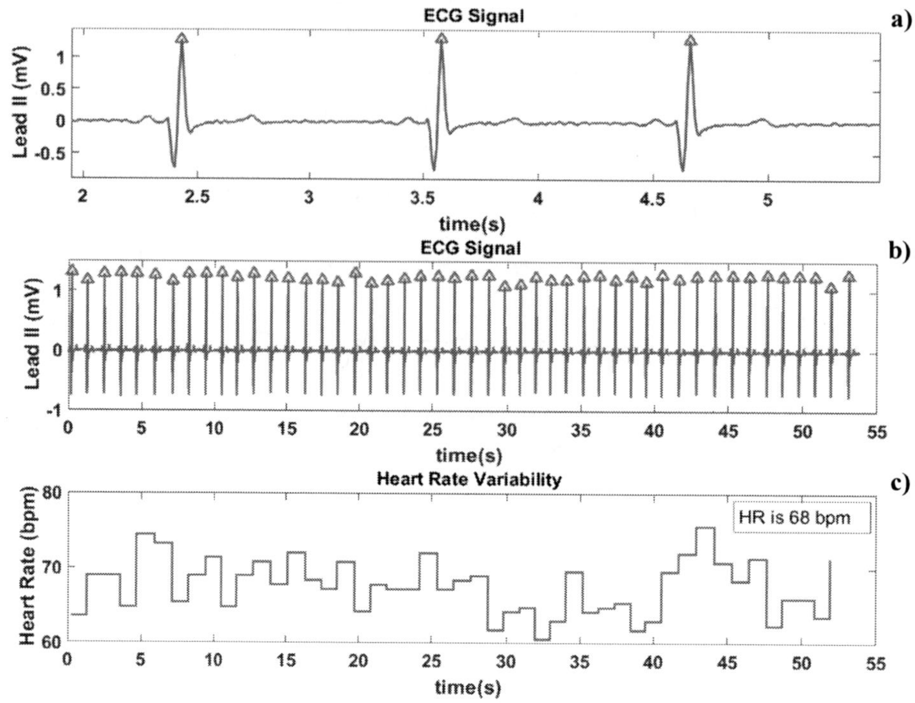

Fig. 2. Example of the ECG signal (lead II) acquired on a human volunteer: a) the detail of the signal, b) the one minute record, c) the instantaneous value of the heart rate determined from the ECG

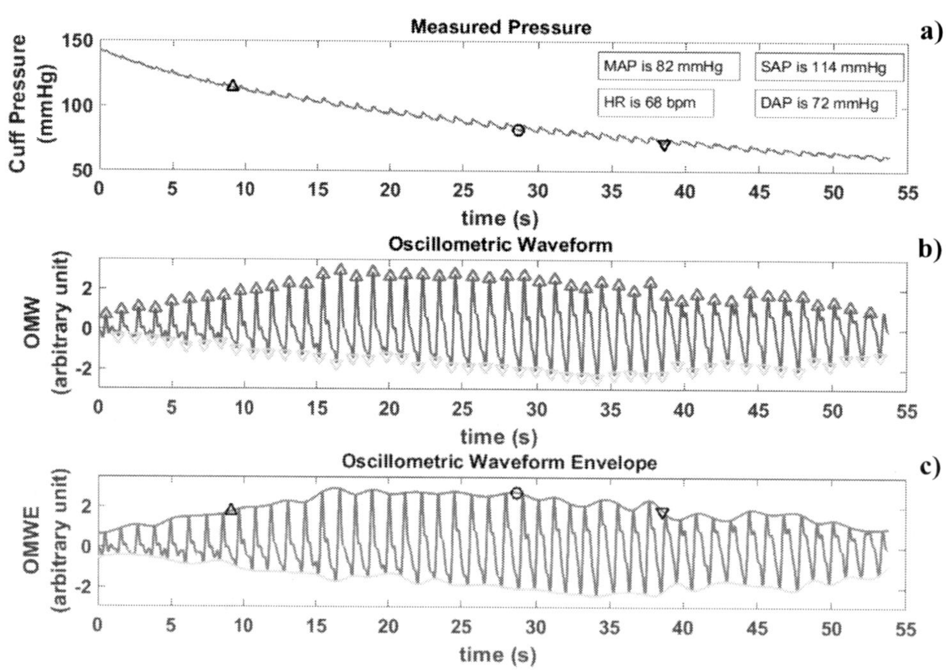

Fig. 3. Example of the blood pressure signals acquired on a human volunteer: a) the cuff pressure acquired during the deflation of the cuff, b) the oscillometric pulsations, c) the oscillometric waveform envelope

shown in Figure 3b, the local extremes of the signal are highlighted by red and green triangles. Consequently, the oscillometric waveform envelope is shown in Figure 3c. The mean arterial, systolic and diastolic pressures determined from the signal envelope are highlighted by a black circle and black triangles, respectively.

IV. CONCLUSION

The paper presents the partial results of the research in progress. The design and realization of a device for non-invasive measurement of ECG and blood pressure in veterinary medicine of small animals have been done.

The concept of the device allows not only the measuring of ECG signal and blood pressure but also the possibility to determine additional hemodynamic parameters, such as pulse transition time (a time difference between the R-peak in ECG and a related maximum of the pulse wave in oscillometric pulsations) or pulse wave velocity.

The future steps will contain the evaluation of the device on small animals in clinical practice and the design and implementation of additional signal processing algorithms for enlarging the set of determined hemodynamic parameters.

ACKNOWLEDGMENT

This work has been supported by the grant no. SGS20/167/OHK3/3T/13 of the Czech Technical University in Prague.

REFERENCES

[1] J. Newman, *Hemodynamic*, ser. Encyclopedia of Behavioral Medicine. New York, NY: Springer New York, 2013, pp. 955–957.

[2] J. W. Buchanan, "The history of veterinary cardiology," *Journal of Veterinary Cardiology*, vol. 15, no. 1, pp. 65–85, Mar 2013.

[3] A. Zanchetti and G. Mancia, "The centenary of blood pressure measurement: a tribute to Scipione Riva-Rocci," *Journal of Hypertension*, vol. 14, no. 1, pp. 1–12, Jan 1996.

[4] S. Brown, C. Atkins, R. Bagley, A. Carr, L. Cowgill, M. Davidson, B. Egner, J. Elliott, R. Henik, M. Labato, M. Littman, D. Polzin, L. Ross, P. Snyder, and R. Stepien, "Guidelines for the identification, evaluation, and management of systemic hypertension in dogs and cats," *Journal of Veterinary Internal Medicine*, vol. 21, no. 3, pp. 542–558, 2007.

[5] M. J. Acierno, S. Brown, A. E. Coleman, R. E. Jepson, M. Papich, R. L. Stepien, and H. M. Syme, "Acvim consensus statement: Guidelines for the identification, evaluation, and management of systemic hypertension in dogs and cats," *Journal of Veterinary Internal Medicine*, vol. 32, no. 6, pp. 1803–1822, 2018.

[6] M. Forouzanfar, H. R. Dajani, V. Z. Groza, M. Bolic, S. Rajan, and I. Batkin, "Oscillometric blood pressure estimation: Past, present, and future," *IEEE Reviews in Biomedical Engineering*, vol. 8, pp. 44–63, 2015.

[7] J. Jilek and T. Fukushima, "Oscillometric blood pressure measurement: the methodology, some observations, and suggestions," *Biomedical Instrumentation & Technology*, vol. 39, no. 3, p. 237, May 2005.

[8] A. R. Bodey and J. Sansom, "Epidemiological study of blood pressure in domestic cats," *Journal of Small Animal Practice*, vol. 39, no. 12, pp. 567–573, Dec 1998.

[9] M. Mika, W. Toshifumi, F. Kouichi, M. Hiroto, W. Yoshito, and T. Mitsugi, "A clinical evalution of blood pressure through non-invasive measurement using the oscillometric procedure in conscious dogs," *Journal of Veterinary Medical Science*, vol. 59, no. 11, p. 989, Nov 1, 1997.

[10] A. T. Ginty, *Heart Rate*, ser. Encyclopedia of Behavioral Medicine. New York, NY: Springer New York, 2013, pp. 951–952.

[11] D. Borchevkin, "Method of photoplethysmography diagnostics of domesticated animals cardiovascular diseases," *Journal of Veterinary Science & Technology*, vol. 7, no. 1, 2015.

[12] A. Dupre, S. Vincent, and P. Iaizzo, *Basic ECG Theory, Recordings, and Interpretation*, ser. Handbook of Cardiac Anatomy, Physiology, and Devices. Totowa, NJ: Humana Press, 2005, pp. 191–201.

[13] M. Martin, "ECG interpretation in small animals 3. practical guidelines," *In Practice*, vol. 24, no. 5, pp. 250–261, May 1, 2002.

[14] National Semiconductors, (2020, Oct.) "MP3V5050, 0 to 50 kPa, differential, and gauge pressure sensor," 2018. [Online]. Available: https://www.nxp.com/docs/en/data-sheet/MP3V5050.pdf

[15] Freescale Semiconductor, (2020, Oct.) "Noise considerations for integrated pressure sensors," 2005. [Online]. Available: https://www.nxp.com/docs/en/application-note/AN1646.pdf

[16] Analog Devices, (2020, Oct.) "AD8232 single-lead, heart rate monitor front end," 2020. [Online]. Available: https://www.analog.com/media/en/technical-documentation/data-sheets/ad8232.pdf

[17] G. W. Mauck, C. R. Smith, L. A. Geddes, and J. D. Bourland, "The meaning of the point of maximum oscillations in cuff pressure in the indirect measurement of blood pressure–part ii," *Journal of Biomechanical Engineering*, vol. 102, no. 1, p. 28, 1980.

[18] B. G. Celler, A. Argha, P. N. Le, and E. Ambikairajah, "Novel methods of testing and calibration of oscillometric blood pressure monitors," *PloS one*, vol. 13, no. 8, p. e0201123, 2018.

[19] J. Pan and W. J. Tompkins, "A real-time QRS detection algorithm," *IEEE Transactions on Biomedical Engineering*, vol. BME-32, no. 3, pp. 230–236, 1985.

Performance Evaluation of High-Accuracy Time Synchronization Sensor Device Using Indoor GNSS Time Information Delivery System for Structural Health Monitoring of Buildings and Civil Infrastructures

Narito Kurata
Tsukuba University of Technology
Tsukuba City, Ibaraki, Japan
e-mail: kurata@home.email.ne.jp

Tsutomu Sano, Makoto Ishii
ENABLER Ltd.
Minato-ku, Tokyo, Japan
e-mail: t.sano@enabler.co.jp, ishii@enabler.co.jp

Satoru Ishida, Masaki Tanaka
Hitachi Industry & Control Solutions, Ltd.
Taito-ku, Tokyo, Japan
e-mail: satoru.ishida.xr@hitachi.com,
masaki.tanaka.hc@hitachi.com

Abstract—**The purpose of this research and development is to realize structural health monitoring for increased efficiency in the maintenance of buildings and civil infrastructures, and observations to prepare for natural disasters, such as earthquakes. The most difficult and interesting issue is the realization of inexpensive time-synchronized measurements. It is necessary to install numerous sensors in a building or civil infrastructure and to acquire measured data whose time synchronization is ensured. Although Global Navigation Satellite System (GNSS) time information is generally only available outdoors, the authors designed a system capable of using GNSS time information indoors. This system can deliver time information to a building by using existing TV coaxial cables. The authors further developed a sensor device able to receive indoor GNSS time information and to add high-accuracy time information to measured data. This paper describes the development of a sensor device that adds high-accuracy time information to measured data by using a system to deliver GNSS time information indoors. The performance of the developed sensor device equipped with a mechanism for receiving GNSS signal-based time information was verified from the results of a shaking table experiment. It was shown that it can be applied to structural health monitoring of buildings and civil infrastructure and seismic observation.**

Keywords; time synchronization; GNSS; structural health monitoring; earthquake observation.

I. INTRODUCTION

Japan has suffered serious damage from natural disasters, such as the Great Hanshin Earthquake and the Great East Japan Earthquake. While technologies are being developed to reduce damage at the time of a disaster, one of the most important issue to be addressed is the automation of operations, such as the structural health evaluation of buildings and civil infrastructures after earthquakes, and assessments of damage situation of cities. Because structures, such as houses and other buildings and infrastructures, such as expressways and bridges have deteriorated over time, the automation of inspection for their maintenance is an urgent social issue. To automate such inspection and error detection, data collection is required, using sensors. In order to analyze the data collected by the sensors and so evaluate the structural health of buildings and civil infrastructures, time synchronization between the sensors must be ensured.

In general, dedicated wiring or a wired or wireless network is used to ensure time synchronization for the sensors installed in a building or other structure. Installing wiring over multiple stories of a building is neither easy nor cheap. Because space for wiring and locations for sensors are limited, it is virtually impossible to install sensors in arbitrary locations inside a building. When a wireless network is used, wiring is no longer required. The application of a wireless network is therefore being anticipated now. Applying wireless sensor network technology, the authors developed a sensor device specifically for structural health monitoring and earthquake observations, and verified its performance in a skyscraper [1]–[3]. In a wireless sensor network system, time synchronization was realized through the transmission and reception of wireless packets between sensors [3]. However, with wireless sensor network technology, it is impossible to cover every floor of a skyscraper, or a long structure, such as a bridge, or an extensive area of a city.

Despite these limitations, the problem can be solved fundamentally if the sensors installed in various locations can autonomously hold accurate time information. Using a clock of ultra-high accuracy, namely a Chip Scale Atomic Clock (CSAC) [4]–[6], whose delay time is radically short compared to other devices, such as crystal resonators, a prototype was manufactured of a sensor device that autonomously holds accurate time information [7][8]. Improvements were then made to develop and commercialize the prototype, and a sensor device for practical use was developed [9]. In order to apply the developed sensor device to earthquake observations, a logic was implemented to detect the occurrence of an earthquake and store data of an earthquake event only. The functioning of the logic was checked by a shaking table experiment [10] and the logic was applied to an actual building [11]. The sensor device's ability to autonomously hold accurate time information was confirmed, and it was shown that it could be applied to such operations as structural health monitoring and earthquake observations. Autonomous time synchronization sensing using CSAC is the most effective method. In addition, research into and development of a miniature and inexpensive CSAC is underway, and it is expected that a CSAC that can be mounted in a smart phone will be realized. However, the CSAC available at present is quite expensive, which hinders its widespread use.

For a device, such as a sensor to acquire high-accuracy time information, a Global Navigation Satellite System (GNSS) can be used. A GNSS, such as the Global Positioning System (GPS), Global Navigation Satellite System (GLONASS), or Galileo Satellite Navigation Network (Galileo), measures positions and delivers time information by using signals emitted by satellites. A sensor with a mechanism capable of receiving GNSS signals can add high-accuracy time information to measured data. However, GNSS signals are available only in outdoor places where satellites are not blocked from view. Sensors installed inside a building cannot use GNSS signals. For that reason, the authors designed a system in which signals acquired from an antenna installed on the roof of a building are delivered indoors; GNSS signals can then be used indoors as well as outdoors. The authors also developed a sensor device able to receive indoor GNSS signals, and equipped it with a Micro Electro Mechanical System (MEMS) acceleration sensor.

In Section II of this paper, previous researches into time synchronization methods are described, to show the originality of this research. Section III describes the system for delivering GNSS signals indoors. Section IV describes in detail the development of a sensor device with a mechanism for receiving GNSS signal-based time information. Section V describes a shaking table experiment conducted to check the performance of the developed sensor device, and shows that good acceleration measurement and high-accuracy time synchronization between sensors could be realized.

II. STATE OF THE ART

A time synchronization function must be provided to sensor devices to be used in the structural health monitoring of buildings and civil infrastructure, or for earthquake observations. If time-synchronized data sets are not acquired, time series analysis using phase information cannot be performed. For example, it will then not be possible to perform a mode analysis of a structure, or analysis for structural health evaluation, or a wave propagation analysis of seismic waves traveling through the Earth's layers. Many previous studies have been conducted of time synchronization sensing, such as the use of GNSS signals using satellites, and the Network Time Protocol (NTP) intended for time synchronization on the Internet [12]. In addition, as a technology for realizing high-accuracy time synchronization indoors, there is the IEEE 1588 Precision Time Protocol (PTP). In PTP, with an Ethernet cable used for a common Local Area Network (LAN) and others set as a transmission path, a synchronization accuracy is realized of one microsecond or less, using time packets. However, when affected by fluctuations of packet delay or by packet loss due to congestion in a LAN, PTP has difficulty in providing a stable synchronization accuracy. PTP also faces multiple other problems due to the amount of delay being corrected by exchanging packets, such as the limited number of PTP devices that can be connected to the master station, and PTP not being deployable under a Wide Area Network (WAN), in which the amount of delay fluctuates greatly. Some studies realized time synchronization by making use of the wireless sensor network characteristic of small propagation delay. For example, time synchronization protocols, such as Reference Broadcast Synchronization (RBS), Timing-sync Protocol for Sensor Networks (TPSN), and Flooding Time Synchronization Protocol (FTSP) are being studied [13]–[15]. Although these technologies are used for many purposes, they are not the most appropriate method for sensor devices used to monitor the structural health of buildings and civil infrastructures, or earthquake observations. To be specific, as mentioned previously, GNSS signals can be used outdoors only, and the NTP's time synchronization accuracy is not adequate. A time synchronization method using wireless technology is highly convenient, but does not guarantee that wireless communication is always possible. In particular, if wireless communication ceases when an earthquake occurs, it becomes impossible to perform sensing with time synchronization ensured.

In this research, the authors developed a sensor device that retains accurate time information, based on a system capable of using GNSS signals indoors. Even when a huge number of sensors are installed in a building, provided accurate time information can be added to data measured by each sensor based on indoor GNSS signals, time synchronization between sensor data can be ensured simply by collecting data by any method and sorting it by using the time information. Data sets whose time synchronization is ensured by the sensor device developed in this research can be used for analysis of the structural health of buildings and civil infrastructures, or the earthquake observation.

III. INDOOR GNSS TIME INFORMATION DELIVERY SYSTEM

Time synchronization using GNSS, of high accuracy and over a vast area, is widely used in mobile communications. For positioning by GNSS, clock synchronization between GNSS satellites and a GNSS receiver is required, which makes it possible to measure the distance between each satellite and a receiver. In other words, positioning using GNSS is realized by highly accurate synchronizing of the controlled atomic clocks mounted in each artificial satellite orbiting the Earth and the clock of a GNSS receiver on the ground. First, the distance (pseudo-distance) between each satellite and the relevant receiver is measured. A pseudo-distance can be obtained by measuring the difference between the time a signal departs from each satellite and the time the receiver receives it. An atomic clock is mounted on the GNSS satellite side, so that the time of day is always kept with high accuracy. The clock of the GNSS receiver is inexpensive, and is synchronized with the satellite time. After the clock synchronization is completed, the use of only one satellite is sufficient for acquiring the time. From the GNSS receiver, Pulse Per Second (PPS) signals are output based on the timing of satellite synchronization.

In an environment where GNSS signals can be received, the GNSS receiver can perform high-accuracy time synchronization and positioning, but cannot be used in an indoor area where GNSS signals cannot be delivered. The authors designed an indoor GNSS time information delivery system that realizes high-accuracy time synchronization by delivering GNSS signals indoors. Specifically, GNSS signals are received on the roof of a building, and delivered as broadcasting into the building by using the transmission path of an existing system, such as a common antenna TV system or cable TV system. A transmitter is installed at any location from which the delivery of GNSS signals into the building is desired, and the signals are sent. The GNSS receiver receiving these signals reads position and time information and outputs high-accuracy synchronization signals (PPS signals). By mounting a GNSS receiver on each sensor device and implementing a mechanism to add high-accuracy time stamps to measured data, it becomes possible to collect data sets whose high-accuracy time synchronization is ensured from indoors. Measured data with accurate time stamps added can be grouped into data sets whose time synchronization is ensured simply by collecting data by any method, such as 3G, 4G, 5G, Wi-Fi, and Ethernet.

The transmission path of a CATV system or cable TV system in a building is used to deliver indoors high-accuracy times synchronized with GNSS satellites. As shown in Figure 1, an indoor GNSS time information delivery system consists of D1 on the roof, D2 inside the building, and D3 at the terminal (a transmitter for delivering GNSS time information indoors). D1 shown in Figure 1 receives a signal from the GNSS satellite, frequency-converts the synchronized time signal, and transmits it into the building. D2 receives time signals from D1 and demodulates them into high-accuracy time synchronization signals (PPS signals). D3 receives data from D2, adjusts the timing, and sends time information to a sensor device. Time information sent from D3 is received by a sensor device to add high-accuracy time information to measured data. By using a hub, it is possible to connect multiple D3s under D2. In addition, by incorporating the transmission function of D3 into D2, space can be saved.

IV. DEVELOPMENT OF SENSER DEVICE ABLE TO RECEIVE INDOOR GNSS SIGNALS

Structural health monitoring of buildings and civil infrastructure is evaluated by analyzing acceleration data from sensor devices that ensure time synchronization. Structural health and damage after an earthquake can be detected by analyzing changes in the natural frequency of the structure and inter-story deformation of the building. A sensor device normally consists of components, such as a CPU that controls measurement, an analog sensor, analog filter, A/D converter, memory, and network interface. In this development, to reduce the risk that noise will enter during measurement, a sensor device was developed with a digital sensor mounted on it instead of an analog sensor. Tables I and II show the specifications of the sensor device and the mounted digital three-axis MEMS acceleration sensor, respectively. The acceleration sensor is a low-noise and low power consumption type, capable of high-resolution vibration measurement. Furthermore, minimal offset drift over temperature, and long-term stability enabling precision applications with minimal calibration are provided.

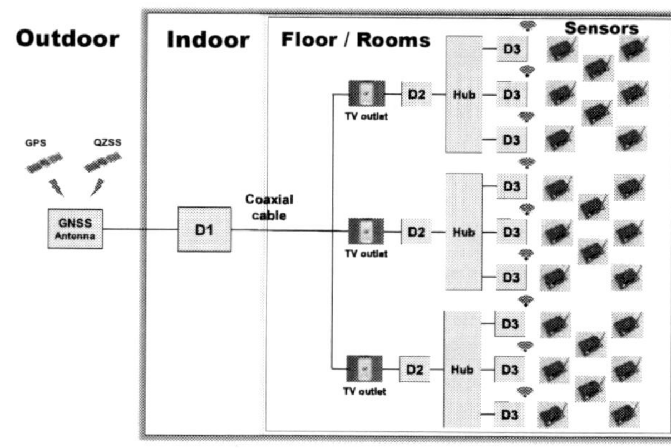

Figure 1. System configuration.

TABLE I. SPECIFICATION OF SENSOR DEVICE

GNSS module	FURUNO/GF-8801
Frequency	1555.983-1610.202 MHz
Center frequency	1597.926 MHz
FGGA/CPU	Zynq2 (CPU Dual-core ARM Cortex-A9)
RAM	SDRAM 512Mbyte
ROM	Serial-FLASH 128Mbyte × 2
Power supply	14 W (Typ.)
Size	102（W）× 172.5（D）× 40（H）
Weight	1.65 kg

TABLE II. SPECIFICATION OF MEMS ACCELERATION SENSOR

Model	ADXL355
Measurement direction	3
Maximum acceleration (± G)	2
Outside dimensions (mm)	6 × 6 × 2.1
Consumption current (μA)	200
Stand-by power consumption (μA)	21
Sensitivity	256,000 LSB/G ± 8%
Noise characteristics	22.5 μG/√Hz
ADC Resolution	20 Bits
Operating temperature Range (°C)	-40 - +125

A crystal oscillator is used for the CPU of the general sensor device. However, when an attempt is made to receive indoor GNSS signals and perform measurement while correcting the time information of the CPU, a delay occurs because the clock accuracy is too high. Therefore, in order to add GNSS signal-based time information directly to data measured by a sensor through hardware, the authors developed a mechanism equipped with a dedicated integrated circuit, a Field-Programmable Gate Array (FPGA), to manufacture a sensor device. Because an FPGA is programmable, it is also possible to embed logic for an operation, such as earthquake detection using measured data, while adding GNSS signal-based time information to measured data.

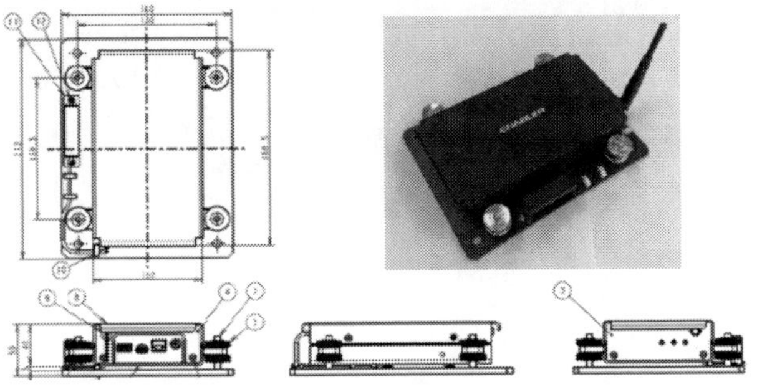

Figure 2. Sensor device.

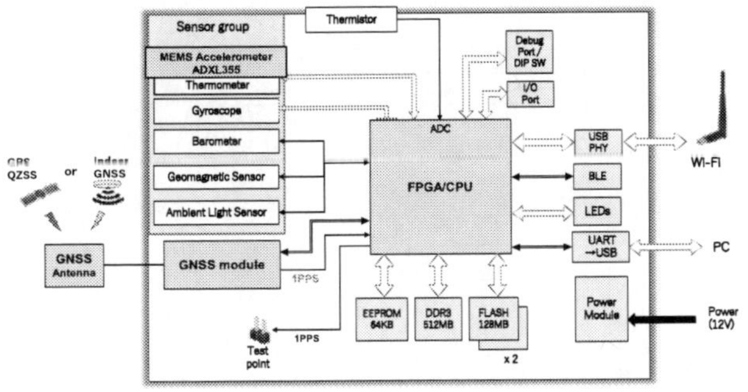

Figure 3. Hardware block diagram.

The sensor device consists of such components as a GNSS receiver, FPGA, CPU, memory, local storage, and network interface. The FPGA controls the sensor's measurement while generating time stamps using GNSS signal-based ultra-high accuracy time information. Measured data is stored in the memory, then sent to the network via Ethernet or wireless communication. Data can be collected using a wired or wireless method. Figures. 2 and 3 show details of the sensor device.

V. PERFORMANCE EVALUATION OF THE SENSOR DEVICE ABLE TO RECEIVE INDOOR GNSS TIME INFORMATION

A shaking table experiment was conducted to evaluate the measurement performance and time synchronization performance of the sensor device developed in Section IV. During the shaking table experiment, measurement was performed with the digital three-axis MEMS acceleration sensor incorporated in each sensor device. Figure 4 gives an overall view of the experiment system. A red circle indicates the indoor GNSS time information delivery system, a yellow circle indicates the sensor device and shaking table, and a blue circle indicates the shaking table control system. As shown in Figure 5, the indoor GNSS time information delivery system consists of D1, D2, and D3. As shown in Section III, D1 receives a signal from the GNSS satellites and frequency-converts the synchronized time signal and sends it into the building. Since the purpose of this experiment was to evaluate the performance of the sensor device, the GNSS satellite was not used, and the time signal was generated by the GNSS simulator and input to D1. D2 receives time signals from D1 and demodulates them into high-accuracy synchronization signals (PPS signals). D3 receives data from D2, adjusts the timing, and sends time information to the sensor device via the antenna in Figure 4. The sensor device receives time information sent from D3 and adds high-accuracy time information to measured data.

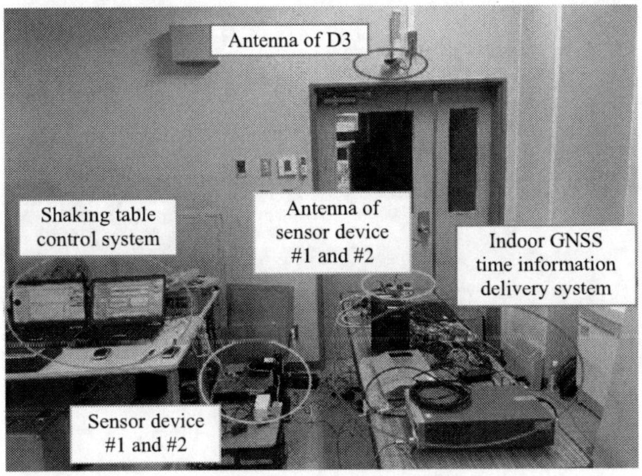

Figure 4. Overall View of Experimental System.

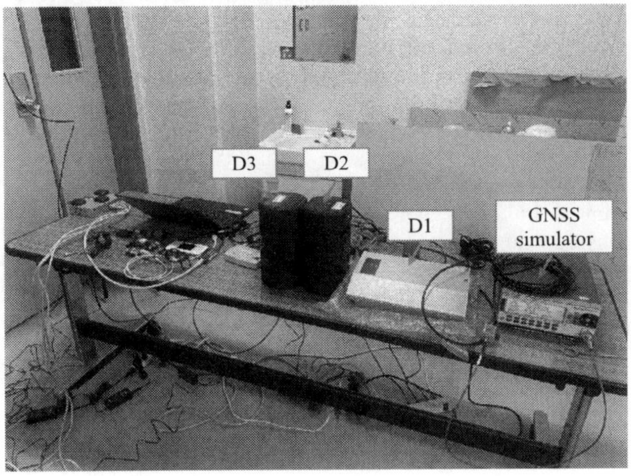

Figure 5. Indoor GNSS Time Information Delivery System.

A. Sweep Input Experiment

As shown in Figure 6, two sensor devices and a servo acceleration sensor for comparison were fixed to the shaking table, and the same vibration was applied to compare the results of measurement. The natural frequencies of houses, small buildings, and skyscrapers range from 0.1Hz to 10Hz. In addition, the dominant frequency of seismic motion has a similar frequency component. Therefore, the frequency band from 0.1 Hz to 10 Hz was used as the test target. Two types of input waves were prepared to vibrate with a large acceleration amplitude in each frequency band. In the experiment, 0.1–2.0 Hz and 2–10 Hz swept sine waves (Figure 7) were set as input waves to vibrate the shaking table. The measurement sampling frequency for each sensor device was set to 100 Hz.

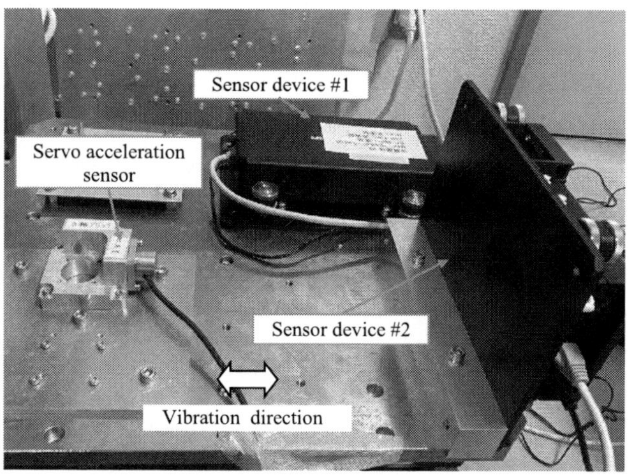

Figure 6. Sensor Device and Shaking Table.

Vibrations were applied to the horizontal direction of sensor device # 1 and the vertical direction of sensor device # 2, and measurements were taken with the sensor device and the servo-type acceleration sensor for comparison. Figure 8 shows the results of Fourier amplitude spectrum ratios calculated for acceleration waveforms measured by the sensor device #1 and the servo acceleration sensor. Compared to the servo acceleration sensor, the amplitude of the sensor device #1 was flat in the 0.1–2.0 Hz and 2–10 Hz bands, showing that the MEMS digital acceleration sensor mounted in the sensor module has good performance in terms of components in the horizontal direction. Figure 9 shows the results of Fourier phase spectrum ratios calculated for the acceleration waveforms of sensor devices #1 and #2 on the shaking table. If there is no phase delay between the sensor devices, and if time synchronization is ensured, the Fourier phase spectrum ratio must be near zero in all vibration frequency bands. In the figure, phase delays within 0.001 seconds are plotted in dotted lines. It can be seen that time synchronization within 0.001 seconds could be realized between the sensor modules.

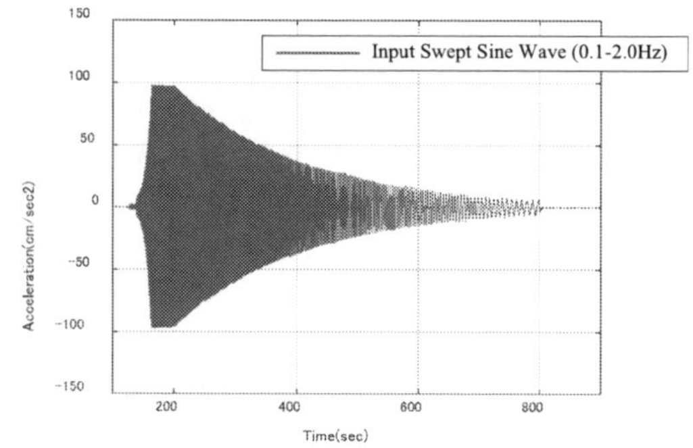

(a) 0.1-2.0 Hz

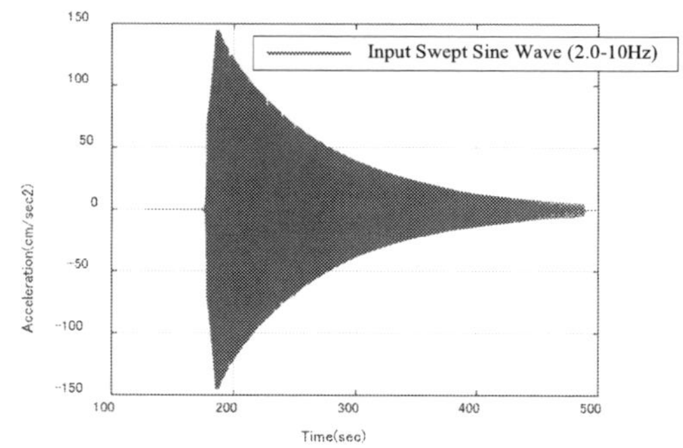

(b) 2.0-10Hz

Figure 7. Input Swept Sine Waves.

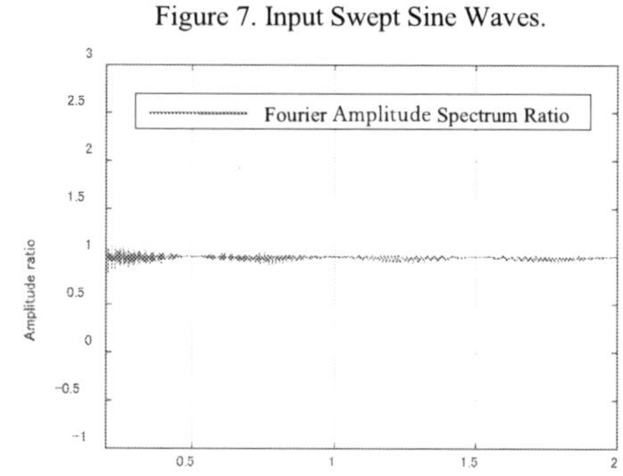

(a) 0.1-2.0 Hz sweep

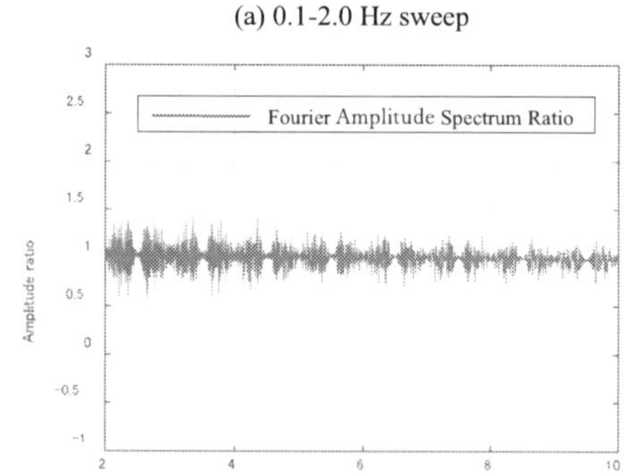

(b) 2.0-10Hz sweep

Figure 8. Fourier Amplitude Spectrum Ratios of Sensor Device #1 Compared to Servo Acceleration Sensor.

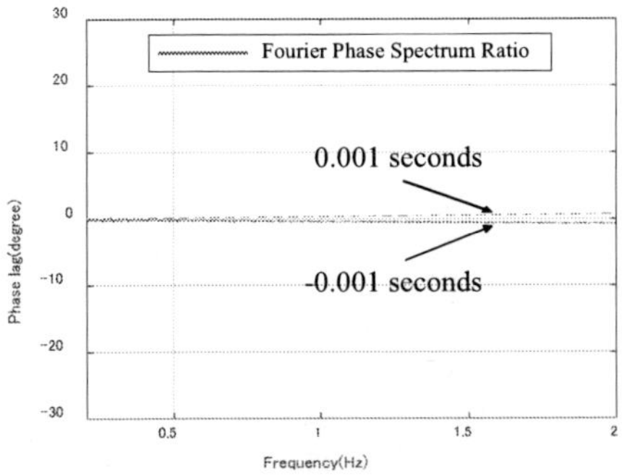

(a) 0.1-2.0 Hz sweep

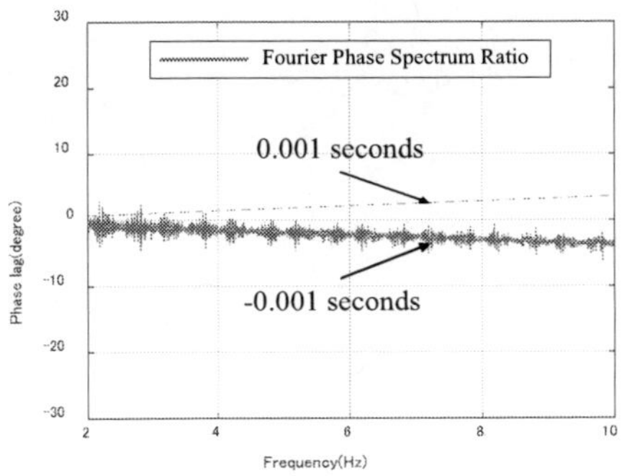

(b) 2.0-10Hz sweep

Figure 9. Fourier Phase Spectrum Ratios of Sensor Device #2 Against Sensor Device #1.

B. *Seismic Wave Input Experiment*

In order to evaluate the measurement performance and time synchronization performance when inputting seismic waves containing random vibration frequency components, the shaking table was operated using seismic records measured at the Kobe Local Meteorological Office during the Great Hanshin Earthquake. Figure 10 shows the measured time-history waveforms of the horizontal sensor device # 1, the vertical sensor device # 2, and the servo accelerometer for comparison.

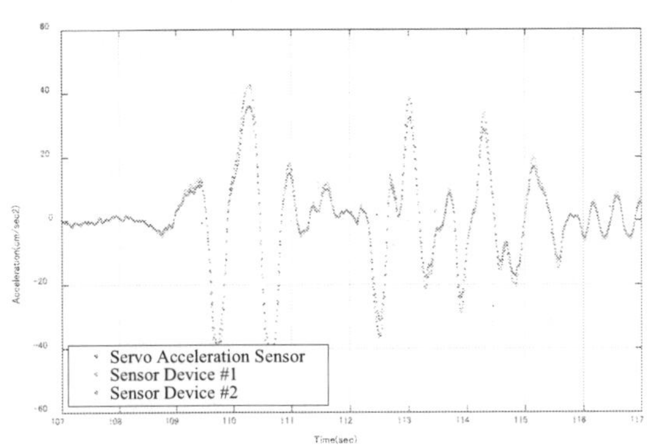

Figure 10. Seismic Wave Input Experiment.

The results in the three cases matched, confirming that the developed sensor device has a good measurement performance, equivalent to that of the servo acceleration sensor, and that time synchronization between two sensor devices was ensured.

VI. CONCLUSION

For the purpose of application to the structural health monitoring of buildings and civil infrastructures, or to earthquake observations, this paper reported a sensor device that adds high-accuracy time information to measured data by using a system to deliver indoor Global Navigation Satellite System (GNSS) time information. A system for delivering GNSS time information indoors was described first. The development of a sensor device with a mechanism for receiving GNSS signal-based time information was then explained in detail. The results of a shaking table experiment conducted to evaluate the basic performance of the sensor device were presented. From the results mentioned above, the measurement performance and time synchronization function of the developed sensor device were verified, to show that it could be applied to such automatic operations as structural health monitoring of buildings and civil infrastructures and earthquake observations. Verification using an actual building is now scheduled to be carried out.

ACKNOWLEDGMENT

This research was partially supported by JSPS KAKENHI Grant Number JP16K01283 and JP19K04963.

REFERENCES

[1] N. Kurata, M. Suzuki, S. Saruwatari, and H. Morikawa, "Actual Application of Ubiquitous Structural Monitoring System using Wireless Sensor Networks" The 14th World Conference on Earthquake Engineering (14WCEE) IAEE, Oct. 2008, pp. 1-8, Paper ID:11-0037.

[2] N. Kurata, M. Suzuki, S. Saruwatari, and H. Morikawa, "Application of Ubiquitous Structural Monitoring System by Wireless Sensor Networks to Actual High-rise Building" The 5th World Conference on Structural Control and Monitoring (5WCSCM) IASCM, July 2010, pp. 1-9, Paper No. 013.

[3] M. Maroti, B. Kusy, G. Simon, and A. Ledeczi, "The Flooding Time Synchronization Protocol" The 2nd International Conference on Embedded Networked Sensor Systems (SenSys '04) ACM, Nov. 2004, pp. 39-49, ISBN:1-58113-879-2.

[4] D. L. Mills, "Internet time synchronization: the network time protocol," IEEE Transactions on Communications, vol. 39, Issue 10, pp. 1482-1493, Oct. 1991, doi:10.1109/26.103043.

[5] B. W. Parkinson, and J. J. Spilker Jr. eds, Global Positioning System: Theory and Applications, Vol. I & II. American Institute of Aeronautics and Astronautics (AIAA), 1996, ISBN: 978-1-56347-106-3.

[6] S. Knappe, et al., "A microfabricated atomic clock," Applied Physics Letters, vol. 85, Issue 9, pp. 1460-1462, August 2004, doi:10.1063/1.1787942.

[7] Q. Li, and D. Rus, "Global Clock Synchronization in Sensor Networks," IEEE Transactions on Computers, vol. 55, Issue 2, pp. 214-226, Jan. 2006, ISSN: 0018-9340.

[8] R. Lutwak, et al., "The Chip-Scale Atomic Clock - Prototype Evaluation" The 39th Annual Precise Time and Time Interval (PTTI) Meeting ION, Nov. 2007, pp. 269-290, ISSN: 2333-2069.

[9] N. Kurata, "Disaster Big Data Infrastructure using Sensing Technology with a Chip Scale Atomic Clock" World Engineering Conference and Convention (WECC2015) WFEO, Dec. 2015, pp. 1-5.

[10] N. Kurata, "Basic Study of Autonomous Time Synchronization Sensing Technology Using Chip Scale Atomic Clock" The 16th International Conference on Computing in Civil and Building Engineering (ICCCBE2016) ISCCBE, July 2016, pp. 67-74.

[11] N. Kurata, "An Autonomous Time Synchronization Sensor Device Using a Chip Scale Atomic Clock for Earthquake Observation and Structural Health Monitoring" The Eighth International Conference on Sensor Device Technologies and Applications (SENSORDEVICES 2017) IARIA, Sept. 2017, pp.31-36, ISSN: 2308-3514, ISBN: 978-1-61208-581-4.

[12] N. Kurata, "Improvement and Application of Sensor Device Capable of Autonomously Keeping Accurate Time Information for Buildings and Civil Infrastructures" The Ninth International Conference on Sensor Device Technologies and Applications (SENSORDEVICES 2018) IARIA, Sept. 2018, pp. 114-120, ISSN: 2308-3514, ISBN: 978-1-61208-660-6.

[13] J. Elson, L. Girod, and D. Estrin, "Fine-Grained Network Time Synchronization using Reference Broadcasts" The 5th Symposium on Operating Systems Design and Implementation (OSDI'02) ACM, Dec. 2002, pp. 147-163.

[14] S. Ganeriwal, R. Kumar, and M. B. Srivastava, "Timing-sync Protocol for Sensor Networks" The 1st international conference on Embedded networked sensor systems (SenSys '03) ACM, Nov. 2003, pp. 138-149.

[15] K. Romer, "Time Synchronization in Ad Hoc Networks" The 2nd ACM International Symp. on Mobile Ad Hoc Networking & Computing (MobiHoc'01) ACM, Oct. 2001, pp. 173-182.

Comparison Between Electrical Impedance and Optical Spectroscopy for a Field Soil Analysis

Olga Chambers
Faculty of Electrical Engineering, Trzaska 25,
Ljubljana 1000, Slovenia
email: olga.chambers@fe.uni-lj.si

Janez Trontelj ml.
Faculty of Electrical Engineering, Trzaska 25,
Ljubljana 1000, Slovenia
email: janez.trontelj2@guest.arnes.si

***Abstract*— In this paper, we performed a comparative analysis of the electrical impedance and optical methods performance for a field soil characterization. The study was optimized by reducing the texture variation and the influence of the unknown soil elements that are not in the focus of this research. The research dataset was created using pure soil from two agriculture farms and fertilized with fertilizers selected by farmers. The impedance spectrometer developed in our laboratory was used to perform the impedance measurements between 30 kHz and 14 MHz showing promising results. Optical measurements were performed within the ultraviolet-visible-near infrared (UV-VIS-NIR) range. The obtained results indicate that it is possible to perform low-cost soil analysis with high accuracy for a field fertilization analysis.**

Keywords- fertilizer analysis; soil analysis; impedance sensor; spectral analyser.

I. INTRODUCTION

The development of the fast and accurate soil characterizing sensors has been recognized as a crucial problem in nowadays agriculture. Several strategies with different degrees of success have been proposed to predict soil properties in a field [1][2]. Literature indicates a different degree of the accuracy for sensors that usually depends on the soil properties variation and sensor specifications [3]. Soil texture variation is the most common problem for agriculture sensors, leading to large datasets with an expensive chemical analysis that significantly increases the research cost [4]. Thus, the commercial AgroCares scanner is based on the reflectance spectroscopy and uses a large dataset to provide only brief information about soil nutrients, i.e., low, medium, and high. Therefore, a compromise between strategy and price must be found concerning the measuring time and accuracy. The most advanced technologies in agriculture use multi-sensor systems that include expensive ion-selective sensors [5]. This sensors type has high cost and requires a chemical solution that is not suitable for real-time measurement in a field. Alternative sensors, such as optical reflectometry and impedance spectroscopy, have relatively low cost and do not require chemical support. Unlikely, they are sensitive to soil moisture level, microelements variation, ambient temperature, humidity, etc. Optical reflectometry is the most common method mentioned in the literature that operates on the whole Ultraviolet-Visible-Near Infrared (UV-VIS-NIR) range.

Nevertheless, some researchers indicate the unstable performance of this method. Luleva et al. [6] showed the influence of the soil texture on the position of the potassium absorption centre. They also reported that samples with high clay content results in a smaller change in absorption. The electrical impedance method is less accurate for soil nutrients detection and is commonly used for soil moisture analysis or quantitative analysis when other components are neglected [7]. Pandey et al. [8] reported their results for soil-nitrates detection in a real-time application indicating the impedance method great potential for in-suite measurements.

Our research aims to integrate a low-cost solution suitable for real-time field applications with high accuracy. Therefore, the comparison between impedance and optical methods performance was studied. To minimize the influence of the texture and unknown microelements (that are not in the focus of this research), the fertilized soil's characterization was performed using soil from a field. The fertilized soil samples with different nutrition levels were achieved using only fertilizers defined by farmers. Following the literature recommendations, soil samples were prepared in the laboratory and measured using electrical impedance and optical methods. Finally, the classification-based validation approach for soil collected in two entirely different locations in Slovenia was performed to compare the methods' effectiveness. Due to the non-uniform soil properties, it is common to perform a set of measurements in different locations to reduce variability. Therefore, the final validation accuracy was achieved based on a set of repetitive measurements for each soil sample.

Section II describes research datasets, set-ups for electrical impedance and optical measurements, method for soil properties prediction using classification-based approach. Electrical impedance measurement was performed using laboratory designed soil spectrometer. This spectrometer is small and easy to use. Its impedance Application Specific Integrated Circuit (ASIC) was implemented by using the CMOS process. A programmed microprocessor enables the communication between ASIC and personal computer. Finally, results of the soil properties prediction are shown and discussed in Section III.

II. Materials and Methods

This section describes the research dataset and instruments used for soil measurements. All measurements were performed in the laboratory under controlled conditions. To eliminate the impact of external factors, the ambient temperature near 22℃ and relative humidity under 40% are kept constant.

A. Dataset

The research datasets, i.e., Dataset A and Dataset B, consist of soil samples collected from two different agriculture farms in Slovenia. The pure soil samples are collected from a 0-30 cm top-soil surface. Each sample is air-dried for one month, grounded, and then sieved through a 2-mm sieve to provide a dry base for experiments. Following recommendations in literature and farmers requirements, a simple system for nutrient-level classification and coding shown in Table I is created and used for model parameters learning. Using this system and chemical characteristics, codes for each soil sample were obtained with respect to the amount of phosphorus, potassium, and magnesium (see last columns in Tables II and III).

TABLE I. A simplified system for soil nutrients level Coding.

Score, mg/100g	Grade
0 - 10	0
11 - 20	1
21 - 30	2
31 - 40	3
> 40	4

The commonly used agricultural fertilizers selected by farmers were used to prepare samples with a different nutrition levels. Each fertilizer was diluted in a deionized (DI) water and then mixed with an air-dried soil in various concentrations. Tables II and III provide information about soil chemical characteristics performed by a certified laboratory at the Agriculture Institute of Slovenia [9]. The chemical analysis results shown in tables indicate an entirely different fertilizer impact on the soil chemical properties, with an observable correlation between the added fertilizer concentration and nutrient change. Thus, a medium level of a nutrient in the soil corresponds to roughly 0.05% of fertilizer. A 0.1% concentration of fertilizer leads to a high level of a nutrient that is also confirmed in literature [10].

TABLE II. Chemical characterization of the soil samples from Dataset A.

Soil ID	Added fertiliser	P, mg/100g	K, mg/100g	M, mg/100g	Code
1	none	3.9	6.4	23	002
2	0.05% F1	14	6.4	24	102
3	0.05%P+0.05% F2	16	15	25	112
4	0.1%K	4.2	44	23	042
5	0.1% F1+0.1% F2	39	47	23	342
6	0.05% F3	7.8	14	22	012
7	0.1% F3	12	17	22	112

F1: Triple super phosphate (P2O5 -46%); F2: potassium sulphate (K2O - 50%); F3: Potassium phosphate (14% P2O5, 28%K2O, 2%MgO).

TABLE III. Chemical characterization of the soil samples from Dataset B.

Soil ID	Added fertiliser	P, mg/100g	K, mg/100g	M, mg/100g	Code
1	0.05%F1	18	13	25	112
2	0.05%F2	10	20	25	012
3	0.05%F3	11	15	29	112
4	0.05%(F1+F2+F3+F4)	23	23	30	222
5	0.1%F1	23	16	25	212
6	0.1%F3	11	16	34	113
7	0.1%F5	11	14	24	113
8	none	10	17	23	012

F1: calcium phosphate (P2O5 -26%, CaO - 40%); F2: potassium sulphate (K2O - 50%); F3: magnesium sulphate (MgO - 25%, SO3 - 50%); F4: potassium sulphate (K2O - 60%); F5: organic mass minimum 70%.

B. Soil electrical impedance measurement set-up

This paragraph describes the laboratory set-up for the measurement of soil samples. Measurements were carried out from the moist soil. Therefore, the dry soil samples were mixed with the predefined amount of the DI water (i.e., 60% of the dry soil sample base) to obtain soil samples with the same moisture level. The obtained soil samples were then placed in a 3D-printed holder with approximate dimensions of 20 x 10 x 10 mm (Figure 1). The soil holder was designed to hold small soil moisture samples of approximately 5 g.

The workspace set-up for impedance measurement is shown in Figure 1 that includes an impedance spectrometer interfaced with the personal computer (PC) for data processing and storage. The measuring process was controlled using a graphical user interface developed in Matlab software [11].

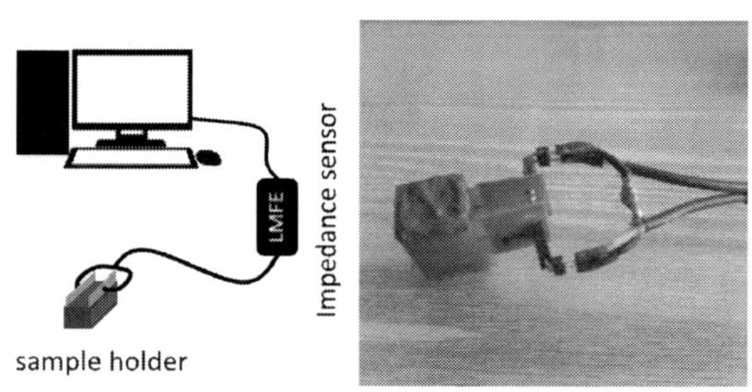

Figure 1. Photography of the set-up for electrical impedance measurement and sample holder with soil. (a) set-up workspace for measurement; (b) sample holder with the soil.

The impedance spectrometer's architecture is split into three main sections: analog, processing, and sensor. The Analog section measures soil electrical impedance. The spectrometer generates AC current with user-set frequency and sends it in the soil through sensor electrodes. The resulting imaginary and real components of the impedance are then digitized and send to the PC via the universal serial bus (USB).

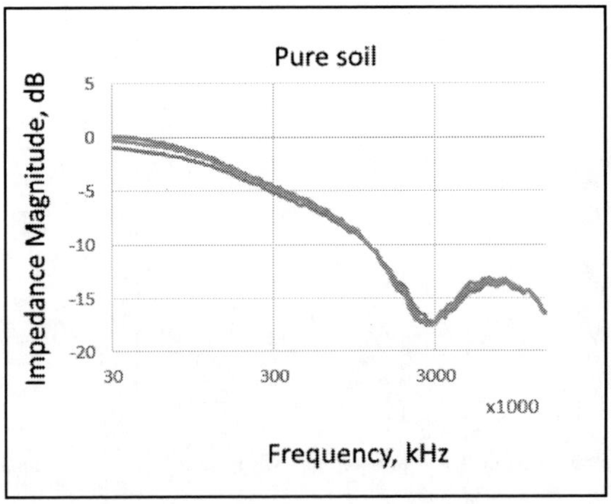

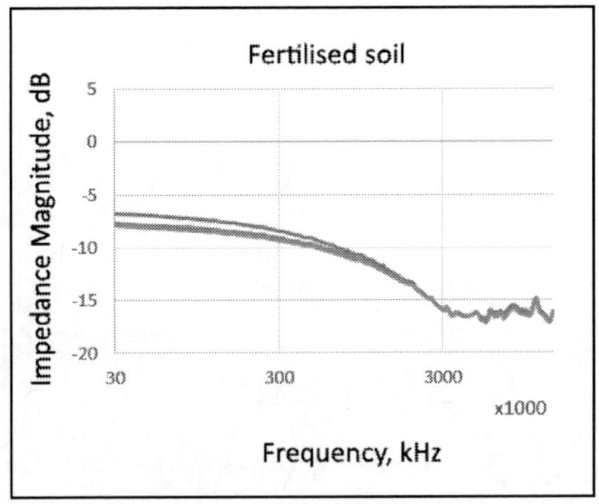

Figure 2. Impedance magnitudes of three pure soil sub-samples and three fertilized soil sub-samples respectively.

Spectroscopy measures resultant voltages when a constant current is applied at different frequencies. The 122 frequencies selected between 30 kHz and 14 MHz enable a good fit of the whole frequency domain's impedance signal. Figure 2 shows impedance magnitudes plots corresponding to three sub-samples of the pure soil and impedance magnitudes plots corresponding to three sub-samples of the fertilized soil over the selected frequency range. As expected, measurements of sub-samples collected from the same soil are very similar. A small deviation can be explained by non-ideal manual sample preparation that can be improved by an automatic sample preparation. As the frequency increased, the impedance of the samples dropped obviously. It can also be noted that the lower fertilizer content is associated with higher impedance amplitude. Our earlier research indicates that soil solutions' primary information can be achieved from impedance magnitudes alone [12] that is also observed for soil characterization in our study. Therefore, the only impedance magnitudes are used in the following analysis.

C. *Soil optical measurement set-up*

This paragraph describes the set-up for the light reflectance measurement. A deuterium-halogen light box was used as the light source. The light reflectance from the sample was measured by placing 5 g of air-dried sieved sample into a quartz glass petri dish three mm-diameter, as shown in Figure 3. The set-up includes a fiber-coupled spectrometer FCR-7UV200-2-ME from Avantes that is fixed perpendicularly to have a 3 cm distance between the probe and samples. The light from a light source is sent through six illumination fibers to the sample, and the reflection is measured by a seventh fiber in the center of the reflection probe tip. The AvaSpec-ULS2048CL-EVO-RS and AvaSpec-HSC-TEC perform the light measurement in the ultraviolet, visible, and near-infrared regions of the electromagnetic spectrum, i.e., 200-2500 nm. Spectra normalization was performed by dividing soil reflectance spectra by the white body reflectance spectra used here as a reference.

Soil spectral measurements were collected from seven randomly selected points for each air-dry sample. Figure 4 shows seven plots corresponding pure soil in the UV-VIS range and NIR range, separately. It can be seen that the UV range between 200 to 400 nm is less informative than the VIS range and does not provide any characteristic variations that can be seen visually. The normalized signal in the VIS range appears with a bias having shape variation and peaks appearance that can be characteristic for different soil properties. The obtained plots indicate good repetitiveness of the measurements corresponding to the same soil. The small variation between measurements can be explained by a non-uniform soil surface resulting in a reflectance angle variation.

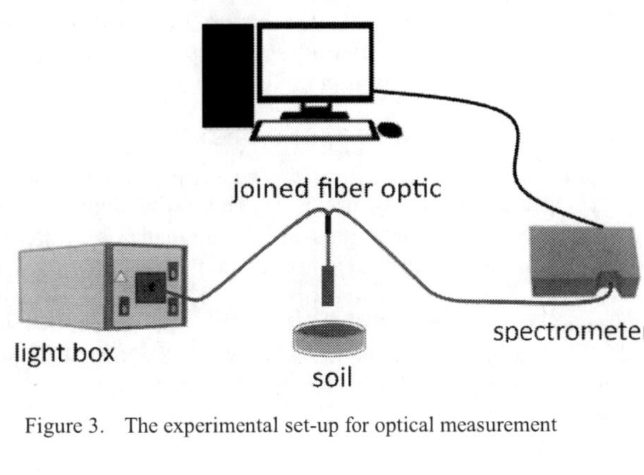

Figure 3. The experimental set-up for optical measurement

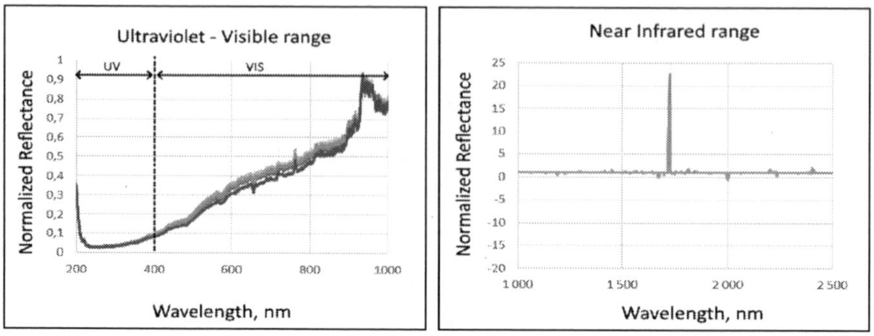

Figure 4. Normalized spectra plots obtained for pure soil in the UV-VIS range and NIR range.

D. *Soil properties prediction*

The principle of the soil's properties prediction is based on identifying the measurement from the research dataset. This measurement has shape variation as close as possible to the shape variation of the test measurement belonging soil, which characteristics need to be predicted. Then, chemical characteristics of the identified measurement are used to indicate the properties of the soil. The leave-one-out principle [13] is applied to validate the classification accuracy, where each sample is excluded from the dataset and used as a testing set. The rest of the samples are then joined in a training set.

The classification procedure consists of feature extraction and machine learning. Several feature extraction methods, such as' regionprops', moment invariants, etc., are proposed in the literature. However, each particular task requires a complex analysis to estimate the optimal features enabling the best classification of high-dimensional data. Thus, classification based on a principal component analysis (PCA) [14] is used in this research allowing the most optimal performance, where fixed threshold Th=0.2 was applied on the feature weights to reduce irrelevant features (Figure 5). The PCA maximizes the expected classification accuracy reducing feature vector. The decision tree procedure was used for machine learning to estimate parameters characterizing the training set [15].

III. RESULTS AND DISCUSSIONS

This section demonstrates the effectiveness of the electrical impedance and optical methods for identifying the soil samples in research dataset A and research Dataset B using a classification-based approach. Measurements were performed using set-ups described in Section II for electrical impedance and optical methods. Thus, 21 feature vectors corresponding to 7 soils from Dataset A and 24 feature vectors corresponding to 8 soils from Dataset B were obtained during electrical impedance measurement. During optical measurement, 49 feature vectors corresponding to 7 soils from Dataset A and 56 feature vectors corresponding to 8 soils from Dataset B were obtained. Tables IV and V show the results of the leave-one-out classification for research datasets with entirely different characteristics. Classification results from the corresponding optical method are shown separately for the UV-VIS range and NIR range to investigate their effectiveness for the soil properties prediction. As can be noted, the optical approach enables more accurate sample identification when the electrical impedance is less accurate. The incorrect identification of the soil samples with different amounts of the phosphorus can be observed. This can be explained by a small difference between measurements corresponding to pure soil and soil with added potassium fertilizer. In this research, it was observed that the impedance response of the phosphorus fertilizer is the smallest compared to other fertilizers under analysis. The NIR range showed results that are also less accurate than the VIS range. Therefore, it is possible to provide a characterization using only the VIS range.

Figure 5 shows the weights of the dataset values for different methods. The essential features for classification using the UV-VIS range are concentrated near the NIR range. Features corresponding electrical impedance magnitudes can also be easily observed and detected near the domain end. Therefore, using feature selection procedure it is possible to significantly reduce frequencies and wavelengths required for accurate analysis. The fixed threshold in our analysis was selected based on the visual inspection and enabled good delineation between informative and uninformative features. Nevertheless, for different set-up it is possible to detect threshold invisibly based on the statistical analysis of the all feature weight. For this purpose, the automatic Otsu method can be used [16].

TABLE IV. CLASSIFICATION RESULTS FOR DATASET A.

method of data capturing	P, mg/100g	K, mg/100g	M, mg/100g
El. impedance measurements	77%	71%	100%
UV-VIS range measurements	90%	84%	100%
NIR range measurements	90%	81%	100%

TABLE V. CLASSIFICATION RESULTS FOR DATASET B.

method of data capturing	P, mg/100g	K, mg/100g	M, mg/100g	
El. impedance measurements		75%	96%	100%
UV-VIS range measurements		80%	91%	93%
NIR range measurements		75%	92%	88%

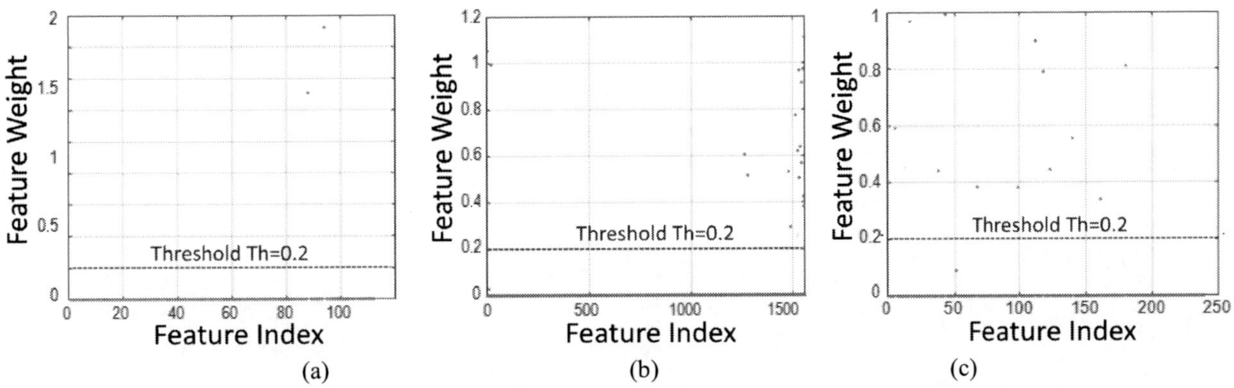

Figure 5. Feature weights corresponding (a) frequency domain, (b) UV-VIS range, and (c) NIR range

The classification results obtained for soils located in entirely different Slovenia locations indicate the potential of the sensors for a real-time field fertilization analysis. The difference between classification accuracy obtained for Dataset A and Dataset B can be explained by the fertilizer difference used in the analysis. Thus, a different chemical solution may have different influence on the measurements when performing measuring.

Due to the obtained results, it can be concluded that there is possible to obtain the low-cost sensor for soil fertilisation characterisation. Feature selection procedure significantly reduced the wavelength range and frequencies in our analysis without classification accuracy lost. Thus, the final price of the sensor would be also reduced.

All measurements were carried out under controlled laboratory conditions in order to perform accurate methods performance comparison. This is a critical step when selecting sensor for implementation. The atmospheric factors, such as rain and wind, has obviously significant influence on the methods that will be discovered in a future work.

IV. CONCLUSION

The results obtained in this research indicate the potential of both electrical impedance and optical method for accurate soil analysis and nutrients identification alone when performing characterization within a field. Due to the high sensitivity of the electrical impedance measurements to the various factors, such as texture, temperature, etc., it is critical to minimize their influence on the classification procedure. The feature extraction using principal component analysis enables detecting the most informative frequencies and wavelengths for a low-cost real-time sensor implementation. Only the VIS range for optical spectroscopy is required. The electrical impedance method in this research performs better for magnesium identification and less accurate for phosphorus due to the different impacts of the fertilizer on the measurements.

REFERENCES

[1] A. Bah, S. Balasundram, and M.H.A. Husni, "Sensor Technologies for Precision Soil Nutrient Management and Monitoring", American Journal of Agricultural and Biological Science, vol. 7, pp. 43-49, 2012.

[2] G. Pajares, "Advances in sensors applied to agriculture and forestry", vol. 11, pp. 8930–8932, December 2011.

[3] V. I. Adamchuk, J. W. Hummel, and M. T. Morgan, S. K. Upadhyaya, "On-the-go Soil Sensors for Precision Agriculture.", Computers and electronics in agriculture, vol. 44, issue 1, pp. 71-91, July 2004.

[4] A. K. Rêgo Segundo et al., "A Novel Low-Cost Instrumentation System for Measuring the Water Content and Apparent Electrical Conductivity of Soils", Sensors, vol. 15, Issue 10, pp. 25546-25563, October 2015.

[5] W. S. Lee et al., "Sensing technologies for precision specialty crop production", Computers and Electronics in Agriculture, vol. 74, issue 1, pp. 2–33, 2010.

[6] M. I. Luleva, H. van der Werff, V. Jetten, and F. van der Meer, "Can infrared spectroscopy be used to measure change in potassium nitrate concentration as a proxy for soil particle movement?", Sensors (Basel), vol. 4, issue 4, pp. 4188-4206, 2011.

[7] U. Lazuardi and S. Rahmondia, "Low Cost Soil Sensor Based on Impedance Spectroscopy for In-Situ Measurement", AIP Conference Proceedings, American Institute of Physics, April 2015, vol. 1656, issue 1, pp. 040005(1-9), ISBN: 978-0-7354-1298-9.

[8] G. Pandey, R. Kumar, and R. J. Weber, "Real Time Detection of Soil Moisture and Nitrates Using On-Board In-Situ Impedance Spectroscopy", 2013 IEEE International Conference on Systems, Man, and Cybernetics, Manchester, 2013, pp. 1081-1086, 2013, doi: 10.1063/1.4917112.

[9] Agriculture Institute of Slovenia. [retrieved: October, 2020] Available online from: http://arhiv.kis.si/pls/kis/!kis.web?j=EN

[10] M. Sirsat, E. Cernadas, M. Fernandez-Delgado, and R. Khan, "Classification of agricultural soil parameters in India", Computers and Electronics in Agriculture, vol. 135, pp. 269 – 279, 2017.

[11] The Mathworks, Inc., Natick, Massachusetts. MATLAB version 8.5.0.197613 (R2015a), 2015.

[12] O. Chambers, A. Sešek, R. Ražman, J. F. Tasič, and J. Trontelj, "Fertiliser characterisation using optical and electrical impedance methods", Computers and Electronics in Agriculture, vol. 155, pp. 69-75, 2018.

[13] K. Anbumani and R. Nedunchezhian. Soft Computing Applications for Database Technologies:

Techniques and Issues. Hershey, PA: IGI Global, 2010. http://doi:10.4018/978-1-60566-814-7.

[14] Yang, W., K. Wang, and W. Zuo. "Neighborhood Component Feature Selection for High-Dimensional Data", Journal of Computers, vol. 7, issue 1, pp. 161-168, January, 2012.

[15] W. Y. Loh, "Regression Trees with Unbiased Variable Selection and Interaction Detection", Statistica Sinica, vol. 12, pp. 361–386, 2002.

[16] Nobuyuki Otsu. "A threshold selection method from gray-level histograms". IEEE Trans. Sys. Man. Cyber. Vol 9, issue 1, pp. 62–66, 1979.

Monitoring Outdoor Air Quality Using Personal Device to Protect Vulnerable People

Luca Rampini, Fulvio Re Cecconi
Department of Architecture, Built Environment and Construction Engineering
Politecnico di Milano
Milan, Italy
e-mail: {luca.rampini, fulvio.rececconi}@polimi.it

Abstract—**World Health Organization considered air pollution the most dangerous threat to human health. This paper presents a novel system to mitigate risks derived from polluted air by introducing a portable device for vulnerable people able to detect hazardous pollution concentration and to suggest healthy behaviors. Along with the device, a tailored web server application, called Monitoring Outdoor Quality of Air (MOQA), is developed. The application will make the data collected from the device's sensors more readable and will provide citizens with air quality information. That information will alert vulnerable people about air pollution hazards and let them take actions consequently. This system can reduce the health risks derived from air pollution for the weakest population in the short-term.**

Keywords-Outdoor Air Quality; Pollution Sensor; CO_2 Sensor; Machine Learning; Sensor reliability.

I. Introduction

SLow Onset Disasters (SLODs) are continuous, low intensity, and high frequency events that represent a serious risk for the health of people [1][2]. Among SLODs, the World Health Organization (WHO) declared air pollution as the biggest environmental threat [3]. Hence, developing a system that helps the whole community to mitigate the risks arising from polluted air would be of great benefit to everyone.

Air pollution is caused by a range of factors including transportation, agriculture, waste, anthropogenic activities (e.g., respiration), construction, and building operations. Indeed, 39% of global energy-related carbon emissions are related to the building sector [4]. Within this context, Built Environment scenarios, that have low capacity to deal with heat absorption and rejection are more prone to expose their hosts (people) to SLODs.

Moreover, the impact of air pollution on people is well documented, revealing that some demographic categories might be more disadvantaged than others. This vulnerable population comprehends toddlers [5], elders [6], and those suffering from respiratory issues (e.g., allergies, asthma) or cardiovascular problems [7]. Considering that 1) the arousal frequency of SLODs' evidence is larger in urbanized context [8], 2) more than half of the world's population lives in urban areas [9], handling strategies should be a priority.

The effects of interactions between humans and their Built Environment (BE) have been studied for a long time [10]-[12]. At the same time, it is well documented the influence of BE in affecting the intensity of SLODs [13]-[16]. Consequently, this trine relationship among people, BE and SLOD, represents a complex mechanism to depict.

In Europe, researchers have been studied the progression of SLODs, identifying where these disasters are more prone to take place or to have a larger effect. For instance, the work in [3] reported Italy as one of the most critical areas of Central Europe, where the worst conditions have been shown for the municipality of Milan. Therefore, this territory represents a useful case study to test procedures that might reduce air pollution effects.

Currently, air pollution can be noted and predicted but is harder to mitigate. This study aims to reduce risks derived from polluted air, by introducing a system that might help to protect vulnerable people. Exploiting the novel field of Citizen Science [17], in which ordinary people contribute information for scientific research, a wearable device has been made. The device can measure data about CO_2, Particulate Matter (PM), and Total Volatile Organic Compounds (TVOCs), and send them to a tailored web server application, called Monitoring Outdoor Quality of Air (MOQA). Looking to the application, vulnerable people might understand when the quality conditions of the air are dangerous for their health and consequently, take precautions. In a short-term period, the actions taken by alerted people can mitigate the risks deriving from the most extreme dangers, reducing the incidence of pollution on the weaker population [18].

This study is unique in the following ways: i) to the best of our knowledge, this is the first research that comprehends the introduction of tailored software and a personal portable device that can retrieve air quality data; ii) the involvement of others citizen to collect air quality measurements, exploiting the principles of Citizen Science; iii) the implementation of an alert system to increase the safety of vulnerable people by mitigating the risks derived from air pollutants concentration event.

The rest of this paper is organized as follows: Section II presents the background of this research. In Section III are reported methods and tools, that comprehend hardware and software description. Those instruments will be deployed in a case study described in Section IV. Finally, the conclusion and future works are discussed in Section V.

II. Background

Typically, air quality is monitored by stationary monitors, able to measure pollutants as well as temperature and relative humidity. However, these monitoring stations are difficult to operate, bulky, and expensive. Each instrument can cost from about 6000 euros to tens of thousands euros [19], in addition to a relevant amount of resources to be dedicated to maintenance. Moreover, those monitors are sparsely distributed in specific locations, therefore, they might represent pollutant levels, that vary a lot spatially and temporally [20], only in limited areas near the stations. Hence, recently, there has been an emerging trend of using low-cost, portable sensors to provide air quality data as an alternative monitoring option. Indeed, compared to the more expensive air monitors, the introduced personal sensors had an overall cost of less than one hundred euros. Those sensors are easy to deploy, operate, and maintain, thus present significant characteristic to be used at multiple locations [21].

However, low-cost sensors generate data with lower precision and accuracy than those registered by monitors [22], thus several studies develop calibration models deploying Machine Learning (ML) techniques to improve the performance of the low-cost sensors. For instance, Alhasa et al., used a Multi-Layer Perceptron (MLP) to calibrate three EC AlphaSense sensors, obtaining an r score in the range of 0.89 to 0.92 [23]. Among different ML algorithms, Neural Networks (NNs) and ensemble methods (e.g., XGBoost) produce the best results, with the former performing generally slightly better than the latter, albeit requires greater efforts in tuning the hyperparameters [24].

III. Methods and Tools

The method adopted in this study is represented in Figure 1, reporting the Research Schema. The first step involves volunteer who collects data as a part of a scientific inquiry, adopting the principles of Citizen Science. This information is useful to depict the effects given by the interactions between humans and the built environment, which can influence SLODs trend. The measurements are collected exploiting the usability of the mobile software application and low-cost sensors devices. The portable device, unlike the stationary monitors, could provide representative data for a whole urban area, helping to form a clearer picture of pollution field trends.

To facilitate involved citizens' work, a tailored mobile software application is introduced to retrieve and store the data measured by the portable device. To calibrate and validate those data, a measurement campaign was carried out near the air quality monitor sensors situated in Città Studi. The data gathered with this system are then compared with those collected by the ARPA (Agenzia Regionale per la Protezione Ambientale) station.

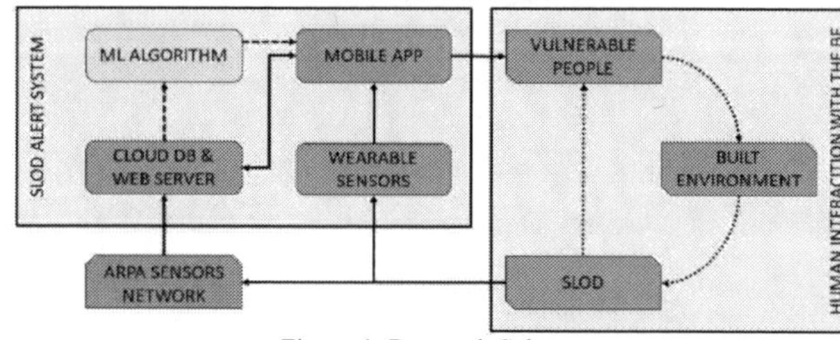

Figure 1. Research Schema.

The calibration is carried out by an Artificial Neural Network (ANN) that takes the data from low-cost sensors as input and transform them into corrected measurements using ARPA dataset.

The ANN has allowed increasing the precision of the device's measurements, reducing the difference with the pollutant level measured by the station. Once the model is trained, citizens can measure air pollution in different areas using the data corrected by the ANN and, in case of a dangerous situation, modify their behavior (e.g., bring their inhaler or decide to remain at home). Finally, in the next sub-sections are described the hardware components used to build the portable device, the developed software application, and the data taken from the regional open data repository.

A. Hardware

To accomplish the objectives of the Research Schema, this study introduced a portable device able to measure pollutant levels in the air as well as atmospheric information such as temperature and relative humidity. The main board of the device is an Arduino, whereas the following sensors measure information about air quality:

- 1 SparkFun Environmental Combo Breakout - CCS811/BME280 - SEN-14348: this sensor measures Temperature, Relative Humidity (RH), Atmospheric pressure as well as pollutants' amount such as equivalent CO_2 (eCO_2) and Total Volatile Organic Compound (TVOC). The eCO_2 output range is from 400 to 8192 ppm, whereas the TVOC output range is from 0 to 1187 ppb.
- 1 PM sensor SDS011: this sensor detects PM in the air. The PM output range is from 0 to 999 $\mu g/m^3$ and the humidity working range of the sensor is 0-70%.

The core part of the wearable device is shown in Figure 2.

Figure 2. Core sensors of the portable device.

The device makes a measurement every 90 seconds and sends it to the web application via wi-fi.

B. Software

To collect, store, and visualize data measured by the device, this research has introduced a new cross-platform application called Monitoring Outdoor Quality of Air (MOQA).

To fetch data and send them to the server, the users should be registered via email and password. The database used is a Relational DataBase Management System (DBMS), which guaranteed the fundamental properties for a database of this type: i) atomicity, ii) consistency, iii) isolation and, iv) durability. The entity-relationship diagram (Figure 3) shows the main sources of the application.

To encourage widespread adoption of the app, a Graphical User Interface (GUI) has been developed and the features of the application are divided by screens as follows:

- Authentication: the user log-in the application by his/her email and password;
- Arduino: the user has a quick view of the last data retrieved by the wearable device. Besides, it is also possible to send and store the data to the remote server;
- Map (Figure 4): this screen displays the data coming from the Arduino board (blue circles) and ARPA dataset (red circles) on a map. The radius of a circle depends on the value of the data associated;
- Chart: the user can see the data coming from the Arduino board and ARPA dataset on a line plot. Moreover, a table with a computation of the quartile deviation is provided;
- Filter (Figure 5): The user could pick the measure to visualize. Once the category is selected, the user can choose the time range and whether to show the ARPA data corresponding to a defined station;
- Settings: the user can change his/her personal information, as well as edit the IP address and port where Arduino is available.

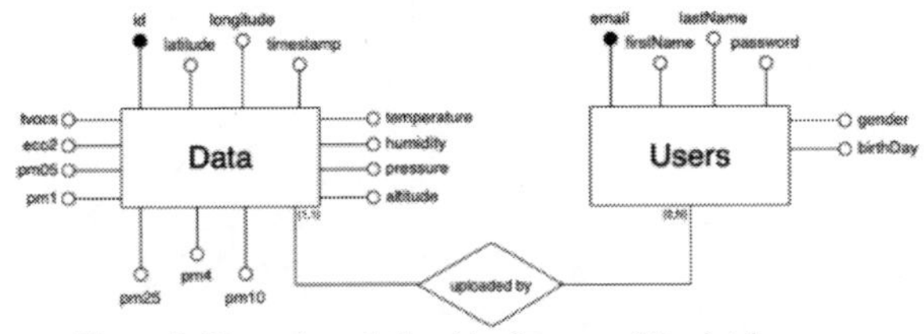

Figure 3. The entity-relationship diagram of the database.

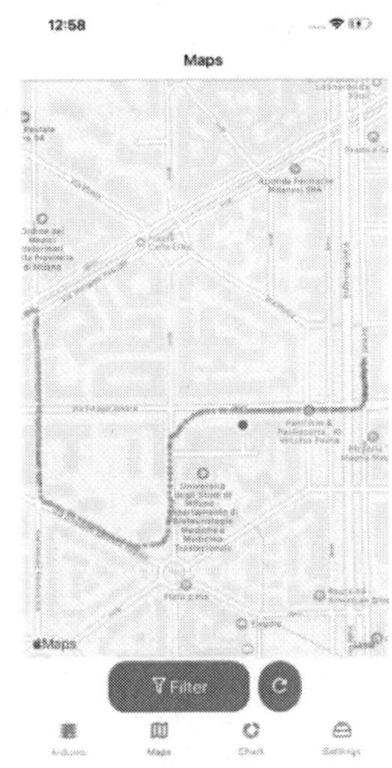

Figure 4. MOQA map screen.

In Figure 6, it is shown the use case diagram, taken from the documentation available on the GitHub repository of the MOQA application [25], that shows the flow of operations triggered by an actor, which could be the user or the system that wants to perform a task. Inside the diagram, the actions colored in light blue are performed by the application whereas the green one represents the data source.

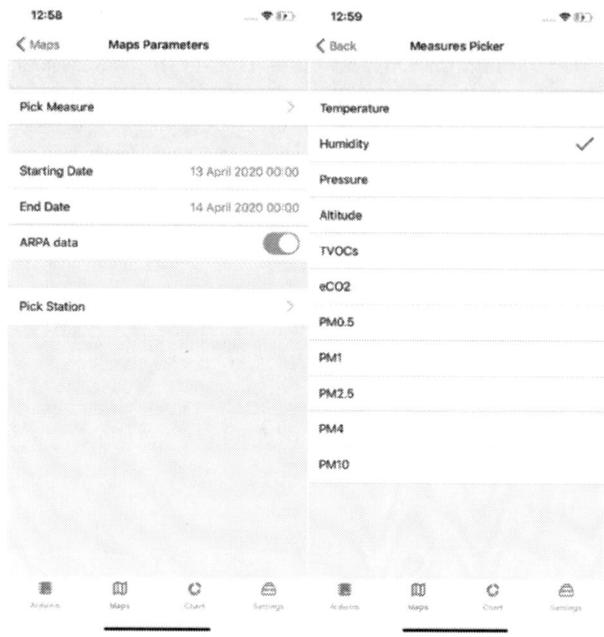

Figure 5. Filter screens.

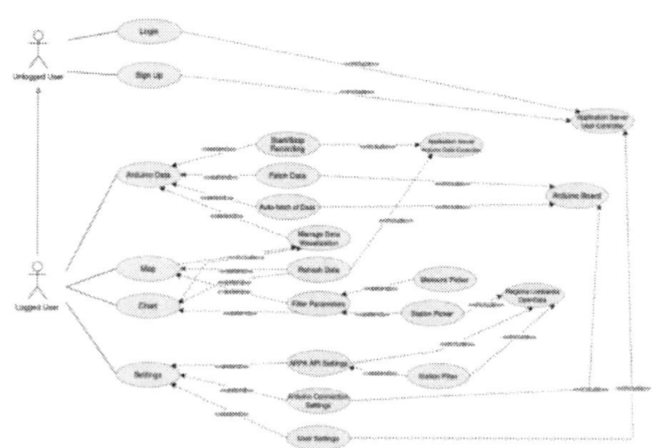

Figure 6. Use case diagram of the system [25].

The major benefits driven by MOQA will be its usability and its data reading easiness that allows non-expert users to monitor air quality conditions.

C. ARPA Data

The data collected with the portable device are compared to those downloaded from the Lombardy Region's open data repository (ARPA Lombardia). This database is quite extensive and contains all the measures registered by the stations, divided into yearly historical series. Each yearly dataset for each Air Quality (AQ) station is composed of approximately 2.5 million records. Therefore, data for all the available AQ sensors have been cleaned, removing negative or absent values, and keeping only the validated (VA) records. The analysis of the data provided by ARPA can provide useful insights about how the pollutants are distributed throughout the year and what affects them. For instance, in Figure 7, it is reported the analysis of PM10 data distribution from 2017 to February 2020. It is clear how the PM10 concentration is dependent on the heating period in Italy for climate zone E: 15th October to 15th April as stated by the DPR n. 74/2013. Indeed, in those periods, the total amount of PM10 exceeds the threshold of 50 µg/m3 set by the European Environment Agency [26].

IV. RESULTS

The portable sensor had been tested against a reference one, i.e., the monitor situated in Città Studi and managed by ARPA, to verify its reliability. More than five hundred measures of CO2, temperature, and relative humidity of the two sensors included in the portable device were used in the test.

Figure 8 shows a comparison between the simultaneous reading of the portable sensor and a reference sensor. The difference between the measure of the reference sensor and the portable one is computed according to the following formula:

$$\Delta CO_2 = {(CO_{2,r} - CO_{2,p})}/{CO_{2,r}} \quad (1)$$

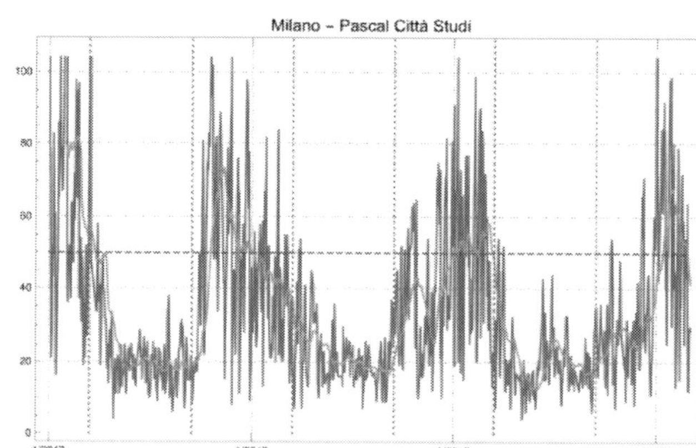

Figure 7. PM10 from 01/01/2017 to February 2020 registered by the AQ station Pascal Città Studi (ARPA). The blue line represents the daily average, whereas the orange line shows the 1 month moving average.

Where:
ΔCO_2 is the difference between two measures
$CO_{2,r}$ is the reference sensor measure
$CO_{2,p}$ is the portable sensor measure

The reliability of the sensor is not suitable for most scientific applications, since during the test period 73.64% of the ΔCO_2 were either bigger than 50% or lower than -50%.

The difference between the reference and the portable sensor readings may depend on many factors. Among these, temperature and relative humidity can influence the data collected by the device. Figure 9, it shows the difference between the two sensors CO2 measures as a function of the difference between temperature and relative humidity readings. For instance, in some temperature conditions,

Figure 9 highlights a direct correlation between relative humidity and CO2 error.

To calibrate the device's sensor to the monitor's measures a deep learning model is implemented. The ANN designed is a feedforward neural network [27] with an input layer, three hidden layers and, an output layer. The net uses two types of hidden layer: a) linear layer, i.e., a trainable, fully connected net layer that computes w·x+b, where w represents the weights, x the input features, and b the bias; b) Tanh layer, i.e., a layer that applies the hyperbolic tangent function to its input. The net has twelve neurons on each layer except for the input and the last two layers. To train the network, 80% of the available data were fed to it, whereas the remaining 20% has been used for test evaluation.

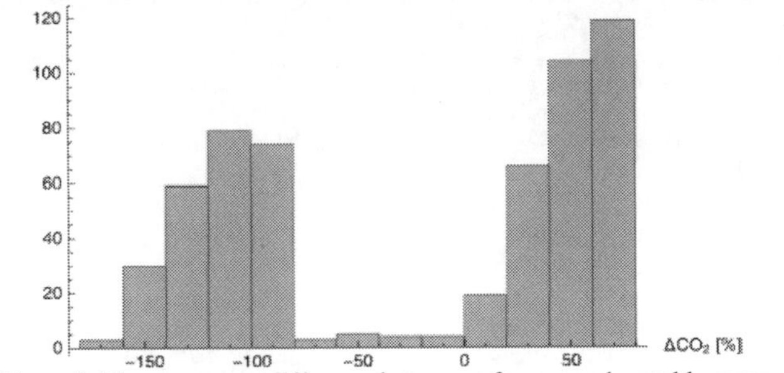

Figure 8. The percentage difference between reference and portable sensor readings.

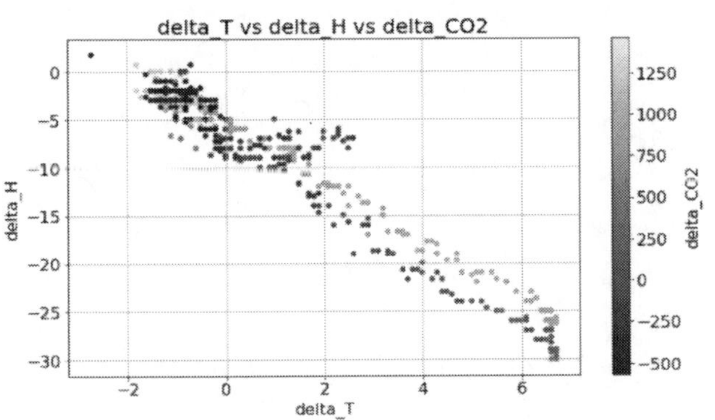

Figure 9. Differences in CO_2 sensor readings (color scale) as a function of the difference of temperature (X axes) and relative humidity (Y axes).

The performance of the network on the test dataset is shown in the scatter plot in Figure 10. The trained net performs very well since the Pearson's correlation coefficient computed for actual and forecasted CO2 is R2=97.59.

Summing up, the ANN allows for much better precision. As reported in Figure 11, the difference between portable sensor's measures improved using the ANN and the ones of the reference sensor computed according to (1). The ΔCO_2, in this case, is between -5% and +5% in 92.97% of the readings, hence the errors that occurred with non-calibrated data are almost canceled. Moreover, most of the incorrect correlations are around 900 ppm values (both predicted and actual), thus a further investigation on that aspect might hone the results. In conclusion, the data adjusted by the network might be used to make measures in different zones far from the reference station and thus, help to depict polluted areas dangerous for vulnerable people.

V. Conclusion and Future Work

Although SLODs are among the major causes of death, few studies have been carried out on their diffusion in the built environment, especially in big cities. There are too few air quality monitoring stations in cities to understand the exact relationship between pollutants and the built environment. A crowdsourcing data collection on SLODs may help to solve this issue, but low-cost sensor devices are needed.

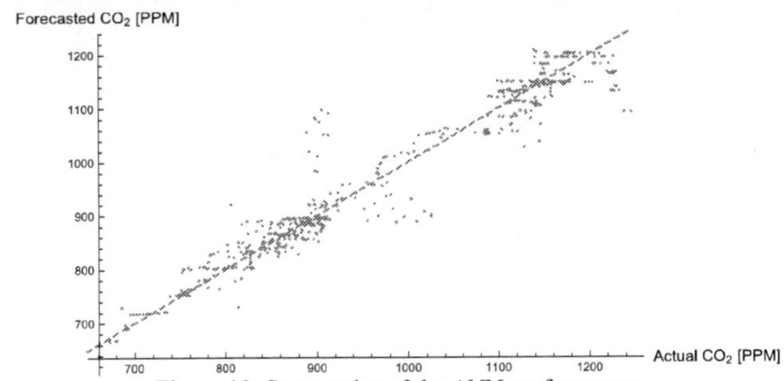

Figure 10. Scatter plot of the ANN performance.

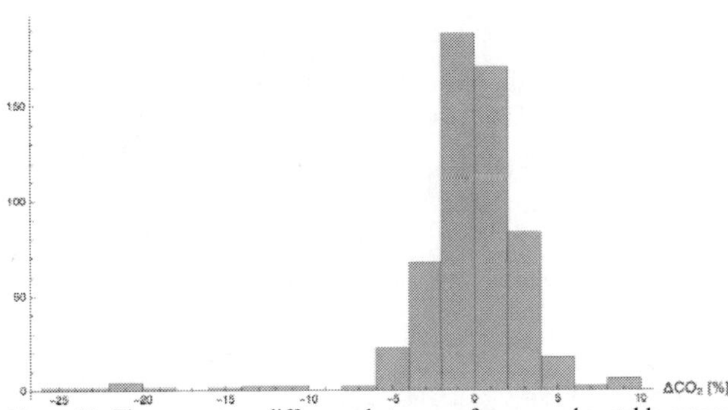

Figure 11. The percentage difference between reference and portable sensor readings after ANN correction.

Thus, a portable air quality monitoring device had been made. The small and cheap device and the bespoke mobile application allowed for citizen involvement in collecting data, but their reliability appeared to be too low during a test with reference sensors. To overcome this hurdle, ML had been used to calibrate the portable sensor. This approach proved to be effective and the data collected from citizens are now sufficiently reliable to continue with the next stages of research.

Future works will include the implementation of a warning system inside the mobile application that will alert vulnerable people in case of dangerous conditions and make them act accordingly. This step will help non-expert users to be aware of the risks without the need to have a thematic knowledge of air pollution and pollutants threshold levels.

Meanwhile, the work on the portable device will continue and will be twofold: i) optimization of the hardware (better connection, a 3D printed shell, on board software optimization, etc) and ii) try to improve machine learning performance by deploying further approaches with higher model complexity.

ACKNOWLEDGMENT

The authors would like to thank Mathays Giudici for his valuable work in the development of the mobile application.

FUNDING

This research was partially funded by the MIUR (the Italian Ministry of Education, University, and Research) Project BE S2ECURe - (make) Built Environment Safer in Slow and Emergency Conditions through behavioral assessed/designed Resilient solutions (Grant number: 2017LR75XK).

REFERENCES

[1] J. E. Jackson et al., "Public health impacts of climate change in Washington State: Projected mortality risks due to heat events and air pollution," Clim. Change, vol. 102, no. 1–2, pp. 159–186, 2010, doi: 10.1007/s10584-010-9852-3.

[2] J. Y. Lee and H. Kim, "Projection of future temperature-related mortality due to climate and demographic changes," Environ. Int., vol. 94, pp. 489–494, 2016, doi: 10.1016/j.envint.2016.06.007.

[3] World Health Organization, "Ambient Air Pollution: A global assessment of exposure and burden of disease," 2016.

[4] WorldGBC, "About Green Building," World Green Building Councils, 2020. [Online]. Available: https://www.worldgbc.org/what-green-building.

[5] P. de Prado Bert, E. M. H. Mercader, J. Pujol, J. Sunyer, and M. Mortamais, "The Effects of Air Pollution on the Brain: a Review of Studies Interfacing Environmental Epidemiology and Neuroimaging," Current environmental health reports, vol. 5, no. 3. pp. 351–364, 2018, doi: 10.1007/s40572-018-0209-9.

[6] R. B. Devlin, A. J. Ghio, H. Kehrl, G. Sanders, and W. Cascio, "Elderly humans exposed to concentrated air pollution particles have decreased heart rate variability," in European Respiratory Journal, Supplement, 2003, vol. 21, no. 40, doi: 10.1183/09031936.03.00402403.

[7] R. J. Delfino et al., "Traffic-related air pollution and blood pressure in elderly subjects with coronary artery disease," Epidemiology, vol. 21, no. 3, pp. 396–404, 2010, doi: 10.1097/EDE.0b013e3181d5e19b.

[8] EPA, "Urban heat island basics," in Reducing Urban Heat Islands: Compendium of Strategies | Heat Island Effect | US EPA, 2008, p. 22.

[9] World Urbanization Prospects: The 2018 Revision. 2019.

[10] N. Garin et al., "Built Environment and Elderly Population Health: A Comprehensive Literature Review," Clin. Pract. Epidemiol. Ment. Heal., vol. 10, no. 1, pp. 103–115, 2014, doi: 10.2174/1745017901410010103.

[11] A. Forsyth, J. Michael Oakes, B. Lee, and K. H. Schmitz, "The built environment, walking, and physical activity: Is the environment more important to some people than others?," Transp. Res. Part D Transp. Environ., 2009, doi: 10.1016/j.trd.2008.10.003.

[12] S. Srinivasan, L. R. O'Fallon, and A. Dearry, "Creating Healthy Communities, Healthy Homes, Healthy People: Initiating a Research Agenda on the Built Environment and Public Health," American Journal of Public Health, vol. 93, no. 9. pp. 1446–1450, 2003, doi: 10.2105/AJPH.93.9.1446.

[13] I. D. Stewart and T. R. Oke, "Local climate zones for urban temperature studies," Bull. Am. Meteorol. Soc., vol. 93, no. 12, pp. 1879–1900, 2012, doi: 10.1175/BAMS-D-11-00019.1.

[14] R. Paolini, A. G. Mainini, T. Poli, and L. Vercesi, "Assessment of thermal stress in a street canyon in pedestrian area with or without canopy shading," in Energy Procedia, 2014, doi: 10.1016/j.egypro.2014.02.177.

[15] E. Jamei, P. Rajagopalan, M. Seyedmahmoudian, and Y. Jamei, "Review on the impact of urban geometry and pedestrian level greening on outdoor thermal comfort," Renewable and Sustainable Energy Reviews. 2016, doi: 10.1016/j.rser.2015.10.104.

[16] N. Colaninno and E. Morello, "Modelling the impact of green solutions upon the urban heat island phenomenon by means of satellite data," in Journal of Physics: Conference Series, 2019, doi: 10.1088/1742-6596/1343/1/012010.

[17] R. Lukyanenko, A. Wiggins, and H. K. Rosser, "Citizen Science: An Information Quality Research Frontier," Inf. Syst. Front., vol. 22, no. 4, pp. 961–983, 2020, doi: 10.1007/s10796-019-09915-z.

[18] H. Chen et al., "Effect of air quality alerts on human health: a regression discontinuity analysis in Toronto, Canada," Lancet Planet. Heal., vol. 2, no. 1, pp. e2–e3, 2018, doi: 10.1016/S2542-5196(17)30185-7.

[19] A. Cavaliere et al., "Development of low-cost air quality stations for next generation monitoring networks: Calibration and validation of PM2.5 and PM10 sensors," Sensors (Switzerland), vol. 18, no. 9, 2018, doi: 10.3390/s18092843.

[20] Y. Xiong, J. Zhou, J. J. Schauer, W. Yu, and Y. Hu, "Seasonal and spatial differences in source contributions to PM2.5 in Wuhan, China," Sci. Total Environ., vol. 577, pp. 155–165, 2017, doi: 10.1016/j.scitotenv.2016.10.150.

[21] D. M. Holstius, A. Pillarisetti, K. R. Smith, and E. Seto, "Field calibrations of a low-cost aerosol sensor at a regulatory monitoring site in California," Atmos. Meas. Tech., vol. 7, no. 4, pp. 1121–1131, 2014, doi: 10.5194/amt-7-1121-2014.

[22] R. Jayaratne, X. Liu, P. Thai, M. Dunbabin, and L. Morawska, "The influence of humidity on the performance of a low-cost air particle mass sensor and the effect of atmospheric fog," Atmos. Meas. Tech., vol. 11, no. 8, pp. 4883–4890, 2018, doi: 10.5194/amt-11-4883-2018.

[23] K. M. Alhasa et al., "Calibration model of a low-cost air quality sensor using an adaptive neuro-fuzzy inference system," Sensors (Switzerland), vol. 18, no. 12, 2018, doi: 10.3390/s18124380.

[24] M. Si, Y. Xiong, S. Du, and K. Du, "Evaluation and calibration of a low-cost particle sensor in ambient conditions using machine-learning methods," Atmos. Meas. Tech., vol. 13, no. 4, pp. 1693–1707, 2020, doi: 10.5194/amt-13-1693-2020.

[25] Mathyas Giudici, "MOQA design and technology." [Online]. Available: https://github.com/MathyasGiudici/polimi-dima-moqa-documentation/blob/master/dima-moqa-documentation.pdf.

[26] R. Derwent and A.-G. Hjellbrekke, Air quality in Europe — 2019 report 1994-2019 EEA Report No 10/2019. 2019.

[27] G. Bebis and M. Georgiopoulos, "Why network size is so important," IEEE Potentials, vol. 13, no. 4, pp. 27–31, 1994, doi: 10.1109/45.329294.

Elemental Giant Magnetoresistance (GMR) Sensors for Neuromorphical Applications

J. Gómez, C. Reig, M.D. Cubells
Dept. of Electronic Engineering
University of Valencia
Burjassot, Spain
email: candid.reig@uv.es

F. Pardo, J.A. Boluda, F. Vegara
Dept. of Computer Science
University of Valencia
Burjassot, Spain

S. Abrunhosa, S. Cardoso
INESC-MN
Lisbon, Portugal

***Abstract*—Neuromorphic (bio-inspired) strategies have demonstrated to improve the performance of vision sensors. With the recent advances in sensor integration, such a paradigm can be extended to novel applications. With such a purpose in mind, this paper reports on the design, manufacturing, and characterization of Giant MagnetoResistance (GMR) based magnetic sensor arrays. Preliminary experimental results show that the developed sensors can be integrated, for example, in event driven based magnetic particle tracking systems.**

***Index Terms*—Neuromorphic, GMR sensors, Event Driven (ED), magnetic particles.**

I. Introduction

Bio-inspired approach to sensor design is a new paradigm that is changing the way in which some traditional applications, like artificial vision, are defined [1]. Retinomorphic sensors try to mimic the whole human visual process by considering an Event-Driven representation (ED) of the vision instead of the classical Frame-Driven (FD) one. By following this approach, the output of ED sensors consists of serialized "spiking" signals, grouped in events, which are much more effective where the speed or the bandwidth are constraints. The neuromorphic strategy has already been successfully extended to other human senses such as auditory or olfactory [2]. Developing novel bio-inspired sensors for applications different from human senses is, nowadays, challenging.

The integration of common sensors in specific bio-inspired sensing platforms is not straightforward. Active 'pixels', composed by sensing elements together with the specific electronics are necessary. Consequently, their design involves both electronics and technological issues. In this sense, the potentiality of using resistive sensors (with variations below 1% in sensors for nominal resistances ranging from 100 Ω to 10 kΩ) in ED strategies has been recently demonstrated [3].

The use of Giant MagnetoResistance (GMR) sensors for bio-inspired magnetic field sensors is proposed in this work. GMR sensors are high sensitivity resistive magnetic sensors, CMOS compatible, suitable for low-field detection applications. Their design, fabrication and fundamental characterization is described in the following sections. As preliminary test-benches, current sensing and magnetic particle movement tracking will be explored.

II. Sensor Design

8-element arrays of GMR sensors have designed and microfabricated for preliminary testing the potential of the approach, as described in Figure 1. The sensors were manufactured at the clean-room facilities of the INESC-MN, following a typical four-masks five-lithography-steps, as described in [4]. *Spin-valves* were considered as the sensing elements. Sensors included integrated current strips, aligned with the sensors, for testing purposes. A photograph of a sensor is included as an inset in Figure 1.

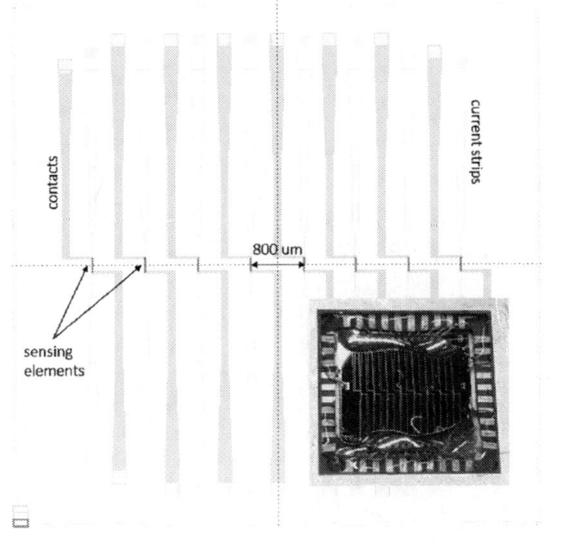

Fig. 1. Scheme of the considered GMR (spin-valves) sensing array with a photograph of an encapsulated sensor.

III. Results

Preliminary tests on so obtained sensors included static characterization (magnetic field and electric current), dynamic measurements, and a scaled proof-of-concept.

A. Static characterization (magnetic field, electric current)

The response of sensing elements versus the applied magnetic field was measured with the help of an automated (GPIB based) testbench, including an electromagnet and a PC. The obtained results are shown in Figure 2. A clean linear behavior is observed in the range of interest, with values of (1160 ± 10) Ω and sensitivities of about (1.65 ± 0.05) Ω/Oe. Analog experiments were performed for measuring the resistance of the sensing elements as a function of the electrical current driving through the integrated strips (10 μm width). In this case, the measured sensitivity was about (1.00 ± 0.05) Ω/mA. Then, 1 mA flowing through a current strips is generating about 0.6 Oe on the below sensing element.

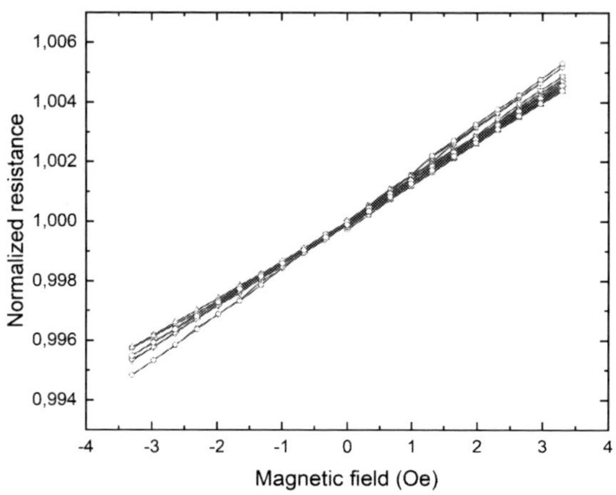

Fig. 2. Typical normalized resistance versus magnetic field of the sensing elements.

B. Current pulses

Dynamic characterization was carried out by applying current pulses to the current strips and measuring the change of the sensing resistors, connected as voltage dividers, with an oscilloscope. Rectangular current pulses (10 mA amplitude, 100 us width) were applied, being the sensing elements biased with a 3.75 mA DC current. Typical results are shown in Figure 3 (four-channels oscilloscope), which are consistent with the static characterization. Fabrication tolerance issues are slightly observed.

C. Small magnet measurements

Finally, small ($\varnothing = 1$ mm) spherical neodymium magnets were placed close to the sensors in order to qualitatively estimate the potentiality of the sensors for detecting moving magnetic particles. Output signals were collected with the oscilloscope, as displayed in Figure 4. The detected field by the sensing elements was in the order of 1 Oe (within its optimal range) and it was conditioned by the distance from the magnet and its orientation. Additional measurements are required in order to give a more precise characterization.

IV. Conclusions and Future Work

Specifically designed spin valve based magnetic sensor arrays have demonstrated to fulfill the requirements for being integrated in sensor systems based on the neuromorphic strategy.

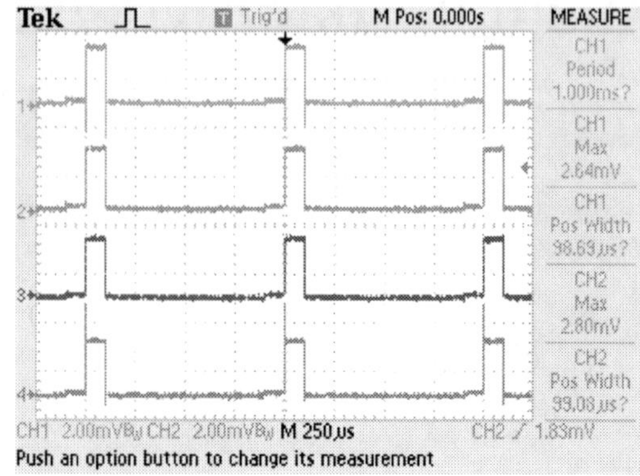

Fig. 3. Oscillograms from the sensing elements being excited by electrical current pulses.

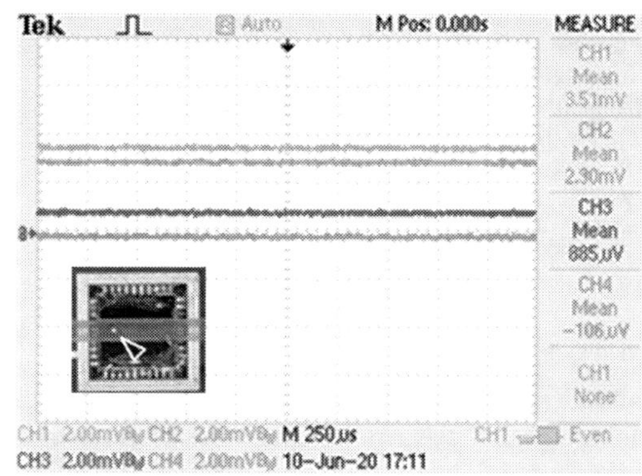

Fig. 4. Detection of a small spherical neodymium magnet ($\varnothing = 1$ mm).

The next steps should include a systematic characterization for optimizing their parameters, mainly those related to power consumption and dynamic response. The development of electrical models and the monolithic integration with specifically designed ASICs should be done in the next future.

Acknowledgement

This work was partially supported by projects TEC2015-66947-R (Spanish Ministry of Economy and Competitiveness) and PID2019-105556GB-C32 (Spanish Ministry of Science and Innovation.

References

[1] N. Wu, "Neuromorphic vision chips", *Science China Information Sciences*, vol. 61, no. 6, p. 060421, Jun. 2018, doi: 10.1007/s11432-017-9303-0.

[2] A. Vanarse, A. Osseiran, and A. Rassau, "A Review of Current Neuromorphic Approaches for Vision, Auditory, and Olfactory Sensors", *Frontiers in Neuroscience*, vol. 10, no. MAR, p. 115, Mar. 2016, doi: 10.3389/fnins.2016.00115.

[3] C. Reig, M.D. Cubells, J. Sanchis, F. Pardo, J.A. Boluda, F. Vegara, S. Cardoso, "Address Event Representation (AER) approach to resistive sensor arrays", in *Proceedings of GMC-ElecEng 2020 (in press)*, 2020.

[4] M.D. Cubells, C. Reig, D. Ramírez, S. Cardoso and P. Freitas, "Full Wheatstone Bridge Spin-Valve Based Sensors for IC Currents Monitoring", *IEEE Sensors Journal*, vol. 9, no. 12, pp. 1756–1762, Dec. 2009, doi: 10.1109/jsen.2009.2030880.

International Academy, Research, and Industry Association (IARIA)
412 Derby Way
Wilmington, DE 19810

CURRAN ASSOCIATES INC.
proceedings.com

ISBN 978-1-7138-2172-4
9 781713 821724